FATAL ERROR

FATAL ERROR

THE MISCARRIAGE
OF JUSTICE THAT SEALED
THE ROSENBERGS' FATE

Joseph H. Sharlitt

CHARLES SCRIBNER'S SONS   New York

Quotations in chapter 9 from "Control of Information Relating to Atomic Energy," by James Newman, are reprinted by permission of The Yale Law Journal Company and Fred B. Rothman & Company from *The Yale Law Journal*, Vol. 56 (May 1947).

Charles Scribner's Sons
Macmillan Publishing Company
866 Third Avenue, New York, NY 10022
Collier Macmillan Canada, Inc.

Library of Congress Cataloging-in-Publication Data
Sharlitt, Joseph H.
Fatal error: the miscarriage of justice that sealed the Rosenbergs' fate/Joseph H. Sharlitt.
p.   cm.
Includes index.
ISBN 0-684-19059-1
1. Rosenberg, Julius, 1918–1953—Trials, litigation, etc.
2. Rosenberg, Ethel, 1915–1953—Trials, litigation, etc.   3. Trials (Espionage)—New York (N.Y.)   4. Trials (Conspiracy)—New York (N.Y.)   5. Capital punishment—United States.   I. Title.
KF224.R6S53   1989
345.73'0773—dc19   89-4290   CIP
[347.305773]

Macmillan books are available at special discounts for bulk purchases for sales promotions, premiums, fund-raising, or educational use. For details, contact:

Special Sales Director
Macmillan Publishing Company
866 Third Avenue
New York, NY 10022

10 9 8 7 6 5 4 3 2 1

Designed by Jack Meserole

PRINTED IN THE UNITED STATES OF AMERICA

CONTENTS

ILLUSTRATIONS

(Following page 146)

PREFACE

Why This Book Demanded to Be Written

The purpose of this book is to pose the question of whether the execution of Julius and Ethel Rosenberg was legal. It concludes that it was not. Since life or death was the ultimate issue in the Rosenberg case, the conduct of our legal system in that case, regardless of the guilt or innocence of the Rosenbergs, remains a matter of grave concern.

Unlike any other book written about the Rosenberg case, *Fatal Error* tells how the Supreme Court of the United States rushed the Rosenbergs to the electric chair in violation of their rights before that Court. The Supreme Court disregarded the law, its own traditions, and violated the rules that govern the conduct of the justices, in its dash to kill this couple. It is a day-by-day account of how our highest court became politicized while deciding the most controversial case in this century. It reveals to the American public for the first time how, in this case, its highest court failed in its responsibilities. The details are dramatic and appalling.

Fatal Error examines the death sentence given the Rosenbergs by Judge Irving Kaufman, probing his words and reasons for the sentence. The judge's own reasoning, expressed in April of 1951, was based on Judge Kaufman's belief that the Rosenbergs put the atomic bomb in Russian hands and ultimately caused the Communist aggression in Korea that resulted in fifty thousand casualties. The realities of what Julius and Ethel Rosenberg did and did not do, and what other spies *did* do *before* Judge Kaufman imposed his sentence on the Rosenbergs, reveal that the judge's theories about the bomb and Korea were based on his own speculations, not on the record before him. Judge Kaufman also had become politicized.

Fatal Error examines, in layman's terms, the law used by Judge Kaufman and the Supreme Court to put the Rosenbergs in the electric chair. What *Fatal Error* discloses is that the government (which prosecuted the Rosenbergs), Judge Kaufman, who sentenced the Rosenbergs to death, and the Supreme Court, which let them die, all used the wrong law. *Fatal Error*'s narrative focuses on the Supreme Court's activities in the last week of the case, in June of 1953, when it was made clear to this Court that the wrong law was about to result in two executions that the correct law forbade. Yet the majority of the Supreme Court disregarded this fact. The intrigues leading to this fatal error highlight the justices' relations with each other. Those intrigues and how they led to the majority's determination to rush to judgment—and two unlawful executions—have not been released from within the sacrosanct provinces of the Supreme Court until now. Those disclosures are extraordinary and disturbing in the highest degree.

All of this took place in the third week of June of 1953. That week may very well have been the high fever mark of an indigenous American disease, McCarthyism. What occurred in the Rosenberg case cannot be judged fairly without reference to the mass anti-Red feeling that had taken hold of this country in June of 1953. *Fatal Error* makes that reference. The reader can then judge the extent to which two courts became politicized and how this resulted in the executions of the Rosenbergs.

This book is not about the Rosenbergs' guilt or innocence. It is concerned with the administration of justice in our country. What it does say is that a gross miscarriage of justice occurred in the Rosenberg case regardless of whether the Rosenbergs were guilty or innocent. No one has ever before told the story of how this breakdown took place, the events and the people that perpetrated the fatal error.

ACKNOWLEDGMENTS

To Jerry Jacobson, Janet Perlman, Charlie and Cordie Puttkammer, Neal Krucoff, Marvin Teplitz, Gary Hesky, Rita Lennox, Kumar Shankardass, and Dan Fenn, without whom this book would never have been written;

to Mary Hesky, who made readable English out of a lawyer's prose,

to Peter and Amy Sharlitt, who helped but never knew it;

to Bernhard Bechhoefer for having faith in his colleague; and

to Fyke Farmer and Marshall Perlin for their extraordinary kindness and assistance.

Finally, I owe a special debt to Ted Perlman and Phil Elman, who bring pride to being a lawyer.

FATAL ERROR

CHAPTER ONE

1

THE ERROR COMMITTED
BY THE COURT

HE CONCLUSION that the Rosenbergs' execution was
illegal is based on an examination of what the law was on
June 19, 1953, when the federal government executed the
two convicted conspirators. The appropriate law on that
date clearly required that the death penalty be specifically recommended by a jury before execution could be carried out in the
Rosenberg case. Because the Rosenbergs were charged, tried,
convicted, and executed under an inapplicable law that did not
require this jury recommendation, no jury ever made such a
recommendation in the Rosenberg case. The law used was a
wrong one, and this was error—legal error. The absence of a jury
recommendation made execution of the Rosenbergs a fatal error,
in every sense of that phrase.

Every one of the numerous judges who reviewed the Rosenberg case before it reached the Supreme Court simply assumed
that the law under which the two were charged, tried, and
convicted was the proper law.[1] One very good reason for this
assumption was that the lawyers for the Rosenbergs had themselves never questioned it.

Indeed, when the case reached the Supreme Court in its final
doom-ridden week in June 1953, the Rosenberg lawyers still had
never questioned the legal basis on which their clients were to be
executed. Not until total outsiders, lawyers for a West Coast
sympathizer who had never met the Rosenbergs,[2] raised the issue

1

and persuaded one justice of the Supreme Court that the imminent execution was illegal did the Rosenbergs and their lawyers belatedly take up this argument.

The argument was a relatively simple one. The Rosenbergs had been charged, tried, and convicted under the Espionage Act of 1917. That act permitted a judge to sentence certain violators of the act (such as the Rosenbergs) to death on the judge's own determination, without requiring any recommendation from the jury. But a new law (the Atomic Energy Act of 1946) had been passed just seven years before the Rosenbergs were executed;[3] it required that spies who passed atomic secrets could be executed only on the recommendation of the jury sitting in the case. From the day that the Rosenbergs were indicted until three days before they were executed, the Atomic Energy Act of 1946, although applicable, was ignored by everyone connected with the case.

The points that went to the heart of the case in its last week and never did get full consideration by the Supreme Court (or any court) were: (1) whether the Atomic Energy Act of 1946 should have been applied to the Rosenbergs' spying, and (2) whether both statutes, the 1917 act[4] and the 1946 act, applied to their conduct. If the answer to either question was yes, the Rosenbergs were executed illegally.

Astonishingly, for any observer who reads the history of this case in the eighties, the Supreme Court not only answered both questions in the negative but also went a good deal further and pronounced the questions themselves insubstantial and not worthy of any court's attention. The Supreme Court's extreme determination was the only way that the Rosenbergs could be put into the electric chair without further delay. And delay was, it seems, to be avoided at all costs.

However, one judge of the Supreme Court not only felt the questions *were* substantial but went further to rule that the later act *did* apply to the Rosenbergs and that the executions were, therefore, illegal.[5] Two other justices of the nine sitting on the Court ruled that the questions were indeed quite substantial and asked for time to have them briefed and studied.[6] But six justices ruled otherwise.[7] The majority prevailed and within eight hours of their ruling, the Rosenbergs were dead. The controversy engendered by this execution has reverberated through the decades as no other in this century.

To dispassionate followers of the case, the most disturbing aspect of this sudden conclusion was the government's rush during that week of June 1953 to execute the two convicted conspirators. Two human lives were at stake. Yet it seemed that the forces of federal justice were mesmerized by the passage of time here and abroad. The reason for this preoccupation with the passage of time was obvious: the case was being used as a vehicle for dissemination in the United States and elsewhere of publicity unfavorable to our government's role in it as prosecutor. International criticism—greater than any in history to that date—of the U.S. government for its handling of the Rosenbergs played a crucial part in the stampede to execution. By the thirteenth of June 1953, the Rosenberg case already had dragged through the courts for nearly thirty-four months.[8] During that time, the Rosenbergs had been given every remedy known to the law, sometimes two or three times over. Moreover, their case had become highly politicized by zealots of the left wing whose goal was far more the discrediting of the United States than it was the freeing of the Rosenbergs.

But all of these considerations pale before a series of pressing facts. First, the immutable reality that two human lives were at stake and time is, by comparison, a paltry commodity when a government is directly dispensing life and death. Second, in the course of that fateful week in June 1953 (commencing on June 13 and ending on June 19, when the Rosenbergs were executed), an entirely new legal argument surfaced *for the first time*. This argument went to the heart of the case. Yet none of the legion of lawyers and judges who had participated in the case had ever made or heard the argument until the week before the Rosenbergs were to die.

Third, that very new argument was raised before Justice Douglas on June 16, 1953, just two days before the Rosenbergs were scheduled to die. Justice Douglas saw merit in it. The next day, on June 17, Douglas entered a stay of the execution of the Rosenbergs (scheduled for the eighteenth) and ordered that this new argument be sent back for consideration by trial judge

Kaufman, thence to the Court of Appeals and back to the Supreme Court, giving the Rosenbergs at least a year more of life. But because the new argument was made to Douglas, a maverick on the Court, and accepted by him, it was doomed before Douglas acted on it. Douglas's earlier conduct in the Rosenberg case—prior to his entry of the stay on June 17—had so isolated Douglas from his colleagues on the Court that even those who might have supported him on the law (and on his stay) were deeply involved in personal disputes with him. Vital votes during that last week were lost, not because Douglas was wrong on the law but because Douglas was making the argument. It is a damning comment on the High Court's conduct during that week that a legal point that had never before been raised, that should have spared the lives of the defendants, that was wholly correct even though scores of judges and lawyers had missed it entirely, was summarily brushed aside by the Supreme Court of the United States because of personal pique of judge against judge. The animus was present. The record demonstrates that it influenced what the Court did. It should not have. It is no wonder that Justice Frankfurter spoke of the Supreme Court's conduct in the Rosenberg case as the "most disturbing single experience I have had during my terms of service on the Court."[9]

Fourth, Attorney General Brownell of the United States, the adversary of the Rosenbergs in this case and a man committed to swift execution of the convicted spies, then engaged, together with Chief Justice Fred Vinson of the Supreme Court, in conduct that violated both the canons of judicial conduct governing all judges and the canons of lawyers' conduct that governed the attorney general. As the narrative for June 16 and 17 in this book sets forth (and as FBI records corroborate), both men met and plotted against Douglas and what he might do while the new argument was pending before Douglas.[10]

Fifth: that was not the full extent of the improprieties of the attorney general and the chief justice. The private notes of another justice indicate that other conduct by both the attorney general and the chief justice—wholly apart from that described above—was aimed directly at nullifying what Douglas might do with the new argument that had surfaced.[10a] As the events of June 16 and 17 reflect, the highest judge and the chief law enforcement officer of the land were engaged in a concerted effort to stop Douglas from acting alone. Douglas had become the target of a totally improper combination of judge and prosecutor (chief justice and attorney general) to prevent—at all costs—Douglas's act of conscience. All of this took place *before* Douglas acted.

Finally, there is substantial evidence that once the Supreme Court had disposed of the last formal attempt of the Rosenbergs' lawyers to sway the Court in the regular manner in which the Court functioned—in the Court's last conference on the afternoon of Monday, June 15, 1953—the justices had agreed that having finally disposed of this monster case that had tormented American justice here and abroad for thirty-four months, no one of them would thereafter reopen the case.[11] And when Justice Douglas, the same Justice Douglas, intervened just two days later, on June 17, to do precisely that on the day before the Rosenbergs were to die, it was no wonder that *Douglas*—and not the Rosenbergs—became the "defendant" before the Court. What Douglas then urged on the Court was not rejected for what it said but in very large part because *Douglas* urged it. It does honor to justices Black, Frankfurter, and Douglas that this final departure from judicial decorum wholly failed to deter those three dissenters when they came to vote their consciences two days later. No such honor applies to the majority of the Court.

One need not be a lawyer to recognize that none of these events was either proper or fair to the defendants, Julius and Ethel Rosenberg. There should have been no private meeting of any kind between the attorney general and the chief justice of the United States to discuss what to do in a case then pending before the Supreme Court in which the attorney general was the major adversary. The attorney general had no business privately urging the chief justice of the United States to influence the conduct of one of the justices in the disposition of a case under consideration by that justice. There should have been no private agreements among the justices *not* to entertain any further petitions in a case—any case—and especially one involving the death penalty.

Yet all of these things happened. As the next section states, the records of the FBI and the justices themselves confirm that they happened.

When Douglas entered a stay of execution of the Rosenbergs on Wednesday, June 17, 1953, the Department of Justice dutifully put in motion the attorney general's and the chief justice's plot: it made the request for a historic special session of the Court already in recess (the third special session in the Court's history). Within one hour—without any notice to the lawyers for the Rosenbergs, who had every right to such notice and to oppose the hasty gathering of the justices—Vinson ordered the Court to reconvene on the next day, Thursday, June 18.[12]

In the accumulation of improprieties that infected the last week of the Rosenberg case, the signal to reconvene the Court for its special session went *from* the Court *to* the Department of Justice. As is shown in the events of June 16 (in the next session), the attorney general and the chief justice had agreed to precisely this course of action on the day before. This was as explicit a signal from the Court that it wished to be reconvened (to undo the mischief that Douglas had done) as it could send forth. It came from the chief justice, who said it in a meeting with the attorney general.

Such signals traditionally are the prerogatives of the litigating adversaries, not of the Court. In all instances, especially the highly unusual one of reconvening the Court out of session, one party takes the initiative, files papers with the Court seeking the Court to act (in this case, to reconvene), and the Court either agrees to or denies the request. But that assumes an unbiased Court. In the case of the Supreme Court of the United States on June 16, 1953, it was not an unbiased court. It personally (in the message of the chief justice personally delivered to the attorney general) sent the signal to the attorney general that it wished to be reconvened. And the attorney general obviously was delighted to oblige now that Douglas had taken his dramatic and—to the Department of Justice—lamentable action. It was no accident that the Department of Justice's motion to reconvene was not served on the Rosenberg lawyers. It was no accident that it was agreed to by the chief justice within an hour of its filing. In the topsy-turvy world of the Supreme Court of the United States on June 17, 1953, it was still another departure from the Court's—from any court's— rules; and it was aimed at putting the Rosenbergs into the electric chair without further delay, whether proper or not.

With Douglas the enemy, with the chief justice acting secretly and in concert with the attorney general to defeat the Douglas heresy, it is little wonder that the new legal argument that brought this all about had no chance. And Douglas himself knew it had no chance when he went public with it—but he could do nothing about it.

Justice Frankfurter was not alone in viewing the case as the most disturbing in his court career. Lawyers who followed the events in the Rosenberg case in its last week before the Supreme Court, both within the Supreme Court and the Department of Justice, consider that last week to be one of the saddest episodes in the recent history of American justice. Lawyers on both sides of the case felt a deep misgiving they have never forgotten. The guilt or innocence of the defendants had nothing to do with their distress over the Court's conduct and that of the Justice Department. Nor was the worldwide fire of partisan fervor on both sides the cause of their dismay. It was, rather, the spectacle of the Supreme Court of the United States becoming politicized before their eyes, with no one having the will or courage to stop it. Justice was rushed. Proper consideration of matters of the utmost importance was not allowed.

The consequences of that last week of the Rosenberg case before the Supreme Court were that the Rosenbergs were executed without ever having the chance to write or argue their brief on the key point of law that had just arisen and the validity of that point has never been tested.

In a sense, this book is the brief that the Rosenbergs were never allowed to write. However, it is written for laymen rather than for a court. Because so many of the elements that today too much disturb the soul about this case occurred during its final week, it begins with a narrative of the events of the week of June 12 to 19, 1953, the last week before the Rosenberg execution. Some of what occurred that week was a reflection of earlier events in the Rosenberg saga. Some of what happened was caused indirectly by events in the Congress of the United States; those are recorded as well. But the human drama of what was said and done by the lowly and the mighty in the hallowed halls of the Supreme Court during those seven days is essential for understanding of the Supreme Court's fatal error.

My first contact with the Rosenberg case was the same as that of millions of Americans: news coverage before and during the trial and the appeals. The entire country lived through the ordeal of June 1953, when the seemingly inexhaustible concern of the courts to give the defendants every measure of justice prolonged its suspense; when the sentimental martyrdom orchestrated by the left wing press and the Communist party around the world had already turned the case into the *cause célèbre* of the decade; and when it seemed that the tragedy of the imminent execution of these two people had subsumed all interest in their apparent guilt. Like millions of Americans quite convinced of the Rosenbergs' guilt, I was nonetheless horrified at the death sentence.

For so many Americans and for me, the reasons for horror were not precise but nonetheless pressing. There was, to begin with, the visceral feeling that no matter what the legal purists might have told us, the Rosenbergs' crime was largely a political crime. Even among enthusiasts for capital punishment, a sentence of death seems appropriate only for crimes of extreme violence; the death sentence for crimes that are political—no matter what the statute says—is very unpopular in this country. Secondly, there was a very strong feeling that this sentence was a part of the times, the McCarthy times. The growing anxieties about what McCarthyism was doing to American life were focused on this case, the prosecution of which seemed to many to be an outcropping of that opprobrious public malady. The words of Judge Kaufman in pronouncing sentence aggravated rather than allayed these anxieties. He blamed the Korean War and its casualties on the Rosenbergs. Without knowing anything about the Rosenbergs or Judge Kaufman, I *had* read the newspapers and knew this to be wrong.

From June of 1953 until the middle of 1972, the Rosenberg

case garnered relatively little public notice. Several books were written asserting the innocence of the Rosenbergs.[13] They received little notice beyond the ranks of those who already held that belief. Occasionally, there was some mention of the case in the press, usually concerning the activities of the Committee to Free Sobell, the only survivor of the affair, but these maneuvers went largely unnoticed. Most Americans felt that Sobell was guilty; his sentence, unlike the Rosenbergs', seemed fair. The curious fact about the attention given the Rosenbergs' case—both during its notoriety in 1953 and then during its rather quick decline—was that none of it pointed toward the element in the case that now seems most disturbing. In the thousands of column inches of front-page coverage given the case in June of 1953, practically nothing was said of the singular reason why three justices of the United States Supreme Court were moved to highly unusual language for them and for the Court when they opposed the government's basis in executing the Rosenbergs. None of the drama of the last-minute intervention of a wholly new point of law filtered through the outcry, the demonstrations, and the controversy of mid-June 1953.

My own discovery of what occurred just before the Rosenbergs went to the electric chair came in mid-1972 when Louis Nizer's and Jonathan Root's books gave the case a new vogue.[14] I was first intrigued, then absorbed, and finally appalled by what I subsequently read.

What follows is an exploration of the events that led—as I am now fully persuaded—to two illegal executions.

CHAPTER TWO

𝟏

THE TRIAL

THE TRIAL of Julius and Ethel Rosenberg took just fourteen court days, starting on March 6, 1951, and ending with a jury verdict of guilty on March 29, 1951.[1] One week later, on April 5, 1951, Judge Irving Kaufman sentenced both defendants to death.[2] Most of the salient facts about the prosecution received worldwide attention in 1951 and have remained well known since. But other highly significant facts about this proceeding have never been brought forward.

Well known in 1951 were the key portions of the prosecution case, which the jury accepted in every detail. The damning witnesses against the Rosenbergs were Mrs. Rosenberg's brother, David Greenglass, and his wife, Ruth Prinz Greenglass.[3] Greenglass was a machinist at the top secret Los Alamos atomic installation during 1944 and 1945.[4] By Greenglass's own testimony (following his agreement to become a government witness and his providing of key testimony in shaping the prosecution against the Rosenbergs), corroborated by his wife and by spy courier Harry Gold, Greenglass passed both to Gold and to his sister and his brother-in-law information concerning the implosion lens, a vital component installed within the atomic bomb dropped on the Japanese at Nagasaki.[5] Greenglass, on the stand, proffered a sketch of the plutonium bomb itself, and testified about it in detail.[6] Gold testified about the receipt of this information from David Greenglass on a trip to New Mexico,[7] and both Greenglasses testified about additional disclosures made to the Rosenbergs while the Greenglasses were visiting their in-laws in New York.[8]

Because the Rosenbergs were charged with conspiracy to spy, rather than spying itself, the identity of who passed what to the Russians was irrelevant to the charge and the proof of the charge at the trial. It was the overall plan to spy and transfer secrets, the conspiracy to do so—in legal terms—that the Rosenbergs were charged with. Accordingly, the plans made by the Rosenbergs with the Greenglasses, and Gold's activities with the Greenglasses, were strong proof of this conspiracy, even though it was clear that Gold (rather than the Rosenbergs) actually did the transmitting to the Soviet couriers.

Gold testified that the disclosures were passed on by him to a Soviet consul in New York.[9] He also spoke of the great value that the Soviets placed on these disclosures.[10] None of this testimony was refuted by anything except the strenuous denials of the Rosenbergs themselves.[11]

The government further offered the testimony of Dr. Walter Koski and John A. Derry. Koski, although not a physicist, was in charge of the machine shop operations where the implosion lens for the Nagasaki bomb was developed. He testified that the Greenglass sketches of the implosion lens (made by Greenglass from memory) were reasonably accurate and could give any observer of them an understanding of the basic principle of implosion.[12] Derry was not a scientist; his function was to act as liaison between Los Alamos and General Leslie Groves, the chief of security for the Manhattan Project. He fully disclaimed any technical background either in nuclear physics or in engineering related to nuclear energy. Yet he then testified that David Greenglass's model of the plutonium bomb (Exhibit 8 at trial) would convey to an outsider the basic principle of the bomb.[13]

Somewhat apart from the Greenglass-Gold-Rosenberg operation was another ring that figured very largely in the trial. Involved in it were one Max Elitcher, a former classmate of Julius Rosenberg's at City College of New York; Morton Sobell, a co-defendant of the Rosenbergs; and Julius Rosenberg. This second group was accused of conspiracy to disclose to the Soviets naval secrets having to do with communications devices.[14]

Elitcher testified that he had been recruited to spy by Julius Rosenberg, and was asked to provide information taken from laboratories where he worked as a civilian employee of the Navy.[15] No actual disclosures of information by Elitcher to either Rosenberg or Sobell were proved, simply the conspiracy to do so. But Elitcher gave damaging testimony on the relations between Sobell and Julius Rosenberg in the conspiracy to leak naval secrets.[16]

It is worth noting that no connection between these two separate rings was made out by the prosecution, except the one common link: Julius Rosenberg. Elitcher and Sobell never met the Greenglasses, nor did it appear that Elitcher or Sobell ever knew of the traffic in atomic secrets from the Los Alamos connection. The Greenglasses, for their part, never knew of the activity of the naval ring operated by Sobell and Elitcher (whom they had never met) and Julius Rosenberg. Rosenberg, the common link to both groups of spies, was used by the government to join both rings in a single trial. None of Elitcher's testimony concerning the naval ring was refuted except by Rosenberg's denials.[17] Sobell never took the stand.

A major portion of the government's case was made up of evidence of the flight (or attempt at flight) by members of both the atomic and naval rings. In graphic terms, Greenglass testified to the instructions and money given him and his wife by Julius Rosenberg, which were to be used in a complicated plan to transport Greenglass and his wife first to Mexico City, thence to Stockholm, and finally past the Iron Curtain to Czechoslovakia and eventually to the Soviet Union.[18] All these preparations occurred after Klaus Fuchs, the German scientist, had been caught in England in 1950 and presumably had named Harry Gold as his courier—or so Rosenberg suspected.[19] Rosenberg's fear was that the FBI would go up the line from Gold to Greenglass and thence to Rosenberg himself, a path that the FBI apparently did follow with the expected results. Rosenberg's awkward attempts to get information on required immunization shots for himself and his family and his visit to a photographer's shop to have passport shots of the family taken were part of the flight testimony offered against the Rosenbergs.[20]

Indeed, most of the case against Sobell had to do with his activities while in Mexico, whence he had fled after the Fuchs disclosures. In 1950, Sobell wandered across Mexico in a meandering course while his family remained in Mexico City.[21] There was little meaning in Sobell's hegira, except the one that the government ascribed to it: Sobell was looking for a way out of Mexico for his family and was searching for a sanctuary. Finally, Mexican authorities, under instructions from the FBI, and acting in their personal, unofficial capacities, took Sobell from his Mexico City apartment and spirited him back to the border, where he was turned over to Department of Justice officials for prosecution.[22]

All of the flight testimony involving the Greenglasses, the Rosenbergs, and Sobell concerned events that took place in 1950 and 1951, long after any of the known acts of spying. Moreover, a great part of Elitcher's testimony concerned events well after World War II, as Elitcher described his continuing postwar relationship with Sobell. The timing of all this has considerable relevance to the legal issues in this case.

In sum, if the jury chose to believe the Greenglasses, Harry Gold, and Max Elitcher, they had no choice but to convict. There was no external evidence of any substance exculpating the Rosenbergs. Since Sobell never took the stand, all that the defense gave the jury were the repeated denials of all wrongdoing by both Rosenbergs from the witness stand. Indeed, when the government tried to get the Rosenbergs to admit membership in the Communist party, when it tried to force descriptions of Communist party activity from either husband or wife, both refused to testify on the Fifth Amendment grounds that the testimony might incriminate them. Sitting, as they did, on the stand and offering, as they did, total denials of participation in either naval or atomic espionage, the Rosenbergs by these refusals severely damaged their case in the jury's eyes, regardless of the legalism that the refusals could not officially be used by the government against them.

The jury obviously believed Elitcher, Greenglass, and Gold and did not believe the Rosenbergs. Among the testimony most effective against all three defendants was the fact that all of the defendants—and the Greenglasses as well—were preparing to flee the country and Sobell had actually done so, apparently to avoid the prosecution now reaching its culmination before the Rosenberg jury. All of the foregoing went directly to the guilt or innocence of the Rosenbergs and Sobell and was never countered by external evidence. Given an abundance of evidence of conspiring to spy by the Greenglasses, by Gold, and by Elitcher, the jury faced only categoric denials from the Rosenbergs. When the government sought to cross-examine the Rosenbergs on their association with the Communist party in order to establish the motive for their conspiracy on behalf of the Soviet Union, there followed a series of invocations by Julius and Ethel Rosenberg of the Fifth Amendment. Observers then and now had little difficulty in accepting the jury finding of guilty as amply supported by this record. For many, that ended the argument on guilt or innocence; for some others, it raised the counterargument that the Rosenbergs had been framed. The resulting dispute has been simmering, but inconclusively, for years. It begins and ends with the evidence offered during the fourteen days of trial. With perhaps two exceptions, nothing of any substance has been added on either side since the trial.

The two exceptions proved to be the bases of an attempt, long after the trial, to *reopen* the case. The first was a console table that was in the Rosenberg apartment. The Greenglasses testified that it was a gift from the Russians and had a hollowed-out interior that Julius Rosenberg used to photograph documents for the Russians.[23] The Rosenbergs claimed they bought the table at Macy's, but testimony from Macy's employees could not prove their claim.[24] The table testimony was strong evidence against the Rosenbergs. The console table was not found by the Rosenberg defense until long after the trial. It then became the subject of an attempt to reopen the trial, which Judge Kaufman denied.

Posttrial evidence is always suspect. It is subject to the accusation that the defense held the evidence back during trial in order to have a basis for a posttrial motion. In this case, proof that the console table (which was never produced at trial) was bought at Macy's as the Rosenbergs claimed would have refuted Greenglass's contention at trial that the table came from the

Russians and was used to photograph documents. This proof would have been important and singular external evidence supporting the Rosenberg denials. But when the table itself was found after trial and became the subject of a Bloch motion for a retrial, Judge Kaufman denied the motion.

One other incident took place during the trial, but outside the courtroom. Irving Saypol, the prosecuting attorney, secured sworn testimony from William Perl, an old Rosenberg friend who, Saypol claimed, would corroborate the Greenglass testimony implicating the Rosenbergs. On March 15, 1951, during the middle of the trial (while Ruth Greenglass was on the stand), Saypol held a news conference to announce the Perl testimony, which got wide newspaper, radio, and television coverage. Since the Rosenberg jurors had not been sequestered (Bloch never requested it), all of the jurymen could have read the story or heard it over the air. Saypol, however, never used Perl. For the Rosenberg jurors, the implication remained that still another witness (whom they never heard or saw) was available to brand the Rosenbergs as spies. The reason that Saypol never used Perl is that Perl, again under oath, recanted his testimony. Perl's changed statements resulted in Perl's indictment, which Saypol announced at his press conference, also announcing why Perl had been slated to testify. The Perl episode was to cause the appellate and Supreme Court judges more pain than any other event at trial.

Emanuel Bloch, the attorney for Julius Rosenberg, received considerable criticism during the trial for a series of questionable defense moves. First, Bloch did nothing about the Perl episode, an omission that caused the reviewing courts to rule that Bloch had waived any objection to it. Second, Bloch had inexplicably moved to suppress from public view David Greenglass's rough sketch—drawn from memory—of the Nagasaki plutonium bomb.[25] Bloch's reason for this astonishing move was Bloch's statement that the sketch was top secret and should, therefore, not be made public. Since one of the defenses available to the Rosenbergs was that nothing that Greenglass, a machinist who had not finished high school, gave to the Russians constituted classified (let alone top secret) information, Bloch's move was then and is today inexplicable.

Bloch also never cross-examined Harry Gold, the courier. In an earlier case Gold had proved to be an inveterate spinner of fanciful tales—to the point where any jury listening to Gold's testimony had to doubt where Gold's real world ended and his fantasy world began. Bloch not only failed to cross-examine Gold, a damning witness, but stated in his summation to the jury that it was clear that Gold had told the truth.[26] Finally, Bloch put both Ethel and Julius Rosenberg on the stand to testify, thus ensuring they would be placed in a position of invoking the Fifth Amendment, with its negative impact on the jury.

Bloch was a fine human being. His devotion to the Rosenberg family, especially to their sons during and after the trial and execution, was laudable. His energy in support of his clients was inexhaustible. But his trial technique was a very different thing, and his deficiencies caused vast controversy during the trial. To this day, the purpose behind Bloch's trial strategy remains a mystery.

Major facts of the trial received no attention in 1951 and have had very little since. The nature of the charge, for example, is not generally known. Specifically, the Rosenbergs were not charged with, or convicted of, spying; rather, they were charged with and convicted of *conspiracy* to spy. Lay observers may miss this distinction and deem it to be one of those meaningless technicalities that lawyers enjoy fighting over, but the distinction had real significance because it enlarged the scope of the case. Among the most significant consequences of the government's choice to proceed with a conspiracy charge (rather than charging espionage itself) was the length and breadth of the conspiracy that the government charged and then had to prove.

The acts of espionage that came out at the trial all took place during World War II. Both the atomic ring and the naval ring passed their information to the Soviets in 1944 and 1945, before V-J Day. There was some evidence that Elitcher's activity continued after the war, but its focus was in Washington in late 1944 and early 1945. If the government had opted to charge the most obvious crimes apparent in the conduct of the Rosenbergs and Sobell, espionage itself, the prosecution would have had the limited burden of proving a very compact set of transactions by both rings carried out within a very short period of time, a period two years or less.

But the government, for very good reasons of its own that will be discussed in another chapter, chose not to prosecute either the Rosenbergs or Sobell for espionage; it chose to charge all three with conspiracy to commit espionage. By so doing, the government opened the door to the singular legal feature of the trial that has been so long ignored. The conspiracy charged by the government indictment began in 1944 and did not end until well into 1950.[27] Thus the government's proof went beyond the war, went beyond V-J Day, and, of significance to the point raised by this book, went well beyond August 1, 1946, the date when the Atomic Energy Act of 1946 went into effect. Had the government's case confined itself to those major acts of wartime espionage that it actually did prove, there would be no doubt but that the Atomic Energy Act of 1946 could not apply. It is an elementary rule of our constitutional law that a criminal statute cannot have retroactive application to anyone or any conduct. But, having chosen to charge the Rosenbergs and Sobell with a conspiracy that lasted well into 1950, the government removed the constitutional argument that the 1946 act could not apply. The 1946 act could and did apply, a conclusion that no one in this tragic drama ever argued to a court until the Rosenbergs were only three days from death.

Another fact about this case that has escaped notice was the government's heavy reliance on postwar (and post–August 1, 1946) conduct in convicting both the Rosenbergs and Sobell. The highly dramatic evidence of flight, which had to do with goings and comings of all of the dramatis personae (the Rosenbergs, the Greenglasses, the Sobells) of the case in 1950 and 1951, made up a substantial portion of the government's case. Moreover, a close reading of the trial transcript discloses that more than 35 percent of the testimony offered by the government dealt with events that took place after August 1, 1946, the date when the Atomic Energy Act of 1946 became effective.

Everything that the prosecution did in the Rosenberg case supports the conclusion that the Department of Justice and the prosecution team (made up of United States Attorney Irving

Saypol, his chief assistant Myles Lane, the bright and already controversial Roy Cohn, and James Kilsheimer) wanted not only a guilty verdict but something more as well. Saypol's decision to try the case himself (rather than allow his principal assistant, Lane, with whom he had a bitter rivalry, to try it) and the assignment of Lane, Cohn, and Kilsheimer to the case were evidence that the government had a strong and special interest in the case. Whether Irving Kaufman sought the case (as some contend), or took it in the ordinary course of assignment of judges, made that strong and special interest ever stronger. Finally, the choice made by the prosecution to charge the Rosenbergs with conspiracy (rather than spying) fit perfectly into the strong and special interest of the government. That interest, evident from the outset of the trial, was to secure the death penalty. The mass of prosecuting talent, the known and bitter anti-Communist bent of two of the prosecutors and the judge, evidenced what the government wanted. And the choice of the charge against the Rosenbergs demonstrated that the prosecution knew precisely how to get what it wanted.

The choice of charge that the government made was not an idle one. The choice to charge conspiracy rather than espionage opened to the government an extensive store of damaging testimony prominently used by the government and of obvious utility in convicting all three defendants. A very large part of that testimony *might* not have been available to the government if it had charged the Rosenbergs with simple espionage occurring in 1944. Certainly, the lurid tale of Sobell's flight, the only flight that any of the defendants or conspirators ever actually made, could have been used by the government against the Rosenbergs only if (1) it charged the Rosenbergs with a conspiracy embracing Sobell and (2) it extended that conspiracy until 1950, when Sobell took flight.

But the result of making this choice was a prosecution of both Rosenbergs and Sobell that was very different from the prosecution for espionage that might have been brought against the three. The conspiracy case that actually was brought in 1950 was far broader, far more incendiary to any sitting juror, and more compelling to jurors than a simple trial for espionage would have been.

Our system of justice commenced its treatment of the Rosenbergs at trial before Judge Irving Kaufman in March and April 1951. It reached its climax in a very different setting.

CHAPTER THREE

✦

SATURDAY, JUNE 13, 1953

THE NARRATIVE of the last week in the lives of Julius and Ethel Rosenberg is dominated by the activities of nine men sitting in the austere marble palace where the Supreme Court in its Olympian majesty dispenses justice. The capacities of the nine men who sat there as justices of the Court were incommensurate with the awesome majesty of their palace, however. In 1953, the Court was a polyglot mixture of retired politicians, lawyer-bureaucrats who had risen through the civil service to the top, and a few genuine intellectual leaders. And even those few—Douglas, Jackson, Frankfurter, and Black—had their lapses. Each had a monumental ego sensitive to real or imaginary slights.

The Supreme Court Building

For the Supreme Court in 1953, the weekly Saturday-afternoon conference of judges was the real nutcracking session. Once each week, the justices met alone in one room. The most recently appointed justice acted as messenger boy, sending out for documents needed by the justices to make up their minds in the cases before them. The individual justices did their deciding here, without secretaries, without clerks, and up against each other. If a justice was bright and energetic, he would shine in the conferences and gather votes for his side of each case. If he was dull-witted or lazy, it would be apparent. Performances at these conferences made or broke a new justice's reputation among his colleagues.

On June 13, 1953, at 10:00 in the morning, the last Saturday conference in the Court term began with Chief Justice Vinson fingering a pile of papers before him. The Court would convene the following Monday, June 15, announce opinions, and then recess for the summer vacation. Fred Vinson was a simple, unpretentious man, slow to burn, slow to excite, relatively slow to follow the path that some of his colleagues in the room skipped along at a much faster pace. Prior to his appointment to the Court, Vinson had served his country well during the war in a series of important jobs assigned him by his close friend, President Truman, culminating in wartime economic czar; Fred Vinson's contributions were loyalty, stability, and patriotism. He could be counted on—and that was his problem. He was predictable. His conservative views on this Court could be counted on in any tally of the votes.

These were the last days of the Roosevelt-Truman Supreme Court. Less than five months before, General Eisenhower had been sworn in as president. Within nine months of that June Saturday, the general-president was to appoint a new chief justice, Governor Earl Warren of California. A whole new era would open for the Supreme Court of the United States.

The Court's personnel seemed due for a dignified closing out of accounts. This Court was old and tired. The chief justice, never a vibrant man, had slowed markedly from his economic czar days. His old colleagues from the Senate, Harold Burton and Shay Minton, were even slower: Burton was visibly afflicted with Parkinson's disease, Minton had a heavy, slow-moving mind that grasped beginnings but little beyond them in any argument. Both were well past seventy. Stanley Reed had a lengthy term as solicitor general (within the Department of Justice) before he was appointed to the Court. Reed and Tom C. Clark, colleagues from the Department of Justice, were not much quicker. Clark was a younger man, but his conservative Texas background had bred into him a wariness of any new judicial moves. The youngest on the Court, he was nevertheless the most conservative.

Vinson, Minton, and Clark were termed by Court followers—not very deferentially—as "Harry Truman's law firm." Truman's views carried inordinate weight with all three; he had appointed them. The two generally voted together on all major issues.

Then there were Felix Frankfurter, Robert Jackson, William O. Douglas, and Hugo Black. They were the "liberals," but they were so split among themselves, so taken up with highly disparate philosophies of the law, that unity among them was rare. Frankfurter was a true intellectual, a lifelong law professor at Harvard, worlds apart from the hurly-burly of the law and, many believed, just as removed from the reality of how the law and the courts affected the lives of ordinary people. Jackson, the former solicitor general and prosecutor at Nuremberg, had a carefully honed legal mind but a hypersensitive ego. Strong, even violent, in his personal likes and dislikes, he was to spend years on the same court with a colleague, Justice Hugo Black of Alabama, to whom, out of some fancied slight and doctrinal disagreements so abstruse that only law professors could understand them, he never addressed a word.

Then there was Bill Douglas. Douglas was a westerner from Goose Prairie, Washington, an outdoorsman, a devoted fisherman and maverick. He was also possessed of a brilliant, incisive, independent mind. He had come East to teach at Columbia and caught the eye of Jerome Frank, among other New Deal talent scouts. Douglas then became one of the early New Deal reformers. He was chairman of the SEC when President Roosevelt appointed him to the Supreme Court in 1938.

One could seldom predict Douglas, though he had clear political leanings. They were consistently Democratic, reflecting the liberal New Deal wing of that party. These beliefs, Douglas's rough-hewn visage and outspoken independence, were all politically attractive. He received considerable support for the Democratic nomination for president in 1952. But the private Douglas was very different. Few could fathom what his basic principles were or where they would take him. And for a considerable number of his acquaintances, the private Douglas, on the Court and off, was far less attractive than the public Douglas.

Bill Douglas had his own very special role in the Rosenberg case. The role had begun eight months before June 13, 1953.

The Supreme Court Building, 9:00 A.M.

That Saturday, June 13, had begun with a blaze of activity in the austere Supreme Court building. Precisely at 9:00 A.M., two of the lawyers for the Rosenbergs had half-walked, half-run up the marble steps and down the silent corridors to the clerk's office. The assistant clerks at the Supreme Court were by now familiar with the Rosenberg lawyers, Emanuel Bloch and Professor Malcolm Sharp of the University of Chicago Law School. Bloch was a warm and humane man who had dedicated his professional life to the Rosenberg case, but whose performance reflected the depth as well as the blunting of judgment that such dedication often brings about. Sharp was a latecomer to the case whose help had been sought when the case went to the appeals courts.

When Bloch and Professor Sharp moved briskly up the marble steps, the Rosenberg lawyers were embarking on their fifth full-scale effort to seek relief from the Supreme Court. In cases where the death penalty is involved, repeated legal efforts in the High Court seeking relief are customary; but Bloch, first alone, and then with Sharp and John Finerty, a volatile Irishman (and veteran of the Tom Mooney case that brought Finerty fame) who also helped on the appeals, had trod and retrod every path that might lead to relief—any relief—for the Rosenbergs with a zeal that was singular. By Saturday, June 13, 1953, the team had made five separate applications to trial judge Irving Kaufman in New York, or to colleagues of Judge Kaufman on that court, all seeking relief for the Rosenbergs. All were summarily denied. They had made five separate applications to the Second Circuit Court of Appeals, and all had been denied. And they had made numerous prior applications to the Supreme Court, and had failed each time: each failure accompanied by a full litany of requests for rehearing or reconsiderations that, in turn, had also been denied. If zeal were the sole criterion of effectiveness in getting a client's conviction reversed, Bloch and his colleagues would have restored the Rosenbergs to their family and friends months before June of 1953. But zeal was only part of what was required, especially in the Rosenberg case.

On that Saturday morning, Bloch and Sharp went straight to the clerk's office on the ground floor of the court building; their purpose was to go from there to Justice Jackson's chambers to press the justice personally to intervene. Bloch's stay papers had been filed the preceding day; with near-automatic precision, the Department of Justice had filed opposing papers within four hours. In the quickening pace of this last week before the Rosenbergs' death, no grass grew under any of the lawyers. Nor did any of them on either side sleep more than a few hours at a time.[1]

Very shortly after 10:00 on that early Saturday morning, three men from the Department of Justice joined the small group in the clerk's office. One was Robert Erdahl of the department's Criminal Division, an expert in criminal procedure who had virtually lived with the government's side of the Rosenberg case since it began. His aide, John Williams, was with him. The third man was the government's top courtroom lawyer, Acting Solicitor General Robert Stern. He was there because it was government practice for the solicitor general to make all representations or arguments to the Supreme Court of the United States, or to choose the person who would. In addition, this particular acting solicitor general had a good deal of knowledge about what was going on that morning because this was the second time that the same arguments had been made to the Court, and Stern had personally been involved in the defeat of the Rosenberg lawyers on the earlier occasion.

When everyone was ready, Deputy Chief Clerk Cullinane began the slow march from the clerk's office to Justice Jackson's chambers. Although this whole exercise was to take place before one justice, and in his chambers, the imperial quality of the Supreme Court was apparent: the lawyers, led by Cullinane, marched in a prescribed order through the empty marble corridors. Justice Jackson had been chosen to hear this argument because he had nominal supervision of cases that came from New York, in the Second Circuit, where the Rosenbergs had been tried.

Newsreel: June 11–13, 1953*

As the lawyers for the Rosenbergs walked to their hearing before Justice Jackson on Saturday, June 13, 1953, there were few dispassionate Americans abroad in the land insofar as the "Red menace" was concerned.

The entire country was embroiled in battles with Communists, real and fancied, all over the world. If there was a predominant mood in this country in June of 1953, it was anti-Communist. That mood was at its peak at that very time, in June of 1953.

It is impossible to assess the rights and wrongs of the Rosenberg case in its final days without placing it in the perspective of this national mood. After all, the Rosenbergs were charged and convicted spies for the Soviet Union. This was the same antagonist that American troops were facing that June across battlefields in Korea. This was the same antagonist that had marched boldly into Eastern Europe in 1944, 1945, and 1946 and had set up totalitarian regimes that gave the lie to President Roosevelt's Four Freedoms. This was the same antagonist that had isolated Berlin in 1948, necessitating an American airlift.

The predominant mood in this country was not based on foreign events alone. In 1947, Harry Truman, a man known for realism and a distaste for cant, had instituted a loyalty program for federal employees. This was a domestic outcropping of the same fears of the Soviets that figured so largely in the history of Europe and the Far East between 1946 and 1953. Before any major politician had uttered a word in anger in 1950, the Red scare was a feature of American life.

---

* All events described in "Newsreel" sections are taken from contemporary issues of the *New York Times* or the *Washington Post*.

In February of 1950, these domestic fears turned to hysteria. In a speech in Wheeling, West Virginia, the junior senator from Wisconsin, a former Marine Air Force flier by the name of Joe McCarthy, had seized on the communism-in-government issue with the zeal of an opportunist smarting under the label of mediocrity that everything he did in Washington clearly carried. Joe McCarthy, under clever guidance from people who should have known him and the times better, was to make communism-in-government a paranoia that Americans will never forget. From his announcement in Wheeling that he had in his hands the case records of over two hundred Communists then employed in the State Department, McCarthy went from half-truth to innuendo to straight lie with unflagging zeal in the next two years. His numbers game about Reds in Washington went way up and then came down, only to go back up again when he felt that the public needed a bit of jarring for McCarthy's own ends. Public servants were not the sole targets of his accusations. Scientists, teachers, state and local officials, all felt the fear of being accused of beliefs that permitted no rational defense. Because McCarthyism was not aimed at Communists at all. It was aimed at those whom McCarthy wished to destroy and aimed at publicizing Joe McCarthy. And in order to do both, the accusation had to be broad enough and vague enough to elude all possible defense, and especially elude it in the columns of newspapers that devoted tremendous publicity to McCarthy's accusations.

Just as the foreign fight against communism reached its peak in June of 1953, so did McCarthyism. Both of these components of the public mood went on for a long time after that. But peace in Korea—just one month after the Rosenbergs died—and McCarthy's public humiliation in the Army hearings just one year later made June of 1953 a high-water mark of anti-Communist feeling in this country.

It may well be said that among other things, Julius and Ethel Rosenberg were phenomenally unlucky. Certainly the unlucky assignment of Judge Irving Kaufman to their case was strong evidence of this. Even stronger was the mood of the public that confronted the Rosenbergs—and the Supreme Court of the

United States—in the last days of this case. At a series of junctures during that last week, events in our foreign confrontations with communism and in the systematized domestic paranoia known as McCarthyism were very relevant to this mood. They both lend perspective to what was happening in the highest court of the land, which proved so thoroughly in that week what Mr. Dooley had guessed long before: the justices certainly did read the newspapers.

Two days before the Supreme Court was to meet in its final conference on the Rosenberg case, a mass of seven thousand Chinese troops had hurled themselves against the American position near the Kaesong Reservoir in Korea. On the day before the Supreme Court judges convened in the Rosenberg case (on June 13, 1953), President Syngman Rhee of Korea stated that the peace proposal for Korea (then under consideration) meant the death of his nation at the hands of the Reds, and newspapers across the land headlined the statement. The Korean attack was then matched by an even more massive offensive of waves of Chinese infantrymen throwing themselves at American (and United Nations) lines on June 13. On June 12, Secretary of Defense Charles ("Engine Charlie") Wilson, fresh out of General Motors, stated in a national interview that it was his opinion that the United States could defeat the Soviet Union if World War III erupted out of Korea.

In the days immediately before June 13, 1953, domestic communism was just as much a part of American anxieties as the armed fight abroad. On June 12, Albert Einstein, already a Nobel laureate, announced to the intellectuals in this country that it was his advice to all of them to refuse to testify if one of the Red-hunting committees of Congress subpoenaed them. Seven teachers in New York City faced firing on June 13, 1953, because of earlier Communist party affiliation. Page 8 of the *New York Times* on that date announced that there was a center of Red activity located near the Los Alamos laboratory without announcing the details of what the Red activity was supposed to be. The magazine section of the *Times* on Sunday, June 14, carried a feature article by Elizabeth Janeway, "Why They Became Communists," delineating the paths of a number of intellectuals into the Party in the thirties and forties.

On June 10, the U.S. government announced that it was purging its libraries at embassies in Germany of all suspected Communist propaganda. That same day, Morris Ploscowe, an eminent New York jurist, stated that organized crime was "Communism's best ally" and that both must be destroyed "if democracy was to survive." On the tenth it was announced in Washington that sixty-two diplomats of various nationalities, all now present in the United States, had been linked to spy cases. The Navy Department warned that "some Navy officers have so taken to heart new security regulations on information that they are hiding routine official papers from one another." A New York movie critic reviewing Clark Gable's *Never Let Me Go* brought the mood to the screen, stating, "It is cheering to have the reassurances that Clark Gable is one fellow, at least, who can still make the Soviet Union tough guys look like absolute monkeys—and does."

On June 17, two former OSS aides defied a congressional inquiry into their leftist leanings. On June 13, the state of Delaware announced that it was requiring all Communists within Delaware to register.

This was the national mood at the beginning of the third week in June 1953, the last week in the Rosenberg case.

The Hole That Douglas Dug for Himself

By that Saturday morning in June 1953, the American public had ceased paying close attention to the Rosenbergs following their conviction and sentencing twenty-six months earlier in April 1951. As the case wended its way higher through the courts, the accepted public view was that the appeals court and the Supreme Court were both being careful because two death sentences had been imposed. But the prevailing public wisdom also believed that the Rosenbergs had been given a proper trial by a fair, if tough, judge. The public fully expected that the death sentences would be carried out after the lawyers had finished making their lengthy, expected noises.

By late 1952, the direct appeals from Kaufman's sentence had already been before the Court of Appeals and the Supreme Court. Apart from a strongly worded dissent by Judge Jerome Frank concerning Sobell, the Rosenbergs got nothing. Similarly, their petition to the Supreme Court for a writ of certiorari—in effect, asking the Supreme Court to accept the case for review on all of its issues and requiring the votes of four justices of the Supreme Court—had been denied. Only Black had dissented. Frankfurter concurred with Black but refrained from dissenting because of his long-standing reluctance to dissent from denials of certiorari.

The public may have lost interest in the Rosenbergs after their trial, but this was not the view within the courts charged with reviewing the Rosenberg case. From October of 1952 on, the public's view that all had gone properly in the Rosenbergs' trial before Judge Kaufman was not shared by at least two of the justices—Black and Frankfurter—of the Supreme Court of the United States. It was not revealed to the public, but for a full eight months prior to the fateful third week of June 1953, the Supreme Court was bitterly divided over whether Judge Irving Kaufman had given the Rosenbergs a fair trial. On one occasion during those eight months, it was Bill Douglas—the same Bill Douglas who stirred the world months later with his stay of execution— whose *negative* vote prevented the Supreme Court from granting certiorari, which, if granted, would have allowed the Supreme Court to take a close and searching look at the controversial events that occurred in the trial before Kaufman.

Later, on another occasion only twenty-seven days before they were executed, the Rosenbergs actually secured the votes of four justices required for a full Supreme Court review of these major issues. But then Douglas reversed himself in a private turnabout in the justices' conference, a turnabout never known to the public but felt keenly by Douglas's brethren on the Court. That Douglas reversal again deprived the Rosenbergs of the four votes required for Supreme Court review.

This Douglas reversal brought down on his head some of the harshest words ever spoken (and recorded privately) by one Supreme Court justice commenting on—and, in this case, bitterly castigating—another. Douglas's volte-face left the Rosenbergs again one vote short. And even this was not the last reversal of conscience by Bill Douglas. Douglas's performance throughout the case stands as one of the mysteries of a case that had more than its share of unfathomable judicial conduct.

What were the queasy feelings that the justices had about Kaufman's trial? Why did Douglas flail about in the eight months before his grand climax stunned the world on June 17, 1953? What happened in those months before Douglas became the apparent hero in June 1953? Two examples provide a vivid backdrop to Bill Douglas's conduct during those eight months that so prejudiced the minds of his colleagues on the Court in that last week of life for the Rosenbergs.

The first example occurred in October of 1952. It concerned whether the Rosenbergs had, in reality, been charged with treason against their country. Treason is a crime defined in Article III, Section 3 of the Constitution; it requires the proof of two witnesses, neither an accomplice to the act of treason. This level of proof of treason had not been made at trial against the Rosenbergs. The Rosenbergs also argued that imposing on them the death penalty without the protection of the treason clause of the Constitution was "cruel and unusual punishment." But the Rosenberg argument had been summarily rejected by Judge Ryan in a motion made after the close of the trial. The Second Circuit Court of Appeals heard this posttrial motion and affirmed Kaufman. But Judge Jerome Frank, a judge of great probity and prestige, had his own qualms. In his opinion, Judge Frank openly requested the Supreme Court to review this point.[2] Four votes were required if the Supreme Court would accede to Frank's request.

Justice Black, who never swerved from his opinion that Kaufman had mistried the case, voted to review. Frankfurter, who had strong notions about the death penalty and cast a gimlet eye over all criminal prosecutions, joined Black, voting for review. Justice Burton said, as recorded by Frankfurter: "This was a death case about which two justices seemed to have strong feelings. He would join them."[3]

The Court was only one vote short of accepting the case for review. But that vote was *not* Bill Douglas's. Justice Frankfurter stated in his private memorandum: "Douglas . . . denys are usually curt and unaccompanied by argument. His 'deny' this time was unaccompanied by argument. But it was uttered with startling vehemence."[4]

Jackson, Reed, Minton, Clark, and Chief Justice Vinson joined Douglas. Four judicial consciences (including that of Judge Jerome Frank) had been stirred, but not Douglas's. The Rosenberg petition was rejected in October 1952 for lack of four votes in the Supreme Court. Bill Douglas's vote would have been that vital fourth vote.

In the spring of 1953, the growing dissatisfaction over Kaufman's handling of the trial would not dissipate inside the marble chambers of the High Court. It boiled up again when the Rosenberg lawyers filed a posttrial motion protesting a Saypol press conference during the middle of the Rosenberg trial. Saypol's conduct in announcing to the world that Perl would corroborate the Rosenbergs' guilt—and then never putting Perl on the stand—would cause more grief to more judges than any other event during the trial. It caused no grief for Kaufman, who denied the Rosenbergs' motion summarily. But when Saypol's conduct came before Judge Swan of the Second Circuit (on appeal from Kaufman's denial), Swan stated flatly: "Such a statement to the press in the course of a trial we regard as wholly reprehensible."[5]

Swan added: "If the Defendants than (upon the trial) moved for a mistrial, it should have been granted."[6] But Bloch had not done so. Swan and his colleagues concluded that this failure constituted a waiver by the Rosenbergs of Saypol's conduct.*[7]

In the Supreme Court, Saypol's conduct brought on a judicial waltz never seen before or since. Bloch filed a petition on March 30, 1953, seeking Supreme Court review of Saypol's conduct. Black was first to make clear to his brethren that Saypol's conduct was typical of what he, Black, had been arguing all along: the trial was unfair. Douglas opted against review, as was expected. Frankfurter's conscience, never at rest in this case, reacted violently—for Frankfurter. Frankfurter wanted review of Saypol's conduct. Clearly lacking four votes to bring Saypol's conduct before the Court for review, Frankfurter wrestled with his conscience through three regularly scheduled judicial conferences trying to decide whether to publish his views in a dissent (a practice Frankfurter did not believe in) when the Court announced the inevitable denial of certiorari. Burton, who often followed Frankfurter, this time voted the other way, against review.

Then the pace picked up. After Frankfurter pleaded for still more time in the *fourth* justices' conference, on May 16, Jackson (Frankfurter's closest intellectual ally on the Court) continued to oppose review but had his own questions. He told Frankfurter: "I cannot imagine that you can be too severe on him [Saypol], to suit me."[8]

Lightning then struck. On May 22, Douglas circulated a memorandum reversing himself—stating that he had changed his

---

* Two comments by members of the Court of Appeals on this point reflect the growing concern over what had occurred at the Rosenberg trial. Once again, Judge Jerome Frank specifically stated that the Saypol point had merit, "and for my part, I believe the Supreme Court should hear it." When the Second Circuit stayed the execution of the Rosenbergs until the Supreme Court could hear the Saypol point, the government objected. Judge Learned Hand, a judge sitting on the Second Circuit and perhaps the most highly respected judge on any court in the land, then rebuked the government in open court: "People don't dispose of lives," he said, "just because an attorney didn't make a point. There are some Justices on the Supreme Court on whom the conduct of the prosecuting attorney might make an impression. . . . Your duty, Mr. Prosecutor, is to seek justice, not act as timekeeper." (Quoted in Robert and Michael Meeropol, *We Are Your Sons* [Boston: Houghton Mifflin, 1975] 187.)

mind. As he commented in his surprise memorandum of May 22 to all eight brethren:

I do not believe that the conduct of the prosecutor can be as easily dispensed of as the Court of Appeals think. I therefore have reluctantly concluded that certiorari should be granted.

Accordingly, I will ask that the order of denial carry the following notation:

"Mr. Justice Douglas, agreeing with the Court of Appeals that some of the conduct of the United States Attorney was 'wholly reprehensible' but believing, in disagreement with the Court of Appeals, that it probably prejudiced the Defendants seriously, voted to grant certiorari."[9]

To any of the justices who had strong doubts concerning Kaufman's conduct at trial, Douglas's memorandum was a bolt from the blue.

Frankfurter now urged a fifth judges' conference in light of Douglas's change of heart. Jackson felt then (and later) that Douglas pandered to his liberal supporters and did so when Douglas was sure he would not have to publicly state his views on the merits of the Rosenberg case. Thus, Jackson felt that Douglas voted for Supreme Court review of *Rosenberg* only when he was sure it would not be granted. Jackson, who felt strongly on everything—but particularly Douglas—then commented to Frankfurter on the Douglas memorandum (quoted above), in words recorded by a startled Frankfurter: "Then Jackson said—I quote from memory, but, I think, with substantial accuracy: 'Douglas' memorandum is the dirtiest, most shameful, most cynical performance that I think I have ever heard of in matters pertaining to the law.' "*[10] Strong words, but stronger ones were to follow.

At the May 23 conference, called to deal with the Douglas memorandum and its effect on the public, Jackson declared that the Douglas memorandum would severely damage the Court. Rather than allow that, Jackson announced, he would vote to

---

* Jackson's volcanic eruption over the Douglas memorandum is hard to understand unless it is placed within the context of Jackson's belief that Douglas was playing to a political constituency. A number of Jackson's statements quoted herein reflect this belief.

grant certiorari and thus prevent Douglas's words from reaching the public.[11] Burton, after receiving a letter from Frankfurter, also voted for review. Douglas, Burton, Frankfurter, and Jackson provided the four votes necessary to accept for review the Rosenberg petition involving Saypol's conduct. The chief justice then went about the chore of setting a date for oral argument. July 6 looked like the best date, given the pressures on the entire Court to expedite its consideration of the case. Burton had booked passage for Europe on July 11, but realizing that he would be engaged in deliberating over the Saypol point at that time, agreed to cancel his plans.[12]

Frankfurter's own notes in his papers best describe what happened next at the May 23 judicial conference:

At about this point, the discussion having gone on for quite some little time, Douglas spoke up. He had been quiet since announcing that he would grant. He ought to say something, he started. What he had written was badly drawn, he guessed. He hadn't realized it would embarrass anyone. He would just withdraw his memorandum if that would help matters.

If Douglas' memorandum was withdrawn, Jackson said, we were exactly where we had been before, and there was no longer any reason for him to change his vote.

And so Douglas, when it became clear that the Rosenberg case would be heard because of the memorandum he had circulated in explanation of his change of position, kept it from being heard. Voting to grant, he effectively prevented the grant. Jackson had made it perfectly clear that the reason for his own change of heart was the memorandum Douglas proposed to print if the grant was not voted. Whatever else Jackson may have said, publication of the Douglas memorandum was for him unmistakably the decisive factor. Withdrawal of the Douglas memorandum obviously would leave no reason for Jackson to change his previous vote in favor of denial.* [13]

With Black ill and not voting, and Jackson changing sides, review was denied. Douglas, in his own way, had again acted to prevent review of the case. Douglas's maneuvering was not

---

* On May 25, two days after the May 23 conference, the Supreme Court dutifully denied certiorari—again. This time based on Bill Douglas's flip-flop.

without further comment from Jackson. Again, a startled Frankfurter heard strong language from Jackson as the justices left the
May 23 conference: "Jackson said to me, and again I quote from
memory, but I believe, accurately: 'That S.O.B.'s bluff was
called.' "[14]

Those words were spoken twenty-five days before Douglas
issued his stay of execution. It is not surprising that when Douglas
did act twenty-five days later, he knew full well that his act would
be received by a hostile Court and that his stay was doomed.
Douglas's own conduct had not helped the Rosenbergs.

Bill Douglas had begun to build an intellectual, indeed moral,
fence between himself and his colleagues. It took eight months
before the third week of June 1953 to do it. But Douglas had
certainly isolated himself on the Supreme Court by that date.

Supreme Court, Justice Jackson's Chambers

When Jackson confronted the lawyers on both sides of the case
at 10:30 on the morning of June 13, 1953, the Supreme Court had
already had its fill of the Rosenberg case. The venture of the
Rosenberg lawyers into Justice Jackson's chambers that Saturday
morning was the fifth time the nine justices had been confronted
with this nightmare. For each of them, the Rosenberg case was
indeed a nightmare. It brought out the worst in some and the best
in others. This case had brought to a boil the personal hostilities
within the Court. Now Bloch had a series of points, all raised by
him since the Rosenberg defeat before the Court on May 25, only
nineteen days earlier.

The points raised by Bloch and Sharp's petition put before
Justice Jackson on that Saturday morning, June 13, were three.
While none disturbed the Court as much as those that led to the
Douglas turnabout and the Rosenberg defeat of May 25, these
new points—in the seemingly inexhaustible supply of legal
disputes that sprang from the conduct of the trial—belatedly
caused a stir within the Supreme Court.

First, Bloch had finally found the console table that David
Greenglass testified was located within the Rosenberg apartment.
In affidavits submitted to trial judge Kaufman, the defense

asserted that the table did not comport with the description given it by Greenglass at trial. The second point had to do with materials that inexplicably had found their way from Greenglass's lawyers' office into Bloch's hands, allegedly demonstrating that Greenglass had made statements to his lawyers and to the FBI that were inconsistent with his trial testimony. The third was a set of affidavits concerning the theft and disposal of a small quantity of uranium by Greenglass from Los Alamos. That theft, the defense claimed, put Greenglass in fear of prosecution and led him to lie on behalf of the government in the Rosenberg trial.

These three points were, when made, the Rosenberg's last gasp. They were put before trial judge Kaufman on June 6, twelve days after the Supreme Court had rejected the major Rosenberg contention on May 25. Indeed, they sounded like a dying gasp. On June 6, the Rosenbergs were to die only twelve days later, on June 18.

Beginning the rush to execution, both Kaufman and the Court of Appeals gave these new points short shrift. Kaufman denied Bloch's motion (based on them) on Monday, June 8. The Rosenberg lawyers appeared in the Second Circuit Court of Appeals on the next day, June 9, to request a stay of the Rosenbergs' execution to allow them to brief these points to that court. The lawyers were directed to argue their case on that very day without briefs, and did. Next day, on the tenth, the Rosenberg lawyers filed a document with the Court of Appeals listing the points they would have briefed had time been given them. On June 11, the Court of Appeals rejected the entire defense submission and ordered the executions to go forward on June 18.

The documents put in Justice Jackson's hands on Saturday, June 13, contained these three points and a request for a stay to brief them. There were other points included, but they were incidental to the three. The points that had been floated before Kaufman on June 6 and sank within a week did not exercise the Court as had Saypol's conduct (which had tied the Court in knots for over a month before the Rosenbergs' defeat on May 25). But belated and redolent of desperation, there they were: three additional points in a case that would simply not disappear, put before Justice Jackson on Saturday, June 13, the same Justice

Jackson whose temper had been signally displayed when the Rosenbergs had suffered their last defeat in the Supreme Court on May 25.

What happened during the next six days in that Court was the climax of the bitter internal strife that hung like a pall over the Vinson Court. Nowhere was that bickering, hostility-laden in-fighting more evident than in the Court's treatment of the con-victed conspirators in their last failing attempts to get the Court's attention. As Emanuel Bloch and Malcolm Sharp marched into Jackson's chambers on June 13, they could not have known that the struggle among the justices during the preceding eight months was a precursor of doom for the Rosenbergs. That internecine warfare within the Court ended in a tragic, ill-advised rush to judgment during six haste-filled days that June of 1953.

In Jackson's chambers, the small procession waited until the justice was ready for them. They then were ushered in, and the lawyers shook Justice Jackson's hand. All of the players in that room were well known to Jackson by that Saturday morning. None of the justices wear robes in chambers, so Jackson was in a light summer suit that hot morning. Chairs had been arranged so that the Rosenberg lawyers would sit to the left of the justice and government counsel to the right.

Bloch began. He explained why he was there with his request. In essence, he was asking for a stay of the Rosenbergs' execution while all of the legal points raised by him since May 25 could be considered by the Court. All of them had been set out in papers before Jackson, and Bloch was terrified that the Court might not act on them on the following Monday. He was equally terrified that the Court *would* act on them without the briefing that Bloch felt was so necessary. In either event, the Court would adjourn without fair consideration of Bloch's desperate arguments. Far more important, the Rosenbergs would die the following Thurs-day night at Sing Sing, and this must not be allowed to happen while the Supreme Court had any unresolved issues about the case before it. It must not happen, Bloch argued, if these issues were brushed aside by the Court without proper briefing. Bloch said that Jackson, or any other justice, could stay the execution himself, which was quite true.

Robert Stern was about to begin when the justice interrupted. He spoke directly to Bloch in short, clipped tones that seemed brusque as the justice's pince-nez waggled with emphasis. Jackson said that the Rosenberg case was already before the full Court for its action; Bloch's request should also be heard by the full Court. He would take the request to the Court for its conference later during the day and ask that the Court include this new request in whatever order the Court entered in the case in its final session that summer, two days later, on Monday, June 15.

To Bloch and Sharp, it seemed like another defeat. They felt they had failed to move Jackson. His words about the Court's ultimate order on Monday sounded foreboding. The lawyers suspected that Jackson was telling them something far beyond what he intended to do with the papers before him. But Bloch and Sharp, so accustomed to adversity, were wrong this time. Jackson had been moved—somewhat. And his conduct at the conference that afternoon reflected this.

Saturday Morning

Late that Saturday morning, June 13, 1953, the scene shifted to a small hotel on the West Side of Manhattan. An important new chapter was added to the drama. Fyke Farmer, the Tennessee lawyer whose theory four days later stayed the execution of the Rosenbergs and caused the Supreme Court of the United States to reconvene, was in a quandary.

Farmer spent that Saturday morning in a futile attempt to get a document into the hands of a federal judge—*any* federal judge— in New York City.[15] Fyke Farmer was a total newcomer to the Rosenberg case. He was an outsider, and since he was a lawyer *and* an outsider, everything he attempted to do for the next six days was clouded by the fact of his *being* an outsider. Farmer had made up his mind months before that the processes of federal justice had gone completely wrong in the Rosenberg case and that he, Fyke Farmer, alone if necessary, was going to do something about it.

It was typical of Farmer to take on the assembled forces of the United States Department of Justice and the fixed opinion of a thoroughly determined judge, Irving Kaufman, in New York City. Farmer was—and is—the quintessential free thinker. Among his various firmly held beliefs were (and are) World Federalism and international control of nuclear energy. He was a firm believer in international control of this great new power science had given to the world.

Farmer had read everything that had been written about our development of nuclear energy, including the Smyth Report of 1945. The Smyth Report was a comprehensive detailing of the American effort to pierce the atom by fission, creation of a chain reaction, and the unlocking of massive amounts of energy for military and peaceful uses. He was conversant (as much as a scientifically knowledgeable layman could be) with the rudiments of implosion, of a chain reaction and other technical aspects of nuclear weapons. He was also a student of the academic exchange of information on nuclear energy before World War II. He understood that there were few, if any, secrets within the international scientific community regarding the *potential* of atomic power. In his quiet but firm way, Farmer doubted that anyone, anywhere, could really give away the secrets of the bomb. When he read Kaufman's sentence while in Europe, he concluded that Kaufman was completely wrong. Again, he was appalled that Kaufman's error involved the imposition of two death sentences. When Farmer returned to the States in 1952, he was determined to do something about it.

Earlier, he had managed a private meeting with President Truman on the question of international control of nuclear energy only to find that the Atomic Energy Act of 1946 was already law and had doomed any semblance of international control of nuclear energy.

The most important facet of Farmer's entry into the Rosenberg case was that Farmer came in as an independent, and very solitary, advocate. He was not part of any committee supporting the Rosenbergs. Farmer's softly spoken statements of conscience were so independent that none of the left wing groups aiding the Rosenbergs ever dared to enlist him among their numbers. Farmer *had* been influenced by a pamphlet published by a Los Angeles radical, Irwin Edelman, entitled *Freedom's Execution,* but that pamphlet's denunciation of the justice being given the Rosenbergs only reaffirmed Farmer's view that the damned-fool Department of Justice and that fool of a trial judge were pronouncing idiocy when they claimed that David Greenglass or Ethel or Julius Rosenberg had given the Soviets the secret of the bomb. And Farmer, who today, in 1988, will not pay the license-tag fee Tennessee levies on his automobile because of his disagreement over how Tennessee spends a portion of that license fee, disagreed with everything he read about the Rosenberg case. Being Farmer, he decided to do something about it.

Farmer was the inventor of the lever that moved the judicial world in the last days of the Rosenberg case. To begin with, he had studied the Atomic Energy Act of 1946 because of his interest in international control of nuclear energy; Farmer was dissatisfied that the United States had opted for closed, secret, internal control of atomic information—which Farmer believed impossible in the scientific world of the fifties. And when Farmer read the Atomic Energy Act of 1946, and then read the published accounts of the Rosenberg case, Farmer concluded that the entire prosecution was misconceived. To Farmer, Kaufman's sentence was not only nonsense, it was a tragic, human error. Edelman's pamphlet may have encouraged Farmer; but everything that Farmer did in the Rosenberg case came out of Farmer's conscience and from no other source or motive.

Farmer spent many days in May attempting to meet with Bloch to try to explain to Bloch that the Rosenbergs had at least two valid defenses under the Atomic Energy Act of 1946. Bloch, the urban cosmopolite steeped in the ideological background to the case (the McCarthy movement), gave Farmer short shrift. To Bloch, Farmer was a Tennessee hillbilly who might detract from the central evil of a conviction and death sentence brought about by this country's anti-Communist paranoia. Bloch and Farmer met once in May 1953. Farmer believes today that when he told Bloch about the Atomic Energy Act of 1946, Bloch never understood what Farmer was talking about. Events proved that to be true.

To Farmer, there were three important events that moved him. One was Eisenhower's denial of clemency for the Rosen-

bergs in February 1953. The second was his meeting with Bloch
in May 1953 that told Farmer that he would get no cooperation
from Bloch. The third was the rescheduling by Kaufman of the
date for execution of the Rosenbergs for the week of June 15.

So Farmer, waiting as long as he felt he could, finally traveled
to New York on June 13, 1953, by himself, using his own money
and with no claim that he represented anyone but Edelman, to do
battle with the conglomeration of fools—or worse—who,
Farmer believed, would perpetrate a tragedy in the week of June
15. When Farmer arrived in New York and went to a modest
hotel on June 13, he was a lone combatant whom Cervantes could
best comprehend. Farmer had no fees, no expense money, to tilt
with *his* windmill. He was burdened by Bloch's clear distaste for
anything he might do. The only thing that Farmer had was his
own stubbornness—and an undertaking from Edelman that
Farmer could put Edelman's name to any pleading Farmer chose
to file. Farmer doubted that this would be of much help. He was
right.

Before Farmer left for New York, he had drafted a sixty-one-
page petition for writ of habeas corpus. It covered every point in
the Rosenberg case that occurred to Farmer. But at page 16, it
covered a point that had not yet been heard—or at least given
serious consideration—by a single judge of the fifteen (including
the nine justices of the Supreme Court) who had read official
papers about this case at least four times before June 13, and had
lifted not a finger about what they had heard. Farmer's fateful
words were:

If the defendants had been prosecuted under the Atomic Energy Act
the death penalty could not have been inflicted for the offense with
which they were charged. As has already been shown [in earlier portions
of the same 61-page document] the penalty for death under the Atomic
Energy Act can only be imposed on recommendation of the jury and
then only when the jury finds that the accused had the intent to injure
the United States.[16]

Farmer then cited the appropriate provisions of the 1946 Atomic
Energy Act. He added:

The indictment in the case at bar did not charge that the defendants conspired with intent to injure the United States.[17]

And, indeed, it had not. The Saypol indictment, drawn under the 1917 Espionage Act, simply alleged that the Rosenbergs had acted "to the advantage of a foreign national." Nor had any *jury* recommended the death penalty. It was Kaufman's *personal,* emphatically pronounced sentence that the Rosenbergs had acted to the advantage of the USSR—a very different matter and worlds easier to prove in this case. Quoted above, Farmer's words, in various papers and arguments, were to dominate all the events remaining in the next six days until the Rosenbergs died just after 8:00 P.M. on Friday, June 19.

The question for Farmer, who might have been a Tennessee lawyer but who fully recognized the combination of forces of the federal government arrayed against him, was what to do with this sixty-one page document now that he and it had arrived in New York City. He had looked at the law carefully—Farmer has always been a stickler for each word of a statute—and found that he had the right to present his document (which was in formal form a writ of habeas corpus, a vehicle for attacking everything that had occurred up to June 13 in the Rosenberg prosecution) to *any* federal judge. Farmer knew personally one such federal judge, Judge Edward Dimock, who sat in New York. Dimock had been on the Reporting Committee of the American Bar Association with Farmer (who was one of Tennessee's representatives on this board of the ABA). On June 13, Farmer called Dimock and said that he wanted to see him. Dimock, who respected Farmer, consented to meet Farmer at his home in Manhattan.

Farmer, who had a country way of getting right to the point, gave a surprised Dimock Farmer's sixty-one-page document. Dimock was visibly shocked by it. He asked Farmer if he had presented the document to his colleague, Irving Kaufman. Farmer said he had not because the statute governing petitions for habeas corpus permitted them to be presented to *any* federal judge, and Farmer told Dimock that Dimock was just as much of a federal judge as was Kaufman.

Dimock understandably demurred. This was not only Kaufman's case. It was Kaufman's most notorious case. Dimock did, however, call Irving Kaufman on the telephone asking what Farmer should do. Kaufman said that Farmer should present his document to Assistant United States Attorney James Kilsheimer (a member of the team of federal lawyers prosecuting the Rosenbergs), who would in turn submit it to Kaufman. Dutifully, Farmer went to Foley Square, the bleak federal courthouse in deep downtown Manhattan, found Kilsheimer and gave Kilsheimer the original sixty-one-page petition. Kilsheimer was then joined by Kaufman's then law clerk—Leonard Sand, now himself a federal judge—and Dimock's law clerk, who were to perform the amenities as instructed by Dimock and then Kaufman. Sand read the document carefully and advised Farmer that Kaufman would take it under advisement—but not when or where.

This was far from enough for Farmer. The statute didn't require that Farmer present his position to an assistant U.S. attorney, or to a judge's law clerk. Farmer, who is as literal on these points as any special pleader to a county court back in Tennessee, believed that he had a right to present his position personally to a federal judge. Not realizing the very special amenities that exist in big city practice, Farmer delayed through Saturday afternoon while Sand and Kilsheimer read his document, and then decided he would do precisely what the statute said to do. He would present his petition to Kaufman.

By this time, it was far too late to do anything on Saturday afternoon. Early next morning, on Sunday the fourteenth, Farmer found from the New York telephone book where Irving Kaufman lived and took to locating his quarry. He felt sure that Kaufman would be at home because it was Sunday, which meant to Farmer that it was not the Jewish Sabbath and therefore Kaufman would be at home. Farmer taxied from his hotel to the impressive apartment on Park Avenue where Kaufman lived, and at precisely 10:40 on Sunday morning, June 14, presented the doorman at Kaufman's apartment with his petition of habeas corpus, all sixty-one pages of it. Farmer engaged in his legal explanation of his right to confront Kaufman and the doorman waited patiently. Finally, the doorman said that he was under absolute instructions not to allow anyone into the apartment to see Kaufman. He would, however, pass Farmer's calling card to the Kaufman apartment.

Undeterred, Farmer returned to his hotel on the West Side of Manhattan and found copies of his petition, an accompanying affidavit he had prepared, and, most optimistically, an order granting the petition, all of which would be submitted to Kaufman.

Farmer then returned to Park Avenue and delivered his documents to the same confused but determined doorman. With the documents, Farmer included a letter to Kaufman. It is dated June 14, 1953, on the simple stationery of the Tudor Hotel. It states:

I am delivering this letter addressed to you to the sidewalk doorman at the hour of approximately 1:30 P.M. with a request that he transmit it to you as soon as possible. I will return to the Hotel Tudor where I am staying and can be reached during the remainder of the afternoon. If for any reason you should deem that the writ and order may not be appropriately drawn and I can be of any further help and assistance to you I will be glad to do so.[18]

Farmer added in his Sunday letter to Kaufman that he had air-mailed, special delivery, a copy of the sixty-one-page petition to Bloch in Washington, where Bloch was awaiting events.[19] In that letter, Farmer related he had asked Bloch to endorse the petition, which was signed by Edelman as "next friend" to the Rosenbergs. Farmer's letter finished by saying that if he had not heard from Kaufman by 8:00 P.M. that evening, he would go to Judge Dimock with the same petition.

The doorman accepted Farmer's package for delivery late on Sunday afternoon. Farmer had as much chance to get something legally meaningful out of the doorman as he had from Kaufman. But the doorman was at least courteous. Not so Kaufman, in Kaufman's own good time.

Thus the opening argument in the legal debate of whether the Atomic Energy Act of 1946 applied to Julius and Ethel Rosenberg took place between a Tennessee lawyer and a doorman on Park

Avenue in Manhatten on Sunday, June 14, 1953. It was a fitting start for what followed.

It should be added that Farmer was very much undaunted. Daniel Marshall, another Edelman recruit, was due to join Farmer on Monday morning in New York. Farmer wanted Kaufman to know this. Farmer had given up all hope of confronting Kaufman. But Farmer did locate law clerk Sand at Sand's apartment in the Bronx; and at 9:30 on Sunday night, June 14, delivered to Sand's apartment still another letter stating that he, Farmer, and his colleague, Marshall, wished to argue Farmer's petition next morning, Monday, the fifteenth. A weary Sand agreed to call Kaufman that evening to inform him.

Conference of Supreme Court Justices, Saturday Afternoon

The conference of the Supreme Court justices on Saturday afternoon, June 13, would have delighted Talmudic scholars. First, Bloch had asked the Court to reconsider the Court's rejection (on May 25) of his earlier petition for certiorari (notable for Douglas's withdrawal of his written blast and Jackson's reversed vote). Delighted to have that squabble behind them, the Court quickly denied reconsideration. But it was far from finished for the day.

Although records of other conferences had been kept by the justices, none have been found for the conference on June 13. Perhaps the votes were so perplexing that no conference notes could explain them. All that was voted on at that conference was announced on what was expected to be the last day before the Court's planned adjournment for the summer on Monday, June 15, 1953.

CHAPTER FOUR

1

MONDAY, JUNE 15, 1953

HERE WERE touches of both tragedy and high comedy in the last session of the Supreme Court of the United States for the October term, 1953, on Monday, June 15, 1953. Promptly at noon, the nine justices appeared from behind the curtained partitions and took their places to read out their last decisions before going on vacation until October. Decision Day was a carefully programmed ritual in the Supreme Court of the fifties. It occurred on those Mondays when the Court was in session; the senior justice on the prevailing side would read the Court's opinion on the cases just decided, followed by the dissents. It was a long oral exercise, with the drama high at the beginning of each opinion until its drift became clear, and then dull for those disinterested in the legal details. No argument was held on Decision Days in the fifties. It was a ritual meeting, and especially so on the last opinion day of the term.

The justices read a few brief opinions that excited no one in the packed courtroom. A full courtroom waited for the announcement that the world waited to hear—the *Rosenberg* decision.

All of the recent events in this controversy pointed to the conclusion that what occurred on that Monday morning in the Supreme Court would be the end of the trail for the Rosenbergs. There was no one in that Court who expected to hear the Court undo the Rosenberg defeat on May 25. The packed room fully expected that none of the justices had given any credence to the recent discovery of the console table. To the reporters and the public, Kaufman's conduct at the trial seemed to be the best issue that the Rosenbergs could raise. Kaufman had, in fact, been a very busy person during the trial, intervening at key points with questions of his own. Invariably, these questions made points for the prosecution, some of them very telling. But a federal judge has the right to voice his opinion—so long as he makes it clear that his opinion does not bind the jury. Within these limitations Kaufman had not committed error.

No one excepting the justices themselves (and, perhaps, their clerks) knew that Monday morning how deeply troubled at least two of them were over Saypol's and Kaufman's performance. Kaufman as a federal judge was entitled to ask as many questions as he wished so long as they were relevant. And they all were, unfortunately for the Rosenbergs. All of Kaufman's questions during the trial were all too relevant and all too damning to the defendants. No one knew this better than Kaufman, a master at exercising his broad prerogatives within the rules, an expert at flexing his legitimate muscle. Kaufman may have damaged the Rosenberg defense, but he did it very carefully and skillfully within the limits of the law. Saypol's press conference during the trial was even more upsetting. But all of that had been decided at least once—the last time only twenty-one days before, on May 25.

This was in the minds of the observers in the courtroom on that Monday afternoon, June 15. They believed that Bloch had come up with nothing new in all his activity over the past three weeks—since May 25. Everyone in the courtroom believed this. Bloch himself seemed to know it. He was driven to desperation, like a parent compulsively scurrying everywhere for a cure for his dying child. Everyone who knew Bloch lauded his zeal and devotion, more impressive, perhaps, than his agility in a courtroom. On June 15, 1953, in the Supreme Court, no one thought that Bloch had a chance.

As the chief justice addressed *U.S.* v. *Rosenberg,* the massed reporters sitting in the back of the richly wooded room strained forward. They would have to get each word now and get each of them right. Most of them were veterans at the art of getting the words from the bench quickly and correctly. It was a chancy business, the quick telephone call to the newsroom before the written opinion was in hand. But on decision days, it was one of the risks of the business. The printed opinions would not be in their hands until midafternoon; with a hot case like *Rosenberg,* the headlines and stories would be in millions of readers' hands before anyone had actually read the opinion. The reporting all turned on hearing and understanding everything that the chief justice read from the bench.

There were some surprises in what Vinson read. And it was here—far beyond what the reporters noted—that the emerging and obtrusive splits within the Court were disclosed. First, Vinson announced that the request for a stay of the execution of the Rosenbergs had been addressed to Justice Jackson, who had referred it to the entire Court.[1] But Jackson did recommend, Vinson added, that the Court hear oral argument on the stay that very day, the fifteenth, a recommendation that was joined by justices Frankfurter and Burton.[2] This was unusual, very unusual. The Supreme Court rarely heard arguments on stays. As the reporters strained to listen for the remainder of the votes, Vinson announced word for word the Douglas order:

> Mr. Justice Douglas would grant a stay and hear the case on its merits, as he thinks the petition for certiorari and the petition for rehearing present substantial questions. But since the Court has decided not to take the case, there would be no end served by hearing oral argument on the motion for a stay. For the motion presents no new substantial question not presented by the petition for certiorari and by the petition for rehearing.[3]

Douglas had once again marched up the hill and marched right down again. For trained reporters, the words "since the Court has decided not to take the case" gave them what they wanted to hear. It meant that Douglas had joined the stalwarts (Vinson, Clark, and Minton) who had never swayed one inch in rejecting Bloch's attempt to address the Court on his new points, and in denying a stay of execution for the Rosenbergs. The stay had been denied. What came out minutes later was a switch by Burton, who had wanted oral argument on the stay, but voted the other way when it was clear to him that argument lost all meaning if votes for the stay were not there.[4]

What confounded careful observers then and does today is precisely what Douglas was talking about in his brief paragraph. Douglas could not have been talking about the original petition for certiorari in the case because Douglas voted against it, and against rehearing it. What Douglas *may* have been talking about was the fateful May 25 denial of the petition based on Saypol's conduct. One of the other things that the Court did (on June 15) was to deny Bloch's petition for rehearing (Bloch never missed an opening, and never scored on one) of the May 25 decision. But if that is what Douglas was talking about, he did not say so. One very good reason for Douglas's vagueness was his own responsibility for the Court's denial of certiorari on May 25. Douglas had again taken one step forward in his brief paragraph and then two very clear steps back. The good old boys on the Court, "Truman's law firm" (Vinson, Minton, and Clark) had now gotten a bellyful of Douglas's obscurantisms. And Jackson, who was always a good hater, now had further grounds for his own belief that Douglas would always cast a vote to review the Rosenberg case as long as Douglas was sure the full Supreme Court would not do so.

All of the shots that Bloch had fired off after May 25 had gone nowhere. The rejection of Bloch's request for the stay made it entirely clear that the Supreme Court found no merit in any of Bloch's arguments. The Supreme Court was willing to have the Rosenbergs die on schedule on June 18.

The impact of the decision hit the reporters, frantically scribbling to get every word, with groups of them rushing to get to their telephones. While marshals tried to keep order, the courtroom, with the chief justice still talking, turned into a milling mob of human beings straining to get to the doors. In the midst of all this, there was sudden drama in the form of one human being, a lawyer for the Rosenbergs, trying to buck the combined forces of the pushing reporters and the counterpushing marshals—as well as the Supreme Court's rules: John Finerty strode purposefully to the podium. Finerty was a big man. He needed every ounce of his strength to walk over and through a half-dozen reporters who were just as eager to get away from the courtroom as Finerty was to get to its center. As Finerty approached the broad table that extended across the front of the room with the podium in its center, two marshals tried to stop him but Finerty would not stopped. Lives were at stake and he was going to make his request as if this august chamber were just another dingy police courtroom where life and death were handed out by judges every day.

As the two marshals tried to stop him, Finerty shouted directly as the bulky frame of the chief justice departed through the black curtains behind the table. Finerty's sonorous voice could have been heard in Baltimore. As if by magic, the courtroom stilled. Reporters and observers knew they were watching an episode that would be high comedy if the stakes were not life and death. Finerty shouted at the chief justice; Vinson and the other eight justices looked back cautiously from the curtains at the beetle-browed Irishman bellowing at them. Finerty moved orally for a writ of habeas corpus. Vinson wasn't sure he was hearing correctly, and was even less sure that this demoniac performance came from a responsible lawyer, not a crank. But the cautious Vinson erred on the side of being human: he assumed that what was before him was not an outburst but rather a move, however unusual, by a Rosenberg lawyer excited by the morning's events into acting irregularly. While the marshals fought with Finerty and the other justices looked on as if Finerty were undressing publicly, Vinson calmly told Finerty he would have to file his papers with the clerk of the Court. Finerty tore himself loose from the marshals, shoving them bodily across the table reserved for government counsel, and turned on his heel. As he rushed back from the podium into a solid phalanx of lawyers and reporters, which quickly parted in the face of his charge, Finerty's Irish brogue could be heard clearly by Vinson and his colleagues and everyone else in the room. Finerty made it clear that his petition would be filed within the hour.

Finerty was no stranger to controversial cases. He had represented Tom Mooney, the San Francisco labor leader, accused of throwing a bomb on the Preparedness Day Parade in San Francisco in 1917. Finerty had taken Mooney up and through the California courts; he had demonstrated the perjured use of testimony by the California prosecutors. Finerty took Mooney to the Supreme Court, which gave the California courts a severe verbal beating. Largely because of what the Supreme Court said, Mooney walked free, years after he had been jailed.[5]

Two hours later, Finerty had in his hands precisely what the chief justice suggested: a petition for writ of habeas corpus. Smashing against the gilt doors that were closed across the corridor leading to the clerk's office, Finerty let out a bull's cry that could be heard miles away. "How in the hell do I get into the clerk's office?"

Two guards immediately rescued Finerty. The guards opened the doors—not locked, but only seemingly so in Finerty's rush to file. In two minutes, the ornate procedures of docketing a pleading in the Supreme Court of the United States, very much like admitting an emergency patient into the intensive-care unit at an expensive hospital, were completed. Three more deputy clerks appeared and silently stamped the forty copies of the brief document Finerty had in his hand. Other clerks came in from other rooms with questions; all were satisfactorily answered. The deputy assistant clerk counted the copies and found that number satisfactory. One clerk looked at the signatures on the papers and questioned whether Finerty's signature was enough; all the other papers had been signed by Bloch, who was a member of the Supreme Court bar. Finerty was not. But the chief clerk brushed this objection aside and took the forty copies, all stamped and correct, to the waiting justices.

Chambers of Judge Irving Kaufman, Foley Square, New York City

While the news that the Rosenbergs would die screamed across the nation's wires and Finerty bulled his way through the

Supreme Court's bureaucracy, the sideshow in the drama went forward 225 miles north in the chambers of Judge Irving Kaufman in Lower Manhattan. It went forward slowly; Farmer was now joined by Daniel Marshall, a California attorney allied with the California Save-the-Rosenbergs Committee (with strong convictions of his own that both the prosecution and Kaufman had committed serious error at trial). Both cooled their heels from 9:30 in the morning until 2:30 that Monday afternoon. While he was waiting for Kaufman's decision on the papers delivered to Kaufman the day before, Farmer called the clerk of the Supreme Court in Washington to learn whether the Supreme Court had ruled. He was told that the Supreme Court was still sitting and no news would be released until 2:30 P.M.

Precisely at 2:30 that afternoon, Farmer and Marshall got both messages at the same time. Waiting in Kaufman's chambers, both heard on the radio the news that the Supreme Court had ruled against the Rosenbergs. Farmer then called his hotel; Kaufman's office had left word there that his ruling was now available. Farmer and Marshall went to Sand in the courthouse and got it. Kaufman's ruling was notable in charging both Farmer and Marshall with being "interlopers" and "intruders." Bloch had wired Kaufman his unwillingness to join in the Farmer-Marshall effort. Accordingly, Kaufman declared, Farmer and Marshall had no status to add anything to the Rosenberg defense. Kaufman added gratuitously that nothing in the Tennessee attorney's papers (now joined by Marshall) "had any merit." Kaufman added in his order: "It is apparent from the papers that Petitioners and his Counsel have no standing to bring this application. Perhaps this realization has caused them to be so reckless in their charges as to verge upon contemptuousness."[6]

Farmer believed, with considerable justification, that Kaufman had waited to issue his ruling until 2:30 P.M.—when the radio news from Washington told Kaufman that the Rosenberg's final die had been cast by the Supreme Court—before issuing his own ruling.

*　　*　　*

What status did Farmer and Marshall have before Kaufman? On the face of their papers, it said they were acting as "next friends" to the Rosenbergs. That is legal jargon: neither knew the Rosenbergs. Neither represented the Rosenbergs. Bloch made that very clear to Kaufman. Since the question of the status of these "next friends" colored the final five days of the case, it is worth examining. And so is Kaufman's strong reaction to it.

Normally, a "next friend" is the parent suing for a child because in the antiquities of the common law the child could not sue for himself. Throughout the centuries of the common law, the concept has not grown very much beyond that. Certainly, it has never extended to appearing on behalf of criminals with whom there is no family—or other—connection. But there are other ways for outsiders to make their views known in a lawsuit. Acting as "amicus curiae" is one. This is not often done in a trial court, but it is not unknown. To do this, however, one must be accepted by the Court as amicus curiae, and it was very clear to any observer in the Rosenberg case that Judge Kaufman would accept no outsiders in it. In a controversial case, the judge, any judge, simply cannot listen to every courtroom hanger-on who thinks he has a legal theory.

But is this always so? In a capital case, should not a judge welcome all possible arguments, no matter who raises them, in order to be sure this terrible justice is being carried out on solid grounds? While that argument might move other men, it obviously could not move Irving Kaufman. It is impossible to speculate as to just what Kaufman's reasons were. The simplest one is that he wanted no intruders and permitted none, especially since these intruders came in very irregularly.

That explanation, however, may be too simple. Kaufman may have been many things, but he was not stupid. He must have recognized a new and unique argument when he saw it. The Farmer-Marshall brief may have been rough and done in haste (the running of time toward the scheduled execution pressed Farmer hard), but the guts of a new argument were there.

To a shrewd jurist like Kaufman, that argument meant nothing but trouble. It meant, if the argument got currency at all, that Kaufman would be reversed in his most famous case. It also meant that the underlying indictment of the Rosenbergs by the grand jury was defective. That meant, in turn, not only the reversal of Kaufman's judgment and opinion, but an entire new charge, to say nothing of an inevitable new trial. Everything that Kaufman stood for and believed in would have been undercut if these convicted Jewish Communists got this kind of luck with this new point of law. Better to bury it. And the way to bury it was so obvious that anyone could see how, and most certainly a renowned scholar in courtroom procedure (such as Kaufman) saw this clearly.

So, on that June morning in Kaufman's chambers in Manhattan, the argument got buried not only because the wrong people voiced it, but also because of the force of the argument itself.

It should have been easy to push aside formalistic trappings and to announce that with two human lives at stake, arguments that bore on whether those lives should be taken by the government were important, sufficiently so to hear them no matter who happened to voice them. Easy, yes, but so unlike Kaufman and so utterly out of character in the Rosenberg case. And, of course, it was also typical of Kaufman that, when he refused to hear the "interloping," "intruding" attorneys (who verged upon "contemptuousness") who were prepared to present this new legal argument, Kaufman committed no legal, reversible error.

Conference of Supreme Court Justices, 2:00 P.M.

By the time that Kaufman delivered his rough rejection to Farmer and Marshall in New York, there was more rough give-and-take back in Washington within the Supreme Court. All of the justices were desperately tired of the case. This was their last day before recess and vacation. Finerty's blast seemed to the stalwarts to be an aberration. It was far too loud and unseemly. But Finerty did catch the attention of an increasingly disturbed Frankfurter. Frankfurter looked over Finerty's papers very briefly—for less than thirty minutes. In them, Finerty had accused Saypol of knowing use of perjured testimony. No one had ever gone quite that far—even in criticism of Saypol, a prosecutor whose recent conduct comforted none of the justices, including the stalwart naysayers. Frankfurter and Black, a solid alliance formed in the recent weeks of bickering, favored an open argument before the Court on Finerty's issue,[7] now at least the fourth that had surfaced with serious questions about the conduct of the trial. The two justices believed it raised serious questions concerning Kaufman's version of justice. Frankfurter said that he knew something about the Mooney case, and indeed he did. The weary but wary Jackson noted that Finerty had modeled some of his allegations in the papers Finerty had just placed before them on the Mooney papers.[8] Most of the justices understood enough about what the Supreme Court said in the Mooney case, and paid heed.

Douglas then put in his oar. Douglas was adamant. But on which side? He couldn't see, Douglas said, that Finerty had said anything that invoked the jurisdiction of the Supreme Court. Then Douglas added that he was still willing to grant certiorari to the Rosenbergs, but could do nothing whatever for them on what Finerty had written. Few of the justices now either understood or cared what Douglas did or said. But Frankfurter did. He and Douglas engaged in a bitter debate on what had happened in the Supreme Court on *Mooney*.[9]

The records of the Court reflect that the courts rejected Finerty's motion. Black carefully dissented. Frankfurter now walked the tightrope. He ruled that he would not deny Finerty without listening to Finerty argue his points orally to the Court even though, Frankfurter admitted, "the substance of the allegations now made has already been considered by the District Court [Kaufman], and on review by the Court of Appeals for the Second Circuit."[10]

But he added, "Neither can I join the Court in denying the application without more. I would set the application down for hearing before the full court tomorrow forenoon."[11]

In their last law rulings, justices of the Supreme Court had strayed aimlessly across the legal landscape, stopping just short of ordering a public radio debate on the Rosenberg case. The justices were that muddled and that divided. Beyond that, the Court was badly tired and split. Nine fatigued, aging men, some not very resilient, had been confronted with too much of one controversy, both public and private, over too long a time. It had ceased being a Court. It was now nine exhausted judges. The one that felt the strongest, Black, was ill with an ailing gall bladder that was to be removed within days—if they ever got out of the damned courthouse. What happened next is shrouded by time but supported by strong evidence. What the Court did next was as aberrant as anything the Supreme Court had done to date in the Rosenberg case, and its record up to midafternoon on June 15, 1953, was not proud.

The cacophony of the Frankfurter-Douglas debate over *Mooney* stilled. There was quiet from all corners of the conference room. The stalwarts (to whom the Rosenberg case was just another criminal case that had gotten—for reasons they were now beginning to grasp—worldwide attention) wanted rid of it. It was already a blot on the Court. Quietly, Vinson, Minton, and Clark said there was absolutely nothing new in Finerty's papers.

Black dissented. It was expected. He reminded his colleagues that the Rosenberg prosecution had been tainted with error during the trial. Had it not been such an incendiary case, he went on, there was no doubt in his mind that the Second Circuit would have reversed it long before it came to the Supreme Court. What bothered Black more than anything else was the conduct of the trial judge. Judge Kaufman had, Black thought, acted like one of the prosecutors, coming in with important questions to key witnesses at critical times during the trial. Black had always said, and he repeated it on that Monday afternoon, that none of them was, by itself, very hurtful to the Rosenbergs. But the total weight of all of them, all slanted to help the government, had to influence the jury.

Frankfurter, to whom this case had become an enlarging incubus that brought on more pain each time it appeared,* as it

---

* "My brethren may well be forced to have me repeat that the Court's failure to take the case of the Rosenbergs has presented for me the most anguishing situation since I have been on the Court" (memorandum of Justice Frankfurter to the justices' conference dated May 20, 1953, FF Papers); obviously, that anguish had been aggravated by June 15.

had so often in recent weeks, voted strongly that he wanted to hear Finerty. But the vote was 7 to 2 against doing so. Douglas was one of the seven.

Black now warned that none of them in that room was happy with the death penalty in a case like this; none of them was entirely comfortable with the sentence or with the provocative words uttered by Kaufman during the sentencing. Now, Black argued, if any of his brothers had any doubt, now was the time to speak up. Everyone in the room knew all too well the one fact that no one spoke of: the Rosenbergs would die that Thursday at 8:00 P.M. unless the nine men in that room did something about it.

There was the spreading silence that comes when earnest men, tired but humane men, realize that they are deciding that two fellow humans must die. All of the nine men in that room were humane, but they were also lawyers, and they knew what they could do and what they could not do. A bare majority of them sitting there had just as strong a conviction that the Rosenbergs had been given a fair trial as Black's conviction that the trial was unfair. But, by now, the entire Court had had a bellyful of the publicity given the case, especially since much of it came in the form of personal vilification aimed both at them individually and at the Court as a whole by Communists who, they thought, knew or cared nothing about the case. It was time that it all ended. If it ended in the carrying out of a death sentence that none of them could really applaud, that wasn't their business. Only Judge Kaufman had the power under the law to change the sentence, and he had been and remained adamant. The nine of them could act only on error at the trial and, in the view of the majority, there just wasn't any error. The Court and the country would do well to get the Rosenberg case out of the headlines and into the merciful oblivion of legal history.

Moreover, the Court had been given signals by the Department of Justice that the country would, indeed, be well served with a quick and final disposition of the case. The attorney general had commented publicly that the hue and cry from the Communists across the world was doing the cause of freedom no good.

These comments had come back to the Court; after all, its nine members lived in Washington, not in a vacuum. None of them would allow the attorney general's statements to sway his vote one way or the other, but if the vote was already clear, damage being done to the country by this spreading controversy could certainly push the Court to act swiftly and so conclusively that any further delay of the Rosenberg execution would be impossible. On the preceding Saturday afternoon, June 13, there were Rosenberg riots in Paris, and a mob threatened the American embassy in London. It was time, high time, to bring this painful controversy to an end.

Each of the nine justices must have had these thoughts. All nine felt their duty to be clear: the majority to vote nay, Black to dissent, and Frankfurter to ask for oral argument.

What then occurred in the conference room was one of those small digressions in judicial demeanor that means so little at the time but sometimes means so much over the passage of time.

While each of the nine men pondered how this hydra-headed monster could be taken from them, they all decided that it would serve the Court and country well to end the matter right there. All nine agreed they would announce their decision on the Finerty matter that afternoon, a most proper and regular Court procedure. The departure came when the nine justices agreed across the table that none of them would hereafter intervene by himself to delay—for even one moment—the end of the protracted public agony into which the Court had now been drawn. All of them agreed that they were making their last decision on the Rosenberg case that afternoon, and then they all agreed that no one of them would, by himself, reopen the case. The sore from which such poisonous venom had spewed, affecting each of them and their beloved Court, was being closed for good.

It was late in the afternoon, 4:30 by the big clock in the marble center chamber, when the justices left the building. All were torn between relief at having reached a final decision on this prolonged ordeal and unstillable anxieties about the death penalty. None of them thought for a moment that he had committed an impropriety. Yet they all had. And it was that impropriety, very probably more than anything else, that put the Rosenbergs into the electric chair four days, three hours, and forty-six minutes later.

They all had agreed in advance to reject any contention, however just and however persuasive it might be, that the Rosenberg execution was illegal.*

If these men were humane and acted out of concern for the Court, what was improper? The impropriety lies in the essence of our system. Our courts are set up to respond to what the parties before them do. They are not set up, and simply are not intended, to take initiatives on matters not before them. For example, if a trial judge decided after hearing five minutes of one side in a case that justice was all on the other side no matter what was before him, such a decision would be terribly unfair to the first side. Cases often have swung completely around on points made very late in the judicial process, points that were completely untouched in the early stages. For any judges, from local magistrates to justices of the Supreme Court, to agree that they will hear no further arguments of any kind in a case before them is prejudgment, which is improper for magistrates and Supreme Court justices alike.

More important, in a notorious case in which frayed judicial tempers were common, a private agreement by appeal judges not to touch any new argument that *could* come up meant that any lawyer who thereafter raised a meritorious argument fought not only the uphill battle of the argument's merits; he also faced the unseen opposition of the hidden agreement among the judges before him. He also confronted the justices' private annoyance at one of their colleagues who violated the agreement by giving currency to the argument—which is precisely what did happen when Justice Douglas again brought down the ire of his colleagues by agreeing to stay the Rosenberg execution when he heard a completely new argument. The other justices were

* See Justice Jackson's statement to Justice Frankfurter corroborating this understanding, below page 71, and the corroboration made in statements to Philip Elman, below, pages 72 to 73.

outraged by what Douglas had done; the reception given the new argument was seriously, irretrievably jaundiced by distaste over Douglas's action. What he had *previously* done added to their personal disgust.

In a word, private agreements among judges that dispose of serious points of law before they are made do violence to our system of justice. This is doubly true in a capital case. It cuts even deeper in a case where passions ran as deeply as they did throughout *Rosenberg*. While the world went mad in June of 1953 over matters totally irrelevant to the doing of justice, the Supreme Court of the United States should have been the refuge of dispassionate reason. Three justices, Black, Frankfurter, and the mercurial Douglas, provided that refuge. But the majority of the Supreme Court was not that refuge of dispassionate justice in the third week of June 1953. Far from it.

Bloch made one more desperate and futile move that Monday afternoon. After Douglas had returned from his argument with Frankfurter in the justices' conference, Bloch was waiting in his chambers for him. Douglas, not normally a man easy with amenities, invited Bloch in and agreed to listen to him. It appeared very quickly that Bloch had nothing to add. Bloch talked of the indecency of the death penalty. He mentioned that Douglas's travels had taken the justice to Asia. This sentence, Bloch said, would win twenty million Asians to Communism.[12]

Douglas had planned to leave Washington for Goose Prairie at 7:00 A.M. the next morning. More out of personal kindness than anything else, he stated that he would stay on longer and consider what Bloch had said. But he made it abundantly clear to Bloch that the Court's action that afternoon was dispositive of the case regardless of its influence on Chinese communism. Douglas's unusual act of kindness in not rebuffing Bloch that Monday evening may have been the only stroke of luck that Julius and Ethel Rosenberg had been given since they were arrested two and a half years earlier.

New York City, Monday Night, June 15

To Farmer and Marshall in New York, Kaufman's harsh words aimed at them as lawyers in Kaufman's Monday opinion served as a goad. Farmer was more convinced than ever that he was on the right track. No one knew (or, apparently, cared) about the Atomic Energy Act of 1946. The terrible problem was to get someone to listen to it—and to them. Farmer and Marshall knew that they had only three days left.

Late on Monday afternoon, Farmer read in the afternoon papers that Bloch had been allowed in to see Douglas again. Abandoning all plans of going to New Haven to search out the judges of the Court of Appeals (then sitting in New Haven), Farmer and Marshall decided to take the midnight train to Washington. If Bloch could get in to see Douglas after the Court had ruled against Bloch, it was just possible that one of these justices might listen to them.[13]

CHAPTER FIVE

↑

TUESDAY, JUNE 16, 1953

Supreme Court Building, Washington, D.C.

THE TARGET for Farmer and Marshall was Black. Black had dissented from every adverse Supreme Court ruling against the Rosenbergs. At the Willard Hotel, Farmer and Marshall changed a few notations on the petition that Kaufman had rejected, transforming it into a petition addressed to the Supreme Court. Then they taxied to Black's residence thirty minutes away in Alexandria. The lawyers knocked on Black's door for minutes without success. No one was home.

On the way back from Alexandria, Farmer and Marshall decided to try Douglas. Insofar as they knew, Douglas was still in the Supreme Court building, considering Bloch's last-minute appeal of the day before. It was still early on Tuesday morning. They might catch Douglas.

In the Supreme Court building, Farmer and Marshall went to the Lawyers' Lounge, an uncomfortable room where lawyers could do what they do often: wait. There were about twenty reporters there, awaiting word on Bloch's petition. Bloch himself was there. Bloch paid no attention to Farmer. The clerk of the Supreme Court, Harold Willey, appeared and Farmer told him that he had a petition that he wished to put before Justice Douglas.

Formalities had been abandoned in the excitement of the last day. Willey took Farmer's petition without any of the preliminaries of filing and docketing normally required before any document can be put before a justice of the Supreme Court, and disappeared. Very shortly Willey returned. He took Farmer aside in the Lawyers' Lounge and whispered quietly in Farmer's ear that Douglas had asked Willey if Farmer and Marshall represented the Rosenbergs. Willey told Douglas, Willey said, that he did not think they did. Willey told Farmer that Douglas then said that the Rosenbergs "don't care who gets them out of the electric chair." Farmer confirmed that he and Marshall did not represent the Rosenbergs but only Edelman, their "next friend." Willey disappeared again. He was back shortly. Douglas would hear them for thirty minutes at 11:30 later that morning. After the reception they received from Kaufman the day before in New York, both men were indeed surprised.[1]

Promptly at 11:30, Farmer and Marshall appeared at Douglas's chambers. They were ushered in and found three lawyers waiting with Douglas. One was James Kilsheimer of Saypol's staff from New York; the others were aides from the Department of Justice. Douglas introduced the men and turned to Farmer to begin.

Farmer had prepared himself for this precise moment. He told Douglas that two people were about to die, and that no court anywhere had seen the evidence that the Rosenbergs were supposed to have passed to the Soviets. Farmer was speaking of Greenglass's sketch of the Nagasaki bomb, drawn by Greenglass from memory, and his testimony about the sketch, all suppressed on Bloch's motion.

Farmer said that both the sketch and the testimony had never been made part of any record that any appeals court (including the Supreme Court) had ever seen. Douglas was shocked. He asked the government team if what Farmer had said was true. They admitted it was.

Douglas then turned with increased interest to Farmer and asked him to continue. Farmer told Douglas that the entire prosecution of the Rosenbergs had been based on the wrong statute; the Rosenbergs should have been tried under the 1946 Atomic Energy Act. Farmer was quiet and clipped. If they had been tried under the 1946 act, they could not have been sentenced to death without the recommendation of a jury, nor without government proof of an intent to injure the United States. Neither of those was ever done in the Kaufman trial. Farmer made other points, but it was his belief that he had hit home with Douglas from his opening statement.

The government lawyers had little to say. Strangely, after all that had been said by Kaufman the day before, none of them doubted Farmer's right to be before Douglas on the Rosenbergs' behalf. The brief session closed well before the thirty minutes were up. But Douglas had before him Farmer's sixty-one-page petition, and he sat down to read it closely.

Farmer and Marshall went back to the Lawyers' Lounge. There were even more reporters crowded in the room. Bloch was there; again he ignored Farmer.[2]

By noon, Douglas was hungry. It had been a long and surprising morning, one for which the justice had not been prepared. He had his secretary call the Court cafeteria, a small luncheon room in the building that must do for all the lawyers, staff, and reporters during the term. One of the inconveniences built into the Ivory Tower (as the Supreme Court building was scornfully labeled when it was built in the thirties) was its location. Near the Capitol, the building had but one decent but overcrowded restaurant within walking distance where litigants and lawyers could comfortably lunch and confer while appearing before the Court. The justices had their own dining room, but that was closed for the summer on that Tuesday noon when Douglas wanted lunch. It was not unusual for Justice Douglas to eat in the cafeteria; Bill Douglas had been accused of many things, but pomp was not one of them. The attendants had told him that his appearances were the first that a justice, *any* justice, had ever made in the cafeteria.

The place seemed deserted when Douglas walked in. On the first Tuesday of the summer recess, even the tourists had taken their business elsewhere. All the tables except three were closed. Douglas got his sandwich lunch and sat down at the last empty table.

Sitting at the table next to him were Farmer and Marshall, picking at their lunches. Bloch sat by himself at the third table next to the door. For a full twenty minutes all four men sat in silence. Then Bloch moved his bulk between the chairs and left. Marshall and Farmer lingered on, eyeing Douglas carefully. Finally, they both left. Douglas finished his lunch last and departed. Not one word had been spoken among the four men, all of whom were totally preoccupied with the same case. But not with the same questions. Bloch did not yet know—nor did he apparently care—what Farmer had argued to Douglas an hour earlier.

The afternoon passed into early evening.

Bloch was openly exasperated. The fleeting chance that Douglas might modify or even condemn the death penalty would be utterly lost if these meddlers dispelled the mood that Bloch had tried so hard to create in Douglas. They had no business here with their crazy argument. Their sponsor, Edelman, was a fool and a busybody. Worse than that, he was ruining Bloch's last chance.

Douglas was still in his chambers. Farmer, Marshall, and Bloch were in the Lawyers' Lounge. Farmer and Marshall agonized through every minute. Both were tense men (of a very different stamp, Farmer quiet and soft-spoken, Marshall somber and explosive) to whom waiting was exquisite torture.* Bloch slept and read the newspapers, continuing to ignore the presence of Farmer and Marshall. Not a word passed between Bloch and the other lawyers throughout the long afternoon and into the evening.

Early in the evening, Douglas's secretary came through the door of the lounge. The three men started toward her. Motioning them off, she told them that the justice had not finished his deliberations and was going home. There was no point in their staying on at the Court any longer.

Farmer and Marshall taxied to the Willard full of high spirits. Bloch took his separate taxi to the Statler in despair. He was sure that Julius and Ethel Rosenberg had only two days to live.

*   *   *

* Marshall is deceased. Farmer is very much alive.

While Farmer, Marshall, and Bloch waited that afternoon and evening, there were more provocative events taking place within the Supreme Court building. These events received no notice whatever. They remained secret until the FBI released internal FBI documents under a Court order in a Freedom of Information suit brought by the Rosenbergs' sons close to twenty-two years after their parents had been executed. The internal FBI documents confirm that the FBI remained in close contact with the Rosenberg case long after it had left Judge Kaufman's courtroom.

An FBI memorandum from the supervisor of the FBI office in New York, Mr. D. M. Ladd, to a senior FBI official in Washington, A. H. Belmont, dated June 17, 1953, revealed that on Tuesday, June 16 (while Douglas was considering the Farmer-Marshall petition), Justice Jackson arranged a meeting at the Supreme Court on that day between Chief Justice Vinson and the attorney general of the United States, Herbert Brownell. The memorandum reveals that at the meeting, Vinson and Brownell discussed contingency plans, in Chief Justice Vinson's chambers, plans for the Court to put in motion if Douglas took unilateral action on the Farmer-Marshall petition and issued a stay of the Rosenbergs' execution. Because this conduct is as irregular as any in which judges (Jackson and Vinson) and prosecutors (Brownell, the chief lawyer for the United States then seeking the execution of the Rosenbergs) can engage, the FBI memorandum reveals impropriety in *Rosenberg* at the highest level of our courts. For that reason alone, the FBI had no reason to fabricate it; the FBI documents released to the Rosenbergs, grudgingly disgorged, appear accurately to reflect the FBI intelligence on events in those crucial days. Judge Kaufman watching his case like the proverbial hawk was the source of the information given to the FBI.

The FBI memorandum goes farther. Brownell, Jackson, and Vinson, it relates, discussed the unusual strategy of reconvening the entire Court to overturn the stay. The document then reads:

Jackson felt that the whole theory of listening to Farmer's motion was ridiculous and Douglas should have turned it down. . . . Vinson said that if a stay is granted he will call the full Court into session Thursday morning to vacate it.[3]

As the events of the following afternoon, Wednesday, June 17, demonstrated, the contingency plans discussed on June 16 between Chief Justice Vinson and Attorney General Brownell in their meeting while Douglas was deliberating were carried out to the letter.

Formally, under the rules that judges comport themselves, what was improper about Jackson arranging for Vinson and Brownell to meet on the afternoon of June 16? Judicial Canon 17 of the American Bar Association in effect in June of 1953 provides:

Ex parte communication.
A judge should not permit private interviews, argument or communications designed to influence his judicial action, where interests to be affected thereby are not represented before him, except where provision is made by law.[4]

There was no such "provision . . . made by law" excusing the meeting of Vinson and Brownell—arranged by Jackson—on the evening of June 16. It was completely improper. And it was just as improper for Brownell to participate in it, because a parallel provision of the canons for lawyers prohibits these same ex parte communications.[5]

But there was a good deal more awry in that extraordinary meeting of the chief justice and the attorney general arranged by Justice Jackson. There were intensely human motives involved on all three sides.

Both the attorney general of the United States and the two justices had a good deal on their minds when the attorney general sat down on the plush chair in the chief justice's office.

Both Attorney General Brownell and the chief justice were transported beyond ordinary decorum by the maddening Rosenberg case, which seemed at that moment to have the highest court of the nation's judicial system in open turmoil. When Justice

Jackson arranged the meeting for that Tuesday afternoon, the news that Justice Douglas was considering the Edelman-Marshall-Farmer papers was buzzing all over Washington. And Brownell, in his zeal to bury both the Rosenbergs and their case, had taken a step universally considered improper in the courts: as chief lawyer for one party in a legal case, he contacted one of the judges still sitting on the case and asked to see him privately. The various improprieties were now rapidly accumulating. None of the Brownell-Vinson discussion was disclosed to the other side—to the Rosenberg lawyers. In fact, their talk remained secret until twenty-three years later, when the federal government was forced by a Court order to disclose the meeting.[6]

Douglas had accepted the Farmer-Marshall papers some time early that morning and had said nothing to anyone about how he was to rule. By midafternoon, when a flat, quick rejection had not appeared from Douglas's chambers, both Justice Jackson and Brownell felt they had to act. Vinson agreed to meet with Brownell. The conduct of both men just one day later, when Brownell filed a request for the Court to reconvene in an extraordinary special term (with but two precedents in the entire history of the Court), and Vinson granted the request within an hour—with notice to no one, certainly not the lawyer for the defendants—removes all speculation that the FBI had accurate information on what occurred in Vinson's chambers. The two men (Attorney General Brownell and Chief Justice Vinson) discussed contingency plans in case Douglas violated (among the various objectionable things he might do) the Court's private, irregular understanding that no single justice would intervene in the case.

The Tuesday meeting was as improper as any gathering by lawyers could be. It was an ex parte gathering—legalese for one-sided, private, discussion of a case still being argued. The canons of judicial conduct forbade it.

Moreover, the United States government was up to its eyes in an agonizing criminal proceeding with the Rosenbergs. The chief lawyer for the United States was Attorney General Brownell, who, in June of 1953, certainly was no stranger to this case. He had battled for speed in executing the Rosenbergs ever since

Kaufman had made it possible. In talks with President Eisenhower, he had opposed any clemency. He was a confirmed, redoubtable opponent of the Rosenbergs and the chief lawyer for the party who was opposing the spies and intended to execute them. It was totally improper for him to plot—and that is the word—with Vinson when Vinson was chief justice of a Court before whom the Rosenberg case was still pending. To begin with, for Vinson and Brownell to sit down privately while Douglas was deliberating, and for Vinson and Brownell to figure out—together—what they would do if Douglas entered a stay for the Rosenbergs, was a violation of the Canons of Judicial Conduct of the American Bar Association. The basic sense of fairness under which all litigation is carried on in this country was violated by this meeting. This kind of abuse goes straight to the heart of the adversary system and renders it suspect. And all of this was done by the nation's chief law enforcement official, the attorney general of the United States, and its chief judge, the chief justice of the United States, and arranged by his colleague, Justice Jackson.

It was not the last of the strange departures from the rules by the chief justice of the Supreme Court and by the nation's chief lawyer, the attorney general.

To the public, do these legal shenanigans have any importance? To the man on the street, does "ex parte communication" have any real meaning? Is this just lawyers' talk, a special language unrelated to everyday life? In graphic terms, what happened in the Supreme Court that Tuesday, June 16, 1953, was the precise parallel of a hypothetical case that all persons will understand: a son who had gotten into bad trouble by killing a pedestrian while driving drunk. After the young man was tried and convicted and sentenced by the judge to a twenty-year term, his parents' lawyers (or, perhaps, some other lawyers) looked at their law books and found that the state legislature had recently tightened up on all drunk-driving charges, but had decided that a twenty-year sentence *had* to be recommended by a jury. But the son had already been sentenced to twenty years by the judge alone. Lawyers—

either the parents' lawyers or others—went to the judge and told him that his sentence was wrong. But the prosecutor was mad; he wanted the twenty years to stick. So did the judge. So the prosecutor met with the judge *privately* to figure out what to do to prevent any modification in the judge's twenty-year sentence.

That doesn't *sound* fair. It is *not* fair. It is what the ban on ex parte communications (the private meeting between the judge and the prosecutor) is all about. In the Rosenberg case, the judge was the chief justice of the United States and the prosecutor was the attorney general of the United States.

Supreme Court Building, Justice Frankfurter's Chambers

While Farmer, Marshall, and Bloch all waited for Douglas to act, on the same afternoon that Vinson and Brownell were meeting (as arranged by Jackson) to make their contingency plans, more high-level antics had commenced earlier in the day in Justice Frankfurter's chambers. Supreme Court clerk Willey, seemingly omnipresent on that busy Tuesday, called on Justice Frankfurter during the morning. Willey told Frankfurter that Douglas had suggested that Bloch (apparently in his attempt to sway Douglas with the impact of the pending executions on Asian Communists) also should approach Frankfurter with the same argument because of the "shortness of time."[7] Frankfurter viewed this suggestion as something straight out of Gilbert and Sullivan, especially since there was a suggestion by Willey that Bloch might also try to see Jackson with the same argument.[8] Frankfurter dismissed the notion with the comment that if he decided for Bloch while Douglas was still trying to make up his mind, "it would be a pretty how-de-do."[9] Frankfurter said that this was Douglas's matter and there it would stay.

Frankfurter was sufficiently upset over the chaotic approaches being made to various justices that he asked Justice Jackson to come into his chambers. Jackson deemed Frankfurter (and no one else on the Court) to be his intellectual equal, and the give-and-take between the two was informal. Frankfurter repeated to Jackson what Clerk Willey had just told Frankfurter about the approaches being considered by Bloch, not only to Douglas but also to Frankfurter and, possibly, Jackson.

Here, Frankfurter's precise notes of the colloquy are significant:

> Jackson then went beyond what I had said [to Clerk Willey] by stating that it was perfectly understood at conference that in view of the Court's denial of habeas corpus no individual Justice to whom application was made would overrule the Court's determination.[10]

What Jackson said is notable for three reasons. First, Jackson said it was evident that some understanding had been reached by the justices during the conference the prior afternoon, that "no individual Justice to whom application was made would overrule the Court's determination." Second, Jackson's comment is more far-reaching than it appears. When Jackson said it, he knew that the Bloch approach to Douglas (or to Frankfurter, or to Jackson, or whoever else would listen to Bloch) was on a very different issue than had been decided in conference the preceding day. Jackson knew full well what had been decided the day before (the Finerty motion); Jackson knew what Bloch was now attempting had to do with clemency based on Douglas's sensitivity to Asiatic thinking. Jackson, of all the justices, knew that the two issues—yesterday's and today's—were very different. What Jackson was saying is that "no individual Justice to whom application was made would overturn the Court's determination" regardless of what that new application asserted. What was "perfectly understood," at conference, as Jackson stated it, was that the Court's consideration of the Rosenberg case had come to an end. Jackson used words carefully. He could have meant nothing else. Bloch's subsequent attempts to reach Douglas were in violation of what was "perfectly understood" by all the justices at their Monday conference.

The statement has a third significance. Frankfurter did not demur.

There is separate corroboration of what was "perfectly understood" by the justices at their Monday-afternoon conference. It was, indeed, perfectly understood that no individual justice to whom application of any kind was made would overrrule what the Court had determined to be its final action in the Rosenberg case, the denial of the Finerty motion on Monday afternoon, June 15. Yet that is exactly what Justice Douglas did, in response to an argument never before heard in the case, two days later on Wednesday morning.

And what was "perfectly understood" heavily influenced the Court against Justice Douglas's move during the next days. Tragically, this may have been the integral element in a fabric of misconduct of judges and high government officials that deprived the Rosenbergs of a fair hearing on the last two days of their lives.

The separate corroboration is found in the oral history of Philip Elman, a former Frankfurter clerk, Federal Trade commissioner, and lifelong friend of Justice Frankfurter's. Elman was in the office of the solicitor general of the United States when the Rosenberg case occurred, although he had nothing to do with the case. Elman's oral history of his long and historic legal career has been taken by Columbia University and is on file there.[11] Elman's commentary on the Rosenberg case, part his own and part recorded from what he heard from Frankfurter, found in that oral history, is startling. Elman says first:

> The Rosenberg case is the most disgusting, saddest, despicable episode in the Court's history in my lifetime. This has nothing to do with whether the Rosenbergs were guilty or innocent, whether Irving Kaufman should have been impeached for his conduct of the trial, any of those things. I'm thinking about the way the case was handled in the Supreme Court. They were so furious with Douglas.[12]

Elman explains the incensed feeling by Douglas's brethren:

> Black, Jackson and Frankfurter had consistently voted for review on each of the chief petitions for certiorari. Douglas would have been the needed fourth vote to get the case up on review. He voted to deny certiorari, and a motion to hear argument and a stay. Jackson withdrew his previous vote for review.[13]

Against this backdrop, Elman painted the Court's attitude on the last day that the Rosenberg petitions were before them on the preceding Saturday and Monday conferences.

After all the successive petitions were denied, they all agreed this was it; they were not going to entertain further applications, they were going to adjourn for the summer and go off, and that's what they all agreed. They denied the last petition for rehearing.

After they went off for the summer, Douglas entertained this stay application by Fyke Farmer who was not even a lawyer for the Rosenbergs, a stranger to the case. He had this new ground which nobody had ever mentioned before. Nobody knew if it had any merit or not. Looking back at it now, I'm sure it had a lot of merit. The argument is that where there are two statutes imposing punishment for what is essentially the same offense you choose the more lenient. But it was a new argument, nobody had mentioned it before, and nobody knew whether there was anything to it. And what happened, this has been recounted over and over again, all I can say is that from where I sat in the Solicitor General's office, from what I heard from Frankfurter, the Justices were so livid, so furious with Douglas for granting a stay, he became the accused, the Defendant, not the Rosenbergs.[14]

Elman then summarizes:

The whole thing was an absolute shambles, a disaster for the Court—as well as the Rosenbergs, of course. Frankfurter wrote a little dissent in which he was writing really to me and to other friends of his, former law clerks, whose whole faith in the Supreme Court had been shaken. We knew the Supreme Court was one institution that worked the way it was supposed to work, where people got a fair shake, where equal justice under law was more than a slogan. And here the whole thing was falling down and we were shattered. This was our court, The Supreme Court of the United States, for which we had feelings of admiration and closeness. And Frankfurter wrote for us: "This isn't the end, errors are inevitably made but you go on, you don't lose faith in the processes of law."[15]

This condemnation of what occurred in the Rosenberg case is as full as any that could be made. It comes from a student of the Court, an intimate of Justice Frankfurter's, reflects the justice's views, and explains why Frankfurter found the Rosenberg case the most "anguishing" case that he had confronted in his years of service on that Court. It is a damning commentary on what went on in the Supreme Court of the United States when the Court hastily, and without fair deliberation, put the Rosenbergs into the electric chair.

The judicial irregularities did not stop there. Late on the afternoon of the same Tuesday, June 16, Douglas came to Frankfurter's chambers for new advice. It had to do *not* with Bloch, but rather the new lawyers who had put before Douglas a brand-new issue that had never been argued in the case before: the applicability of the Atomic Energy Act of 1946 to the Rosenbergs' conduct. Douglas told Frankfurter that Tuesday afternoon that it had been argued to him by new counsel (Farmer and Marshall) whom Douglas had agreed to hear. Douglas frankly wanted advice from Frankfurter, because Douglas thought that the new point, as belated as it was, had substance. Frankfurter, listening to Douglas, agreed that it looked to him as if it did. Douglas telephoned Frankfurter twice more on Tuesday evening, and finally told Frankfurter that he was going to bed with a draft of his opinion completed. He told Frankfurter that he was relieved that the difficult job had been finished.[16]

CHAPTER SIX

1

WEDNESDAY, JUNE 17, 1953

Justice Frankfurter's Chambers

UT WAS IT? Early on Wednesday morning, June 17, Douglas again telephoned Frankfurter twice. Douglas was now seeking out another justice, Frankfurter, whose wisdom and understanding of how the Court should function meant something to Douglas.

Douglas reported that he had had a busier night than he had told Frankfurter. Douglas reported that he had seen the chief justice for an hour on the night before, Tuesday evening, June 16. Chief Justice Vinson (as Douglas reported to Frankfurter) disputed Douglas's contention that the new point had any merit.[1] Vinson told Douglas that the Rosenbergs at this late date had certainly waived the point, whatever it was. Further, the chief justice said that the two lawyers, Farmer and Marshall, had absolutely no standing to raise this point. They did not represent the Rosenbergs. But Vinson went on to tell Douglas (as Douglas reported to Frankfurter) that "the Attorney General had been in touch with the Chief and had urged that the new matter go to conference."[2]

The substance of this conversation between the attorney general and the chief justice differed from what had been discussed in the Vinson-Brownell meeting (arranged by Jackson) the day before. At *that* meeting, the three men settled on a contingency plan to recall the Court if Douglas acted alone. A *separate* proposal made by the attorney general to the chief justice was the

75

attorney general's urging of the chief justice to convince Douglas *not* to act alone, but rather to submit his new point to a conference of all the justices. Brownell knew he had a majority in the conference of justices; but he also knew that he had no votes of any kind inside the unpredictable conscience of Bill Douglas. Two separate ex parte approaches were accordingly made by the attorney general on June 16; each was received and acted on by the chief justice.

This new suggestion of Brownell's could very well have come from him (along with the other contingency plans) in the Brownell-Vinson meeting the day before. But it is a second private attempt by the attorney general to influence the chief justice (who was obviously open and agreeable to the suggestion) to utilize his influence as chief justice to pressure Douglas not to enter a stay (on his own action) of the Rosenbergs' execution. A request by the attorney general to the chief justice to try to influence a deliberating (and worried) Douglas was just as improper as the contingency plans that Vinson and Brownell (with Jackson's connivance) met to put in place. Indeed, it is more so. It is an ex parte communication (and we now know what *they* are) from the Rosenbergs' leading official adversary, the attorney general, to the chief justice, seeking the chief justice's intervention to influence Justice Douglas on Douglas's vote and disposition of a vital petition then pending in the Rosenberg case before Douglas.

Frankfurter's comments to Douglas were piquant: "Do, I said, what your conscience tells you, not what the Chief Justice tells you. Further, I said, I cannot advise you. Tete-a-tete conversation cannot settle the matter."[3]

It is surprising that Frankfurter himself did not throw up his hands at what was communicated to him. But Frankfurter had not participated in any ex parte communications.

That cannot be said of Jackson, Vinson, and the attorney general of the United States. Apparently, a curious form of slippage occurs when one is elevated to the exalted world peopled by these luminaries. The rules set for all lawyers and judges elsewhere yield to the statesmanlike activities of the highest judge in the land and the chief lawyer for his country. What no judge would do elsewhere and what no lawyer would do elsewhere is, apparently, removed from the practice of ordinary mortals; it is statesmanship. Yet the activities of these high officials affect the lives of litigants as do the activities of all judges and lawyers. What transpired between the chief justice and the attorney general was not statecraft. It was ex parte communication, no more and no less.[4] And it was terribly prejudicial to the defendants in the case.

In practical, nonlegal terms, what did this second approach by the attorney general mean? It meant—in the hypothetical case posed earlier—that the angry district attorney who wanted the angry judge's twenty-year term for the son to remain untouched discovered that new lawyers were approaching a second judge to vacate the sentence because it was not recommended by a jury and therefore not legal. So the district attorney communicated privately with the chief judge in the district and asked the chief judge to use his influence with the second judge to urge the second judge *not* to set the first judge's sentence aside but, rather, to follow another path that the DA felt sure would not touch the original sentence. Since the son's lawyers knew nothing of any of these moves, this was active, private intervention by a prosecuting attorney and the chief judge to influence a judicial result. It was grossly unfair, more so than the private meeting between the DA and the angry judge, to plan what to do *if* the attempt was made to set the sentence aside.

In the Rosenberg case, the angry district attorney (in our hypothetical case) was, in fact, the attorney general of the United States; the chief judge of the district (in our hypothetical case) was, in fact, Chief Justice Vinson of the United States Supreme Court.

Supreme Court Building, Chambers of Justice Douglas

Meanwhile, Douglas had holed himself up for what turned out to be a far longer, tougher job than he'd expected. Helped by just one clerk, the justice read the Farmer-Marshall document three times before he was sure he had it all. On Tuesday afternoon and early Wednesday morning, Douglas got hold of everything he could find on the Atomic Energy Act of 1946. The Supreme Court has "canned" legislative histories of all major acts, files that include all of the committee reports, hearings, and major statements on the floor of both Houses on all bills that become important statutes. Douglas examined the file on the Atomic Energy Act. He found that what Marshall and Farmer told him was true: the Rosenbergs could not be executed under the 1946 act without a jury recommendation. More than that, Douglas found that the indictment in the case was probably faulty to begin with—if, as the two lawyers agreed, the 1946 act applied.

From the very moment that Douglas accepted the Marshall-Farmer papers, he had realized that he was on a lonely track that would lead him to strong public abuse. Once he understood the Farmer-Marshall argument, Douglas knew not only that the death sentence was awry in this case, but the indictment as well. If Marshall and Farmer were right, the government would have to go back to square one. The entire case would have to go back to a grand jury. The Rosenbergs would have to be reindicted; there would have to be an entire new trial: and the trial would probably be before Kaufman, a man whom Douglas did not like. For setting in motion such a painful rerun of the case, Douglas would get personal attacks from every corner of the legal community and from all parts of society. The prospect of personal criticism did not alarm Douglas, but he was understandably worried about other possible repercussions of a retrial. If the sentence were set aside, the Communist press throughout the world would have a field day. The fact that fifteen federal judges in the American system had blundered until one accidentally stumbled upon the truth would be trumpeted around the world as a condemnation of U.S. justice. The next trial would be a circus. It would be held in the eye of a press-radio-television hurricane, and everything that Douglas held dear about American justice would be at its worst in that kind of spectacle. But two people cannot be put to death because the authorities are afraid of the notoriety that would follow the admission of mistakes. Whatever the price, it had to be paid by the Department of Justice in the retrial.

What Douglas liked least about this situation was the antici-
pated reaction of his brethren on the Supreme Court. He knew
full well the animosities that lay only inches below the surface in
the conference room, and not much more deeply submerged in
the hearing room during argument. Douglas's convoluted record
in this case didn't help. He also was aware of the "perfectly
understood" agreement amongst his brethren, the agreement not
to do precisely what Douglas was now planning to do. Perhaps
Frankfurter would not join the others; his standards of personal
propriety were sufficiently high to recognize that not observing
the terms of the justices' private accord was following a higher
road than the justices' agreed path. Black would not join. He had
been committed to the reversal of the verdict in Kaufman's
courtroom from day one. But Jackson would surely visit down
upon Douglas the venom that had heretofore been reserved by
that haughty and egocentric patrician for Black, in a vendetta that
was both public and near-violent. The stalwarts, the good old
boys on the bench from the chief justice through Reed and Clark
down to Burton and Minton, would simply feel betrayed. The
few personal credits that Douglas possessed and could use in cases
where he felt strongly, those small points that came from going
along on those rare occasions when Douglas did go along with
results that concerned him only slightly, would be lost for the
future. Always a loner on this Court, Douglas would become a
pariah in this very building if he violated the "perfectly understood" agreement among his brethren that the Rosenberg case
was closed. And Douglas was particularly sensitive about this
particular case because of his own inconsistent, almost unintelligible record in the Rosenberg case. *That* bothered Douglas,
bothered him terribly.

Supreme Court Building, Lawyers' Lounge, 11:00 A.M.

At 9:00 in the morning of Wednesday, June 17, the reporters
began to gather in the Lawyers' Lounge of the Supreme Court
building. Word of Justice Douglas's consideration of the Farmer-
Marshall document had spread like wildfire overnight. It was on

the national wires, in all of the morning newspapers, and on the front page of the *Washington Post* and *New York Times*. The conversations among the reporters were sporadic. No one had any idea what was in the Farmer-Marshall document; the clerk's office had no copies. The guess among the reporters was that the two lawyers were filing statements from prominent opponents of the death penalty. But no one knew.

Bloch, who had a petition of his own pending before Douglas, was also waiting in the Lawyers' Lounge. But the attention was focused on what Farmer and Marshall had presented to Douglas. Farmer and Marshall were also in the Lawyers' Lounge. Bloch ignored them.

Time passed slowly. At four minutes to 11:00, one of the reporters remarked that the Rosenbergs had exactly thirty-three hours and five minutes to live. The execution was scheduled for 8:00 P.M., Thursday, at Sing Sing.

When the news came that Douglas had actually done it, had entered a stay of the execution, the normally staid and formal room broke into pandemonium. The order reached the clerk's office at 11:00 A.M. and was immediately sent over to the reporters. Every telephone in the Court building was preempted to spread the news.

Douglas's order was concise. He first pointed out that the Atomic Energy Act of 1946 required a recommendation from the jury before any violators of it could be put to death.[5] Then he added a point that appeared for the first time in the Farmer-Marshall papers: under the 1946 act, the additional requirement was imposed that the government must prove that the espionage was done "with an intent to injure the United States."[6] Prior to that time, under the 1917 Espionage Act, all that was required was a showing that the spies intended to benefit a foreign power, a requirement easily proved in the context of nuclear disclosures to the Soviets. Douglas stated simply:

> Neither of these conditions is satisfied in this case, as the jury did not recommend the death penalty nor did the indictment charge that the offense was committed with an intent to injure the United States.[7]

Just as simply he added:

If the Atomic Energy Act of 1946 is applicable to the prosecution of the Rosenbergs, the District Court unlawfully imposed the death sentence.[8]

Douglas recited the government's position:

The Department of Justice maintains that the Espionage Act [of 1917] is applicable to the indictment because all of the overt acts alleged took place before passage of the Atomic Energy Act of 1946.[9]

After noting that "curiously, this point had never been raised or presented to this Court in any of the earlier petitions or applications" and that "this question is presented to me for the first time on the eve of the execution of the Rosenbergs without the benefit of briefs or any extended research,"[10] Douglas made three points disposing of what the government contended:

First, the offenses charged was a conspiracy commencing before but continuing after the date of the new Act [August 1, 1946]; Second, although the overt acts alleged were committed in 1944 and 1945, the Government's case showed acts of the Rosenbergs in pursuance of the conspiracy long after the new Act became effective. Third, the overt acts of the co-conspirator, Sobell, were alleged to have taken place between January, 1946, and May, 1948. But the proof against Sobell, as against the Rosenbergs, extended well beyond the effective date of the new Act.[11]

Douglas added that a substantial portion of the case against the Rosenbergs related to conduct in the conspiracy that occurred after August 1, 1946.[12]

Although Douglas did not decide with finality that the death penalty could not be imposed unless the requirements of the 1946 act were satisfied (that is, unless a jury recommended death, after finding that the Rosenbergs intended to injure the United States), he ruled that the question was substantial, to be decided only after full briefing and argument—so full, in fact, that he ordered the case sent back to Judge Kaufman for his decision on this point. Then it would be taken to the Second Circuit Court of Appeals, and then back to the Supreme Court.[13]

He was giving the Rosenbergs another year of life at the very least.

It was a resounding victory, not alone for the Rosenbergs but for Farmer and Marshall. Coming out of nowhere, they had saved the day with a wholly new argument that a platoon of the Rosenbergs' lawyers and at least fifteen judges—the number who had sat on the case to that point—had either overlooked or completely ignored.

Sing Sing Penitentiary

Both Ethel and Julius Rosenberg heard about it on the radio. The little radio each was permitted was the entire connection with their case and with life and hope for the doomed spies. Bloch had been to visit each of them in a quick trip from Washington on Monday, the fifteenth, and had left them little hope. Bloch was talking about his last approach to Douglas based on the death penalty's being excessive. Regardless of his mistakes in the courtroom, Bloch, a fair and decent man, told the Rosenbergs that there was little chance that Douglas would listen. The last hope, he said, was Eisenhower, and Eisenhower had already spoken once on the case and was known to harbor no sympathy for the Rosenbergs.

Bloch never mentioned the new Farmer-Marshall effort. Prior to June 17, Bloch never once gave the Farmer-Marshall effort any credence. He telegraphed his opposition to it when the Farmer-Marshall petition was before Kaufman on June 14–15. Not once until they succeeded with Douglas did Bloch deal with Farmer and Marshall as anything but intruders or interlopers—to use Kaufman's terms.

On Tuesday, the Rosenbergs heard the radio announce that new lawyers were trying some new tactic that appeared to be on their behalf. Farmer and Marshall meant nothing to them. But they knew of Edelman and assumed that he was a meddler because that was what Bloch had told them. But when hope is lost, any activity at all is light for the blind, and the Rosenbergs' spirits had risen in spite of what Bloch had told them. Now, on Wednesday, when they heard the radio announcement—before the warden came to give them the news officially—Ethel and Julius Rosenberg both wept. It was the first good news of any kind that either had received in thirty-five months, since the day in July of 1950 when FBI men had showed up at their apartment and taken Julius away. Neither had the faintest idea what the Douglas stay was based on; neither understood what the technicalities were that Farmer and Marshall had argued. But the radio news meant all the world to them. They would not have to die at eight o'clock the next day.

Supreme Court Building, Lawyers' Lounge, 11:00 P.M.

Back in the Supreme Court's Lawyers' Lounge a first occurred: Bloch went over to Farmer, threw his arms around him and, amidst clicking cameras, Bloch pronounced a major victory. The sense of what Bloch said made it sound like a joint major victory in which he had participated. Bloch was a heavy, dominant figure who took center stage. Farmer was slight and retiring. But Bloch later acknowledged to his own colleagues on the defense team that he, Bloch, had foolishly ignored Farmer, had called him and Marshall meddlers and that Farmer and Marshall were superior lawyers and Bloch a lesser one. Bloch always had center stage. But Bloch also was an honest and candid man.

Office of U.S. Representative W. M. Wheeler of Georgia

Meanwhile, U.S. congressman W. M. Wheeler of the Fourth District of Georgia was damned mad. Like everyone else in Congress that hot Wednesday in June, he had heard the news from the Supreme Court. For Wheeler, everything stopped; the rush to complete his business so that he could get back to Albany, Georgia, before Congress adjourned for the Fourth of July, all of his chores on the Ways and Means Committee, the powerful taxing committee on which he had a ranking seat; even the reception of delegations from down home that regularly trailed in after lunch—all of the routine occurrences simply receded and disappeared in the face of the new twist in the Rosenberg case. In that damnable order staying the death of the Communist spies, Representative Wheeler was certain that Justice Douglas had subverted the Constitution and laws of the United States.

Representative Wheeler knew that he had to do something about this disgrace, and he had to do it fast so that the whole world would know at once that Justice Douglas was an outcast, a pariah, insofar as all patriotic Americans were concerned.

The question was what to do.

One of the representative's closest cronies in the House, Representative Francis Walter of Pennsylvania, would know what to do. Wheeler was himself a lawyer, true, but a Georgia small-town lawyer more accustomed to dealing with the local railroad or a neighbor's leg broken by an insured but reckless driver than to attacking major legal controversies. Francis Walter, chairman of the House Judiciary Committee, although a Democrat, was a rock of the conservative wing of the House and would know the precise move to fix Douglas's water.

Wheeler called Francis Walter. The chairman was even more aroused than Wheeler. Walter had never trusted Douglas; the justice's ruling in several immigration cases had struck at Walter's pet cause: preserving the nation from hordes of undesirable immigrants, paupers from all those places abroad who wanted to come to the United States. Now Douglas had surpassed himself by saving the Communist Rosenbergs from what they deserved. Walter and Wheeler, both appalled, talked for a long time on the telephone. When he rang off, Wheeler, feeling both righteous and well supported, called his secretary in and began dictating a resolution. He told her that it would be just a rough draft, to be sent over to Francis Walter's office as soon as possible because Walter wanted to go over it quickly. The point was, Wheeler told his secretary, to get the thing written and in the legislative hopper before the day was out.

Twenty minutes later, the secretary began to type. The opening words (after the familiar "whereas" that opens all congressional resolutions) announced that the undersigned members of Congress who were subscribing to this resolution had determined that Justice William O. Douglas had subverted the Constitution and laws of the United States in a manner that required impeachment by the House of Representatives and a trial by the Senate. Wheeler's charge simply cited Douglas's Rosenberg decision and detailed Wheeler's conviction that this decision constituted subversion by giving aid and comfort to the enemies of the United States.[14]

The draft resolution went over to Representative Walter's office an hour later and was filed in the hopper an hour after that. Speaker Sam Rayburn, who knew a legislative aberration when he saw one, but who also read the newspaper headlines every day, assigned the resolution to the House Judiciary Committee, chaired by Representative Francis Walter of Pennsylvania. Rayburn had no other choice.

By the end of the day, nine other congressmen had publicly subscribed to the impeachment resolution.

Statler Hotel, Washington, D.C.

There were more than forty people crowded into Bloch's two-room suite at the Statler. Bloch, who was exhausted, had managed to swallow a couple of Scotch whiskies and was reacting to fatigue, alcohol, and the good news. Farmer and Marshall were not at the party; they had gone off quietly by themselves.

Bloch noisily declaimed that the Edelman lawyers were the best lawyers in the world and that he, Bloch, was the worst. He went on describing the many times that Farmer and Marshall had come to him with their point of law and his blind rejection of each overture. Bloch told his friends that this was a measure of what a pitifully lousy trial lawyer he was.

Gloria Agrin, a young lawyer who had done yeoman service for Bloch in the appeals, was present, still—six hours later— transported by the morning's news. For the Rosenberg lawyers, their families, and the stalwart supporters who had lived together through all of the bad times, it was a first victory, and they were having a liquid celebration.

The party crescendoed at about six. All of the lawyers were

speculating about Kaufman's reaction to the Douglas stay. It would be bloody awful before Kaufman. But they all agreed that the appearance before Kaufman in the fall would be perfunctory, with all of the heavy ammunition reserved for the effort before the Second Circuit. Time spent arguing before Kaufman would clearly be a fruitless waste.

In all the noise, no one heard the telephone for a long time. It was in the foyer of the cell-like Statler suite. Finally, Bloch broke away from friends and answered it. He listened for nearly a full minute before he said a word, and then Bloch's first words were of disbelief. He asked if any opportunity would be given for opposition; then by a shake of his head indicated that none would. He listened quietly for another two minutes. By this time, Bloch's silence and obvious consternation had gathered a small knot of concerned celebrators around him. Bloch's worried look ended the celebration. Finally, he put the telephone down.

The call was from UP. The national wire was already printing the startling news: Vinson had called a special term of the Supreme Court to meet the following day at noon. He had done so on the request of Brownell, filed just an hour earlier. UP's quick check of the justices carried word that at least eight would be in the courtroom. The only justice who was missing and out of Washington was Douglas, and the Supreme Court clerk was trying to find him somewhere driving cross-country to his home in Washington.

The party was over. Gloria Agrin began to cry. The giddy heights of carefree victory at six o'clock, then the terrible anxieties and impending doom coming out of the news at 6:10; it was all too much. Bloch collapsed on the edge of his bed, his head in his hands, his face so white and so fatigued that a group of friends hurried to help him up into a chair. The turnabout seemed to have crushed him.

The partygoers, now quiet, looked at Bloch, speechless in the chair where his friends had put him. The stout lawyer seemed to have aged ten years in ten minutes. There was no chance that the lawyers would be able to do any work that evening. Bloch was in shock. Farmer and Marshall were off somewhere on their own.

Bar Association of the City of New York

Even after the good news from Douglas, Farmer and Marshall were not in a partying mood. They had too much to do. Douglas had given them a second round with Kaufman. But the second round was on a new point, and any second round with Kaufman was not going to be any better than the first.

Immediately after he read Douglas's decision and received Bloch's warm and loud embrace in the Lawyers' Lounge, Farmer talked to Marshall and they headed for the plane back to New York.

Their purpose was simple. Douglas's stay had been granted on but one point: the applicability of the 1946 Atomic Energy Act to the Rosenbergs' conduct. But the sixty-one-page document that Farmer had filed with Douglas had a half-dozen other arguments in it all bearing on what Kaufman had done at trial. Given Douglas's sanction as to one point, Farmer and Marshall wanted to press hard and fast to get all of their other points before Kaufman. Kaufman might refuse to consider them. But he would have trouble in dismissing them summarily. Kaufman had been ordered to review the entire record of the case. He would have some explaining to do, public explaining, if he did not address Farmer's and Marshall's other points. And both of them wanted to force Kaufman to make that public explanation.

The men flew into New York late in the afternoon. Through friends of Farmer, they found they could enlist typing help from secretaries at the Bar Association of the City of New York. They went directly there to redraft their sixty-one-page petition, align it with Douglas's language, and force Kaufman to consider—at least—all of the other points in the original petition. The suppression of David Greenglass's sketch of the bomb from the court record, the suppression of Greenglass's testimony concerning it, the treason issue (that is, it was treason and not conspiracy to spy that the Rosenbergs were really charged with in this case without the constitutional safeguards given defendants in a treason case)—these were only some of the points that the two lawyers were going to press on Kaufman.

While Farmer and Marshall were working with the secretaries from the Bar Association—at six in the evening—word got to the office that Vinson had ordered the entire Supreme Court to reconvene the following afternoon, Thursday, June 18, at 2:00 P.M. to consider the government's petition to vacate Douglas's stay. Within a half-hour, two U.S. marshals appeared in the office in New York, asked for Farmer and Marshall, and told both lawyers that they were directed to appear before the full Supreme Court of the United States the following afternoon at 2:00 P.M. The marshals then made immediate plane reservations for Farmer and Marshall to fly back to Washington early the following morning.

It was a command performance. Farmer and Marshall gave up their work, dismissed the secretaries, went to their hotels and bedded down for the early-morning flight.[15]

Clerk's Office, U.S. Supreme Court Building

The attorney general, the chief justice, and Justice Jackson had planned carefully and well. Following the sequence agreed to among them the day before, the Justice Department filed a motion with the Supreme Court to reconvene itself (for the third time in its 164-year history) by 5:00 P.M. Without notice to any of the Rosenberg lawyers, Vinson acted by 6:00 P.M. to reconvene the Court. Among the things that Farmer and Marshall were later to brood about was whether they had the right to contest the action of the Court in reconvening itself. It was doing so to consider vacating Douglas's stay. There was very good reason to believe that the Court had no legal right to do so.

Home of Joe Rauh

All of the Court was still in Washington with the exception of Douglas, who had entered his stay and then taken off by car through Pennsylvania for the long ride to Goose Prairie, Washington. He knew full well he had shocked the Court and the nation. He also believed he had acted out of conscience.

But his colleagues did not share Douglas's high view of

himself. He had been on both sides of this case, more than just once. There is strong reason to believe that Douglas's own act of conscience was accompanied in his own mind by the belief that it would never succeed. The lone justice was never more isolated. And this time he had violated an agreement that the good old boys had expected to end this nightmare: he had acted alone when it was understood that no single justice would do so.

Frankfurter, whose participation in political affairs outside of the court had brought down criticism on him, had a much stricter view of what was right and proper inside the Court. Frankfurter had strong, negative views about Douglas's overall functioning in the Supreme Court drama that reached its height on June 17. Frankfurter had closed his own house for the summer and was visiting with a former clerk, Joe Rauh, then and now a leader of the liberal wing of the Democratic party, on Rauh's porch that Wednesday evening. Frankfurter's words to Rauh summarized Frankfurter's anger and his feeling of helplessness at the specter of an injustice that was playing out before him. Rauh wrote:

Sitting on our porch that evening, he seemed angriest at Justice Douglas whose actions at earlier stages of the case had not supported a full review of the case and now at the last minute pulled a "grandstand play." He was upset, too, by the hasty action of the Attorney General and the Chief Justice in recalling the Court. His usual feelings against capital punishment were exacerbated by what he believed was the unjudicious conduct of Judge Irving Kaufman in both the manner and substance of the sentencing. Above all, he seemed disconsolate at the hopelessness of winning a majority for a full review of the case.[16]

Frankfurter was, apart from all other things, a highly principled man with a meticulous belief of what should occur in American criminal justice. He knew well how Douglas himself had destroyed the support for his position. And he knew—as he always knew—where the votes on the Court were. It was little wonder that he shared with his friends—more than once—that the Rosenberg case was a low point for him in his years in his beloved Supreme Court.

Perhaps Frankfurter's intellectual colleague, Jackson, saw the reality if not the tragedy of it all. Jackson always believed that

Douglas would vote for a Supreme Court review of the Rosenberg conviction only if Douglas was sure that there were not
enough votes (four) to secure review. Douglas's last act, his
momentous stay, was a perfect example of precisely that gambit.
The pervasive animus and maneuvering that had settled over the
justices when they had two lives in their hands underscored
Frankfurter's despair that evening.

Alexandria, Virginia

Justice Black was in Alexandria having an early dinner; his
doctors had directed him to stay away from food and water after
7:00 that evening because there was a chance that they might
actually operate the following day. A gall bladder operation,
although a miserable business, was not very frightening for a
healthy man like the justice from Alabama. It looked like a good
time to catch up on some light reading; Black already had four or
five novels that he wanted to read during his convalescence
arranged by his bed upstairs.

When the call came from the chief clerk of the Court, Harold
Willey, Black took a few seconds to comprehend Willey's news.
Then his own gorge began to rise. The chief had taken this
unprecedented step without consulting any of his brothers and
without giving the Rosenberg lawyers any opportunity to oppose
the special term. Black was pretty well convinced as he put down
the phone that Douglas's stay, wise or unwise, could not be
touched by the whole Court. Insofar as Black could recall, the
Court had never in its history intervened to vacate the action of a
single justice. But the manner of the Court's reconvening
bothered Black almost as much as it bothered Bloch, Marshall,
and Farmer. And until Douglas died fourteen years later, Black
never knew of the Vinson-Brownell meeting the day before,
where this very contingency had been discussed and planned. Had
he known, Black's annoyance would have turned to controlled
fury, a rare but fearsome facet of the mild Alabaman's personality.

Northwest Washington

Chief Clerk Willey found Jackson in his apartment in northwest Washington. The imperious New Yorker was just as surprised as Black. But his surprise delayed for only a few moments a far stronger emotion: he was delighted. Jackson had been horrified by the Douglas stay; it was a breach of the understanding that the justices had entered into the preceding Monday afternoon. While conduct like this might have been expected from Black, Jackson's arch-enemy on the Court, the fact that it came from Douglas didn't surprise Jackson. Jackson had little respect for the maverick westerner who, thought Jackson, either didn't perceive the historic limits on the Court's powers, or, if he did, ignored them. Besides, Douglas was terribly crude and inelegant. Jackson believed that a seat on the Supreme Court of the United States was not simply an office, but also an assigned role that one played in history's continuing drama. Ideally, one played his role to the hilt: the pince-nez; the rich and elegant prose in his opinions; the fine tailoring; the hatred of certain of his brothers whom he fancied below the salt—all were in the grand manner. Douglas was one of those who, Jackson believed, simply could not rise to the level of the Court's grand, historic traditions.

This stay in the Rosenberg case was a perfect example of it. Granting it for the Edelman bunch, interlopers at best, in defiance of a gentleman's understanding that this very thing would not be done, was poor taste. It must be shown for precisely what it was. The chief justice had acted wisely. Jackson looked forward to the morrow's activities with relish. He knew that Douglas would be taken down a peg or two and could hardly wait until it happened.

A Motel in Uniontown, Pennsylvania

Douglas left the Supreme Court building by car, Wednesday noon, escaping all of the telephone calls that flooded his office when the stay was announced. Then he simply drove west. He knew the roads well; for fourteen summers, he had taken the same route, across Pennsylvania and through Ohio and Indiana to the

Lincoln Highway, stopping to see a friend in Illinois, and then west across the plains to his farm at Goose Prairie, Washington.

He knew that he had just dropped a bomb. A clear majority of the Court would be offended by the stay; Douglas was certain of that. They had all agreed that no one would do it, but he had done it. But none of the rest of them had heard, and read, and thought about the points that Farmer and Marshall had put before him. Uneasy as he was about the reaction on the Court, Douglas was sure that he would have been in misery for the rest of his days had he done anything but grant the stay.

As a precaution, Douglas left a memorandum with the chief justice outlining his itinerary. He was following his route when dusk overtook him in Uniontown, Pennsylvania, just south of Pittsburgh. He saw a motel, stopped and registered, and listened to a symphony while he was moving his bags. Then the announcer interrupted the music and announced that the chief justice of the United States had called a special term of the Supreme Court for noon the next day to review Douglas's stay of execution.

Douglas called his secretary in Washington and confirmed the news. She also told Douglas that she had asked the chief justice if he had tried to locate Douglas and the chief justice said that he had not. Douglas had it in his mind that Vinson would sit over an eight-man Court (with him absent) the next day deliberating his stay. He told his secretary to inform the chief justice that he would be there.[17]

He was tempted to just keep going out to Goose Prairie and let the pygmies in Washington do anything they wanted about his stay. Douglas was sure that the chief justice could not, by himself, convene a special term of court. That required a vote of five justices. Perhaps he should just let them play it out. It would be a gesture appropriate to the contempt in which he held some of the conservatives on the Court—who were obviously behind this action to reconvene—and for the irrational way that Vinson was acting. But, Douglas reasoned, he'd better defend what he had done. Better to get back into the fray. If it was going to be a tough, technical fight, he should be there to try and win it. The Court's procedures were his special preserve. He could make mincemeat out of those lumbering minds who seemed so upset over his stay. With no emotion except perhaps an imperceptible glint of anticipation in his eyes, Douglas went back to the motel desk, told the clerk he would not be checking in, climbed into his car and headed east, back up the mountain road that he had just come down.

The Statler Hotel, Washington, D.C.

For Bloch, it was a time of doubt. He had only the slightest glimmering of the mounting hostility within the Supreme Court concerning the extraordinary events of the day. Indeed, he was not aware of one insuperable hurdle that he faced: the various degrees of outrage felt by the justices against Douglas for violating their secret conference room concordat.

What to do? How to argue? Should Bloch now abandon all of the other arguments that he had made over the years? Was it time to put to rest the unfairness of Judge Kaufman, the console table evidence, the parading back and forth of the issue of membership in the Communist party? Should he limit himself solely to the issue of Section 10 of the Atomic Energy Act of 1946? Most agonizing of all, should he even mention his own continuing belief in the innocence of his clients?

Once the party crowd dispersed, Bloch realized that he was exhausted. It bothered him not at all that two others, Farmer and Marshall, were responsible for the only real break that his clients had ever had before the courts. But the question before him in the twilight fatigue of his hotel room remained: how was he to argue before the Supreme Court of the United States in the unprecedented special session at 2:00 P.M. tomorrow?

The Rosenberg strategists, Sharp, Finerty, Mrs. Agrin, and Bloch, met quietly after the celebrators had left. There was very little talk. Each looked at the others for guidance; they all looked to Bloch for leadership. But Bloch had faced too much; he was exhausted to the point where the very act of speech taxed him. Bloch was through for that day. After a brief discussion, Sharp, Finerty, and Mrs. Agrin left the aging warrior, and gathered without him. But it was a rump session. They all knew that Bloch would have to do the arguing for the group next day. Bloch's present condition made planning impossible. After working out a schedule for the next morning, the three worried lawyers left for their own rooms to spend the night in unrelieved, unproductive anxiety. No one among the four regulars thought of contacting Marshall and Farmer to coordinate their efforts on the following day. Nor did Marshall or Farmer contact anyone in the Bloch camp. The two newcomers felt that their position was clear and that no force on earth could prevent one of them from getting on his feet the next day and speaking out to the Court.

With one last and, apparently, substantial opportunity to save the Rosenbergs in a court session to be observed by the world, all of the lawyers on the Rosenberg side, including the two newcomers Marshall and Farmer, let Wednesday night and Thursday morning slip by without planning what would be said and by whom. Their failure to plan was to lead to another unprecedented event: a near-brawl between lawyers at the ornate lawyers' table in the Supreme Court's palatial hearing room. More importantly, it lost for all time the opportunity to present to the Court in reasoned and orderly fashion the new argument concerning the 1946 act.

But it is very doubtful if the Court would have listened to even the most eloquent and organized argument. It seems clear that every mind on the Court was completely made up by dawn on Thursday, six hours before any lawyer said a word. And it seems just as clear that a majority of the nine were plain mad, mad at Douglas and what he had done. The Lord himself, in morning coat and arguing, could not have produced five votes for the Rosenbergs under those circumstances. And public events continued to prejudice the issue; the Rosenberg luck, although capable of smiling deceptively for a few hours, was still running bad.

Newsreel: June 17, 1953

The first three days in that week heightened the national alarm over the Red Menace. There was outrage on Monday (the day on which the Supreme Court denied the last formal Rosenberg appeal) when the same Court reversed the racketeering conviction of Harry Bridges, West Coast longshoremen leader and accused leftist, causing the government to drop charges against him. The day following Albert Einstein's public advice to American intellectuals to shun the congressional inquiries, Senator McCarthy called Einstein an "enemy of America" for his advice. The senator found himself in conflict with President Conant of Harvard over the reports that certain books were destroyed in embassy libraries in Europe because of their suspected leftist content. Alumni of the Massachusetts Institute of Technology voted moral support for three colleagues accused of testifying falsely before the congressional inquiries on communism. The publisher of the *New York Times* made a commencement speech on Sunday afternoon of that same week declaring that a national amnesty should be given to ex-Reds who "cut their ties by 1948."

A national poll of libraries in the United States revealed that a majority of public libraries did not "curb" books by leftists, while a sizable number of private libraries did. An appellate court in New York sustained the firing of fourteen more schoolteachers who refused to answer questions concerning their political beliefs.

Abroad, there was great alarm voiced in Seoul over the proposed terms of the United States–Red China peace accords under negotiation. But a major new uprising in East Berlin on June 15, involving thousands of residents in that city, gave Americans the first view of violent protest behind the Iron Curtain. Soviet tanks were in action in all parts of the eastern sector of the city. The news of police and Soviet suppression of the Berlin uprising forced the Korean War temporarily off the front pages during the beginning of the week.

CHAPTER SEVEN

1

THURSDAY, JUNE 18, 1953

Supreme Court Building, 2:00 P.M.

AS THURSDAY DAWNED in America, it was far from clear whether the two convicted spies were to die within days, weeks, months, or at all. Washington on that Thursday was in a frenzy of activity centered about the Supreme Court building. A delegation of two thousand Rosenberg supporters had arrived early in the morning from New York; its members spent most of the morning walking the halls of Congress in a fruitless endeavor to bring about a miracle.

All nine members of the Supreme Court were back in Washington, prepared to convene at 2:00 P.M. for the special session. Acting Solicitor General Stern was preparing to argue before the Supreme Court on behalf of the government. On the Rosenbergs' side, the argument was to be a committee effort; Bloch, Finerty, Farmer, and Marshall were all to argue, though they had no plans as to the order of speakers and what each was to say.

On that Thursday, June 18, 1953, Farmer laid before the full Supreme Court for the first time (then or since) the new legal point. The magic words "the Atomic Energy Act of 1946" got their brief day in the headlines. When the sun went down on that Thursday, the argument was over, and so were the lives of the doomed spies who breathed on through twenty-four more hours of borrowed time.

There were, in fact, two other arguments that occupied the

96

combatants in the thronged courtroom all that Thursday after-noon. Besides the question of whether the 1946 act applied to the Rosenbergs, the question of the Court's legal power to undo the act of one of its members was also fought out. And, finally, a third question surfaced as the ramifications of the 1946 act became clear to the Court and the protagonists before it: If the 1946 act applied, would not the government be required to allege and prove an intent by the Rosenbergs to injure the United States— rather than an intent to aid a foreign power, as the 1917 act (under which they had been tried) provided? These apparently identical provisions were really quite different: to aid a foreign country is one thing, to injure your own country can be quite another.

Between 2:00 and just after 5:00 on that Thursday afternoon, the three arguments absorbed all the attention that they were ever to receive from the Court, from the press, and from the lawyers themselves. The process was like major surgery that failed, with the participants quickly burying the corpse.

It is now clear that the Supreme Court was entirely wrong on the answers it gave to each of these questions. Each question will be examined in another chapter. But the mighty significance of the error committed by the Supreme Court during Thursday afternoon when the six controlling justices of the majority clearly made up their minds (if, indeed, their minds had not been made up forty-eight hours earlier when Douglas announced his stay) involves a brief bit of history. For the Court's error grew directly out of events that occurred in a room just two blocks from the Supreme Court chamber, seven and a half years before the arguments on that hot Thursday in June of 1953.

Hearing Room, House Military Affairs Committee, October 15, 1945

It was an unseasonably hot day in October even for Washing-ton. All the windows in the House Armed Services hearing room were open. The heat and the members' total ignorance of what the witness was talking about had got to the chairman first and then spread like a narcotic fog to other members of the commit-tee; the chairman and two of the members were now sound asleep. The witness had not helped; irked by the indifference and then the slumber of his listeners, he droned on in carefully studied detail. The witness was convinced that his was the most important testimony that those politicians had ever heard or ever would hear. Asleep or awake, they would have to hear the message. And then, the witness was confident, they would act. They simply had to.

The witness was a Nobel laureate, Leo Szilard. Out of ill temper rather than ignorance (he knew the witness and his name very well), Chairman Andrew May of Kentucky of the House Military Affairs Committee persisted in calling him "Mr. Sighland" (before the chairman finally fell asleep).

Szilard might as well have been addressing a conclave of deaf-mutes. The Armed Services Committee had already made up its mind on the legislation before it; the personal influence of Chairman May had insured a majority for the bill that the chairman himself had sponsored. With only one or two exceptions, everyone in the hearing room believed that Szilard was wasting the committee's time. Szilard spoke gibberish, accented gibberish; he was obviously a foreigner. Beyond all that, what Szilard was proposing was pure treason—or so the members were convinced. The chairman, in asides that could be heard across the entire hearing room, assured his colleagues sotto voce that Szilard was nothing more than a crazy scientist who had not the slightest notion of what he was talking about. From time to time, members of the committee responded to the chairman's asides with laughter also heard clear across the room while Szilard droned on intently.

The subject before the Armed Services Committee that afternoon was the May-Johnson Control Bill. Chairman May had been joined by West Virginia's Louis Johnson (later to become one of Harry Truman's secretaries of defense) in proposing total military control over all development of nuclear energy. How could anyone doubt the wisdom of it? The bomb had won the war: it had saved a million American lives by preventing an invasion of Japan. The bomb was the greatest military secret in history. As such, it was entitled to every protection the United

States could give it. Anything less then full secrecy was—to May and his colleagues—no less than treason.

Szilard was interrupted and pointedly misunderstood many times during his testimony. The committee was openly rude to him and Szilard knew it. More than that, Szilard's short fuse began sputtering when one of the committee members bluntly told the scientist that he was wasting the committee's time. But Szilard went on and finished his comments in just short of the two hours that had been allotted him.[1]

Szilard's was the first articulation of most scientists' position on the question of control of the atom. Most of the leading atomic scientists had been horrified by the end result of their labors: the bomb. The Europeans among them (Niels Bohr, Szilard, Hans Bethe, Enrico Fermi) had thrown their full energies into development of the bomb because they feared that the Nazis would get it first. When the first chain reaction was triggered in December 1942 in a basement at the University of Chicago's football field, all of them knew it was just a matter of time before this great new phenomenon would be turned into a weapon. For all of them, it was the most painful moral turmoil of their lives, resolved only by the realization that they must get this weapon before the Nazis did.

By late 1944, however, the advancing American armies in Europe had made the astonishing discovery that the Nazis were literally years behind: there was no German atom bomb and there was likely to be none in the near future. When that discovery was made known to the community of nuclear scientists at Los Alamos, Oak Ridge, and Hanford, the moral dilemma of these dedicated researchers was intensified. Almost to the man they were persuaded there was no way that development of a weapon from a nuclear chain reaction could be kept from the international scientific world for a substantially long period of time. Although it was true that the Nazis (and the Japanese) were years behind, there was an inevitability about making up that time that defied security forces, closed installations, and all the barbed wire that had been spread around these installations and around the minds of the scientists within. The scientific principles from which the bomb had been developed were already known to the worldwide scientific community. It was simply a matter of time, a function of the scientific manpower available in isolated research stations around the world, and the time and money given these scientists, before the bomb would be put on paper in a half-dozen laboratories around the world. What happened after that would be the climax of the nightmare: an atomic arms race. The worldwide availability of the scientific know-how to start this arms race was a fact of life, and with some rare but notable exceptions, the scientists saw this tragedy as their own creation. They felt guilty, and they were eager to atone.

The reaction from nuclear scientists at American installations was spawned of idealism and ignorance of the political processes around them. With near unanimity (disputed only by a small group of major scientists), the scientists called out in their own private meetings for international control of the atom. Policing, common agreement among the major powers as to which country could produce atomic devices and for what reason, the intricate details of pooling of highly classified information, all the numbing mechanics of international control of this great force were of little interest to the scientists. What dominated the meetings of atomic scientists in the summer and autumn of 1945 was an overriding necessity: the necessity of international control. It made little difference how this control would be secured, how administered. What made all the difference was the alternative to it: an atomic arms race. These scientific leaders felt that such a race was a moral abomination that scientists had made possible and must now prevent.

In the spring of 1947, a poll was taken of the atomic scientists at Los Alamos. The scientists, Nobel laureates and atomic pioneers, when asked whether the United States should continue the production of atomic bombs, voted 137 nay to 31 aye.

But by October 15, 1945, these same scientists had done very little about their fears. They had spoken of them in small meetings behind the barbed wire at American installations, but there was no organization that spoke for the scientists, no spokesman for them who could go before the Congress. And in this void, their opponents within the military community stole a march on the scientists. The May-Johnson Bill, calling for imposition of close military control (and total secrecy) on all atomic research, had been quietly drafted within the War Department by Assistant Secretary of War Kenneth Royall, with the help of General Groves, the general who had superintended the Manhattan District Project successfully during the war. It had the gloss of scientific acceptance: Dr. James Conant and Dr. Vannevar Bush, former presidents of Harvard and MIT respectively, no less, had joined in support of the bill. Conant's and Bush's proximity to the Washington administration of atomic research during the war (and, thus, their removal from the laboratories) was not calculated to win them support from the atomic scientists who had done the field experimentation that led to the bomb. When they heard of the May-Johnson Bill late in the summer of 1945, the scientists at Oak Ridge, Hanford, and Los Alamos overwhelmingly opposed it. It was late, very late, to do anything about it, but the scientists galvanized quickly. The Federation of Atomic Scientists was formed and leased a tiny office on L Street in Washington. One of its first acts was to send Leo Szilard to testify before the Armed Services Committee chaired by Congressman May in hearings that were pointedly truncated so as to prevent delay in the committee for the War Department bill. Szilard's testimony in October was the first notice to Congress and to the American public that what the War Department had proposed for control of the atom was bitterly opposed by the scientists who had given America the bomb. The lines in this strange legislative battle had been drawn.

What started as an amateur effort by concerned atomic physicists in the halls of Congress soon became a tightly organized lobbying exercise. Financed by nothing more than their own contributions, donating their own time freely, the strange lobbyists roamed the halls of Congress. Szilard, Bethe, Bacher, and Franck—even the twin Zeuses in this scientific pantheon, Fermi and Bohr—buttonholed congressmen with their message:

development of the atom was the greatest humanitarian discovery in recent years, far too important to be left in the hands of the military. More importantly, they informed Congress that atomic development itself, now in its first public emergence but still rudimentary, would be stifled if military secrecy were to be imposed on it.

Early on, these political neophytes developed their strategy: put aside the notion of international control of the atom during these debates; stress the need for peaceful development of this awesome new national resource. It soon became clear to members of Congress that peaceful use of atomic energy would be hopelessly stymied by military controls and secrecy. Academe now spoke out; precious few of the scientists and none of their universities would be willing to engage in research under military controls. The result was as remarkable as it was short-lived. A new bill, the McMahon Bill, sponsored by Senator Brien McMahon of Connecticut, was drafted by the scientists and their lawyer-advisers. This bill shifted control of the atom to a new civilian agency, the Atomic Energy Commission. By July of 1946, this bill had come out of the committee and was ready to replace the May-Johnson Bill, which had been the target of the lobbying scientists for the preceding six months.

The victory for the scientists was short-lived because they had sacrificed too much to get what they wanted. Seeking free academic exchange of scientific information, they had bartered it away for civilian control of development. Neither free academic exchange of scientific information nor any semblance of international control of the atom was built into the McMahon Bill. In their horror at the prospect of an international atomic arms race, the scientists had simply assumed that the civilian leaders of the new agency would be sensible enough to lead American thinking to true international regulation of atomic power. What the scientists got instead was rigorous policing of scientific experimentation and data-gathering under appointed civilians at the new Atomic Energy Commission. Scientists thought they had won civilian control of the atom. But by the time most of them had lived for just a year under the new law, they all knew that the victory was Pyrrhic at best. The scientists soon discovered that, as is the pattern very often in Washington, the officials chosen by Truman for the new commission had transformed the scientists' hopes into a regulatory reality far closer to their fears. Too many of the scientists-turned-politicians were like J. Robert Oppenheimer, of whom it was said by his friend that when Oppie began talking about Dean Acheson as "Dean" and General Marshall as "George," the game was up, and free-exchange-of-information zealots had lost it.

Then, on March 21, 1947, President Truman promulgated his new loyalty order. Scientists who then worked for the Atomic Energy Commission and those who worked under government grants at their own universities now had their pasts paraded in review by gumshoes who enforced the loyalty order. It was a complete turnabout for the scientists. It was the war all over again, but without the incentive to beat the Nazis.

The McMahon Bill, known as the Atomic Energy Act of 1946, was thus an unintended compromise. The scientists got civilian control of the atom at a fearsome cost, dashing hopes of free, scientific development of atomic energy in the United States. The proponents of rigorous policing of atomic research and development won far more than they lost, especially in the day-to-day administration of the new law. But one fact was clear to all sides in the give-and-take. The act that went into effect on August 1, 1946, set the rules for all atomic research and information-gathering from that day on. Just as clear was the fact that the act specified the punishment for violation of those rules.

What did the act say?

What the act said makes very clear the obsessive concern Congress felt in 1946 about theft of any kind of atomic information. The notion that an American scientific breakthrough of any sort could somehow be hidden from competent scientists in other countries was still current. Far from encouraging free scientific interchange of this new kind of knowledge, the act took great pains to prohibit unauthorized disclosure of "all data concerning the manufacture or utilization of atomic weapons, the production of fissionable material in the production of power."[2]

There has been a good deal of argument since the Rosenbergs were executed regarding the secrecy of the information passed by them to the Soviets. The argument is that much of what Greenglass gave Harry Gold was little more than a series of mechanical tricks, hardly more than industrial espionage. The argument, although cogent, is legally irrelevant because of the sweeping nature of the act's prohibition quoted above. Even if the "secrets" passed from David Greenglass to Harry Gold were widely known in 1945, the 1946 act is very clear: disclosure of these "secrets" is prohibited under pain of the penalties of the act.

What were those penalties? They fall into three categories.

The first applies to the disclosure of classified atomic information. Those found guilty of the act of disclosing such information with intent to injure the United States were punished by death or by life imprisonment, *provided either of these punishments was recommended by the jury that convicted the violator*. If the jury did not make such a recommendation, the penalty was up to twenty years' imprisonment and a fine of up to $20,000.[3] Importantly, before the death penalty could be meted out for disclosure of classified atomic secrets, two essentials must have occurred: the jury must have found that the violator intended to injure the United States in making the disclosure, and the jury must also specifically recommend death. On a descending scale, if the jury found that the violator's act of disclosure was coupled with a different form of intent—for example, that of intending to secure an advantage to a foreign power (rather than to injure the United States)—the maximum punishment was twenty years' imprisonment and a $20,000 fine. Finally, if the *intent* of the violator was neither of those above, but the violator had reason to *believe* that injury to the United States or advantage to a foreign power would result from what he did, the punishment was limited to ten years and a $10,000 fine.

The second category of penalties under the 1946 act covered the acts of *acquiring*[4] classified atomic information unlawfully, or attempting to do so. This is the other side of the illegal transaction: the attempt to secure the forbidden data; the first category covered those who unlawfully turned it over. Again, the punishments were on the same declining scale: if such acquisition (or attempt to acquire) was made with the intent to injure the United States, the penalty could be death or life imprisonment if the jury so recommended. The same two essentials must have been present before death could be meted out: a finding by the jury that the violator specifically intended to injure the United States and a specific recommendation by the jury for death. *Without such recommendation,* the punishment, if the intent to injure the United States was proved, was up to twenty years in prison and a fine of up to $20,000. The latter sentence was the limit if the violator's intent (in this case, the illegal acquirer or attempted acquirer) was to secure an advantage for a foreign power. In the acquirer's case, a "reason to believe," rather than a specific intent to injure the United States or secure an advantage to a foreign power, would not suffice. A specific intent to injure or benefit was required for *any* punishment in the second category.

The third category need not involve us here. It dealt with what was, essentially, atomic sabotage. It, too, had the same declining scale of punishments depending on the nature of the intent of the violator. Death could be meted out to a violator whose intent was to injure the United States, but, again, only on the recommendation of the jury; if the intent behind the illegal sabotage was simply to secure an advantage to a foreign power, the limit was twenty years and a $20,000 fine. Again, a specific intent, rather than merely "reason to believe," was required for any of these punishments.

These penalties are very different from those in effect before 1946. The Rosenbergs were indicted, tried, convicted, and executed under the Espionage Act of 1917. All that the jury was required to find under *that* act was an intent to secure an advantage for a foreign power, a much lesser matter, which imposed no great burden on the prosecutors.* And Judge Kaufman, when pronouncing his sentence under the 1917 act, could lawfully send the Rosenbergs to the electric chair without any recommendation

* Section 2(a) of the Espionage Act of 1917 requires (for conviction) that the jury find an intent to injure the United States *or* an intention or reason to believe that advantage to a foreign power would result from the use of illegally secured information. Obviously, it was no burden on the Rosenberg prosecution to establish that the intent of the spy group was to secure an advantage for the Soviet Union.

from the jury. Under the 1917 act, no recommendation of any kind from the jury was even possible.

Significantly, all that the Rosenberg jury found was that the Rosenbergs intended their acts to secure an advantage to a foreign power. Under the scale of punishments of the 1946 act, this jury finding could not have resulted in a death penalty under any circumstances. And it may well be that this is why the prosecution gave such a wide berth to the 1946 act, preferring the easier access to a death sentence under the earlier statute.

There is very little written anywhere on the precise distinction between the two very different intents: the intent to injure the United States in contrast to the intent to secure an advantage to a foreign power. One source on the distinction is Judge Learned Hand, who had said in a 1945 opinion that "injury to the United States" is not as broad as "advantage to a foreign nation." He added:

> While it is true that it is somewhat hard to imagine instances in which anyone would be likely to transmit information . . . which would be injurious to the United States, and yet not advantageous to a foreign power, it is possible to think of many cases where information might be advantageous to another power and yet not injurious to the United States. (*U.S.* v. *Heine,* 151 F.2d 813 [CCA2, 1945])

Judge Hand may have been able to think of many cases, but the imagination of others is not so fertile. A good example, indeed, the sole one that comes to mind without long conjecture, arose in the Rosenberg case itself. There could be no doubt that advantage to a foreign power resulted from every bit of evidence connecting the Rosenbergs to the Soviet consul and to the Communist party. On the other hand, all the activities took place during the war, when the two countries were allies. The advantage to the Soviet Union from disclosures made in 1945 could arguably be both an advantage to an ally and without injury to the United States. *That* argument never got made in the Rosenberg case because the terms of the 1917 act made it irrelevant. But if the 1946 act *did* apply to the Rosenberg case, their pre-1946 conduct would fit neatly into Judge Hand's exception. And if the Rosenberg jury had applied this exception to the facts before it, no death penalty would have been possible for the Rosenbergs under the 1946 act even if the jury had been sufficiently aroused to recommend it.

To complete the history of the Atomic Energy Act of 1946, a word must be said about conspiracy. The federal law regarding conspiracy is a remarkably complicated fabric. But for present purposes—to determine if the 1946 act or the 1917 act applied (or both applied) to the conduct of the Rosenbergs—the federal doctrine of conspiracy can be simplified. We have outlined what the penalties were for individual violations of the 1946 act and what they were for individual violations of the 1917 act.

Both acts made conspiracies to violate their provisions (acts by more than one individual in concerted action to commit violations that the act specifically punished when one person committed them) punishable by the same penalties meted out for individual violations. Thus, under the 1917 act, if the Rosenbergs were found by the jury to have conspired to transmit national defense information, they were subject to the death penalty just as if each of the accused had actually transmitted forbidden information alone. Similarly, under the 1946 act, each of the individual punishments had a parallel and identical punishment for conspiring to do what the act forbade the individual from doing alone.

Under both laws, this had twin effects: first, the act of conspiring to spy—that is, the *planning*—became just as culpable as the spying itself, so long as the planning involved some concrete, or "overt," acts by the conspirators; and, second, the awful force of the federal conspiracy doctrine made the acts and statements of one individual damning against all conspirators so long as the judge somewhere found that a conspiracy existed. This last consequence was to have terrible impact on this case.

But so far as punishment was concerned, the fact that the government had decided to try the Rosenbergs for conspiracy rather than for spying in no way limited the punishment that could be given them. Indeed, because of the damaging flight testimony concerning events as late as 1950, the choice of conspiracy under the 1917 act (rather than spying) was made by the government somewhat transparently in order to maximize its chances of putting the Rosenbergs into the electric chair.

What Congress says in a statute is one thing. What antagonists claim that Congress meant in Court battles that take place immediately after a statute has been enacted is quite another. And what observers say forty-three years later, light-years removed from the furor and confusion of those early Court tests, is still a third thing. The furor and confusion were widely spread in June of 1953 when the Supreme Court took its first look at the criminal penalties in the Atomic Energy Act of 1946 in *U.S.* v. *Rosenberg.*

Normally, it is unfair to take the words of lawyers and pronouncements of a court and test them against the accumulated legal wisdom of thirty-six subsequent years, unfair to the lawyers and to the court, even if the court is the Supreme Court of the United States.

But one of the points that must be made about the Rosenberg case is that the lawyering on both sides was less than Olympian even when judged by 1953 standards. And the conduct of the Court was, as will be shown shortly, tawdry then, and worse in the perspective of the following years.

Thus, it is still quite appropriate to examine what lawyers wrote and said in 1953 and what their opponents in the Department of Justice countered with. After doing that, it is also fair—and certainly necessary for a full understanding of the monumental abuse of the processes of justice as a whole in this particular case—to see what could be and should have been argued and decided in this case, but was not.

Neither what the lawyers wrote in their briefs in the twenty-four hours given them, nor what they said on that Thursday afternoon, was particularly helpful to the Court. The briefs and the oral argument reflect how little all the lawyers and justices could bring to those new issues in such a short time. Fyke Farmer was an exception; he was ready.

Briefs Filed with the Supreme Court

The briefs and oral argument before the Court on that Thursday, June 18, examined in that order, gave the Court's fatal error the inevitability of Greek tragedy. Since the oral argument had fillips of its own, the briefs are discussed first.

Against the backdrop of the two statutes, what precisely did Farmer and Marshall argue?

In their written papers (and late in their argument to the Supreme Court on that Thursday afternoon), both lawyers said a great deal outlining the familiar arguments of which the Supreme Court had long since had its fill before it had ever heard of the Atomic Energy Act of 1946. In their papers, Farmer and Marshall also took a swipe at Bloch.[5] One of the contentions they made, along with the new ones concerning the 1946 act, was that Bloch's conduct of the trial had deprived the Rosenbergs of their rights to adequate counsel as guaranteed by the Sixth Amendment of the Constitution. Farmer and Marshall cited Bloch's absolute refusal to accept any of their arguments concerning the 1946 act (and, indeed, Bloch's telegram to Judge Kaufman to reject Farmer and Marshall's contentions based on that act); and Bloch's still-unfathomable request to Judge Kaufman that his clients be tried *in camera* was also cited, with the courtroom cleared of spectators and reporters during the crucial portion of the trial dealing with the substance of the Greenglass disclosures, Greenglass's sketch of the Nagasaki bomb, and his testimony about the sketch. That request, which confirmed that the information was highly secret and significant, was unwise at the time, and, in hindsight, a major blunder.

In the papers submitted Thursday morning, on the key points regarding the 1946 act, both Marshall and Farmer argued very simply. To them, the death sentence was void because the conspiracy charged against the Rosenbergs

was alleged to have continued from June 6, 1944, up to and including June 15, 1950, and therefore, was renewed after the Atomic Energy Act went into effect,[6]

and accordingly, the defendants

insofar as the transmission of atomic information may have been an object were subject only to the penal provisions of the '(1946)' Act and not the penal provisions of the Espionage Act.[7]

The Farmer-Marshall papers went on to say that since the indictment did not charge the defendants

conspired with intent to injure the *United States,* they were not punishable by death because the Congress in enacting the Atomic Energy Act ameliorated the unprecise and harsh penal provisions of the Espionage Act in so far as they might otherwise be applicable to the transmission of atomic information or conspiring to do so,[8]

and did so by

1. Depriving the courts of any authority to impose offenses of the type under consideration here except upon the recommendation of the jury; and
2. Restricting the power of the jury to recommend punishment for life to cases where the office [*sic*] was committed with intent to injure the United States.[9]

The two lawyers' summary concluded:

The indictment in the case at bar did not charge the defendants with conspiring with intent to injure the United States. (Emphasis in the original)[10]

The Farmer-Marshall papers in the Supreme Court record take up sixty pages. There is very little that transpired before Judge Kaufman that the two lawyers did not address. With the exception of the two points above, nothing was really new. But those two points were totally new, as Justice Douglas and then the entire Supreme Court now fully realized.

The government brief did little to clear the waters. Its brief appeared before the harassed and thoroughly testy justices no more than three hours before the argument convened at 2:00 P.M. The brief reflected the fact that the government was in a bad corner.

The position taken by Justice Douglas in his stay had been one of careful caution: he was far from sure that Farmer and Marshall were correct in their new point. All that Douglas decided was that the points raised were substantial, that human lives were at stake, and that proper judicial consideration should be given to these new arguments before the two lives were snuffed out.

It is extremely difficult to oppose that kind of argument. Almost anything in the law can be deemed "substantial" by adversaries on an argument. The very novelty of the Farmer-Marshall argument pushed hard toward the conclusion that it was substantial. As of June 1953, no Court had *ever* interpreted any of the provisions of the Atomic Energy Act of 1946, let alone the criminal provisions of the new law; and the first hard look at a new law is a matter of great substance in the law if for no other reason than the absence of prior precedents. This special session of the Court took not only the first judicial look at these provisions, but also made the first examination of how they meshed with the closely similar penalties of the 1917 act. That kind of exercise is highly technical and rarely can be dismissed as without substance if there is any real conflict between the language in the two acts, as here there certainly was. The leading legal authority, James Newman, who had written[11] an interpretation of the Atomic Energy Act in the single analysis published prior to the Rosenberg case (in May of 1947), stated so. This same James Newman, who was not personally committed to either side in the Rosenberg case, openly pointed to problems in meshing the conflicting criminal penalties of the 1917 and 1946 acts, concluding ultimately that litigation would be the only way to resolve the conflicts. That very litigation had now erupted through a startling turn of events, and the government was reduced to pretending that the entire exercise was a waste of time, saying so, moreover, in a case in which the outcome would be the death penalty.

It was an awkward position for the government. But such postures are not new to the government, and Acting Solicitor General Stern took up the argument in his brief with enthusiasm. There was no room for the government to argue niceties or nuances; if it did, the Court would probably decide that the new points were indeed refined and technical and, therefore, that the full litany of the briefing and argument through three courts (as Justice Douglas had ordered) was the only prudent thing to do. Fine points, nuances, and technical rectitude were too sophisticated to get this hideous monkey off the government's back.

The government had to come out full blast and say that what the two interloping lawyers were saying was pure rubbish—and get five justices to believe it—if the worldwide clamor that disturbed the attorney general so grievously was to be stilled.

And so, in his brief, the acting solicitor general painted with the broadest possible brush the legal picture to the nine justices. The government could not have prosecuted the Rosenbergs under the 1946 act had it wanted to, Robert Stern began, because their espionage occurred before August 1, 1946; to charge them under that act would be an *ex post facto* indictment barred by our Constitution.[12] Now, he said, the Rosenbergs were also contending that the 1917 act was repealed by the 1946 statute,[13] so that the 1917 act could not be used against them either. The implication raised by the government was clear: if the Farmer-Marshall argument was accepted, the Rosenbergs would claim total immunity for their crimes.[14]

A careful examination of the government brief is much more illuminating than the accounts of anything Stern said. In the brief, the government tried to answer straight-on the extraordinary new argument that had appeared from nowhere. But this brief fell prey to the same difficulty that plagued everything during that week: it was thrown together too rapidly to be able to pin down the issues created by the Douglas stay. And because the questions were not isolated, they were not answered.

The government's entire case rested on the assumption that Congress did nothing in 1946 to limit a prosecutor's full range of options to prosecute spies under both acts. Parsed out somewhat more precisely, the Department of Justice leaned hard on Section (10) (b)(6) of the 1946 act, which did, indeed, state that "the applicable provisions of other laws shall not be excluded" in the enforcement of the new Atomic Energy Act. From this, the department drew the implication that nothing in the 1946 enactment ousted anything in the 1917 act from the statute books. Accordingly, the government's brief argued, this case was not unlike many other criminal situations in which a single act violated more than one statute. The prosecutor could pick and choose, and this, according to the acting solicitor general, is precisely what he had done. Appearing time and again in the government's argument is the phrase "repeal by implication"; the government repeated many times that the law generally does not countenance such repeal—that is, the repeal of an earlier statute simply because a later one seems to deal with the same subject. In such situations, the government asserted, it must be shown from the clear words of the later statute, or the words of debate in congressional committee or on the floor, that Congress intended the earlier act to give way. No such thing had occurred here, the government argued, and a recent Supreme Court case, *United States* v. *Borden,* 308 U.S. 188, decided only fourteen years before, had rigidly applied this rule.[15]

The government's briefs were notable mostly for what they did not argue. The government never admitted that a conspiracy to pass atomic secrets extending long after August 1, 1946, was covered by the 1946 act, and what that admission meant.

Courtroom of the Supreme Court

Promptly at 2:00 P.M., the justices of the Supreme Court appeared through the curtains back of the high bench. As is custom, everyone stood. The clerk recited the oath. The justices and the packed audience sat.

Justice Vinson then announced the convening of the special term of the Court to consider *U.S.* v. *Rosenberg.* The clerk recited the number of the case.

Nothing seemed to proceed with decorum in this case. The moment the number of the case was intoned by the clerk at the front of the courtroom, a stout man arose in the rear row of seats at the back of the courtroom and addressed the Court and the audience in a loud, outraged voice. It was Daniel Marshall. He was upset. For five full minutes Marshall bitingly protested the speed with which the Court had reconvened itself. He said in tones that echoed across the courtroom from the spectators' seats that the issues were not being treated intelligently or even rationally. There had been no time, Marshall declaimed—in a voice that grew with indignation until it could be heard down the corridors outside the courtroom—to understand the issues before the Court, let alone argue them. What the Court was perpetrating, Marshall pronounced, was gross injustice. No one was prepared to do justice that day in that Court, Marshall loudly concluded.

The justices, the clerks, the marshals, the lawyers, and the audience were all shocked. It was an outburst from a spectator in the gallery never heard before in that courtroom and never since. It happened so fast that not even the morning-coated clerks or the blue-uniformed court policemen could stop Marshall.

But Farmer did. Sitting quietly next to Marshall, Farmer waited until his colleague was finished with his outburst. Then, in his quiet Tennessee voice, Farmer told the Court and audience that he, Fyke Farmer, was prepared to argue that day. Marshall and Farmer moved down the row of seats in the audience, went forward and took their places in front of the bar at counsel's table.[15a] On both sides there was a full table.

Outside in the halls, the marble antechambers of the Court building were packed. Leaders of the pro-Rosenberg forces estimated that two thousand of their followers were in and around the building by the time the arguments commenced.

Five lawyers argued to the Court that Thursday afternoon. Observers of the Court commented then that nothing like the free-wheeling bitterness exhibited that day had ever been displayed prior to June 18, 1953.

Acting Solicitor General Stern opened. It was heavy going. Stern took on Justice Frankfurter's main argument almost immediately. The former Harvard law professor was deeply concerned by the possible application of the 1946 Atomic Energy Act to the conduct of the spies. Stern was forthright: "The assumption of the defense is that the case could have been brought under the Atomic Energy Act. If it had been, the case would have been thrown out so quickly the Government would have been a laughing stock."[16]

It was not a practice in 1953 to transcribe oral arguments before the Supreme Court. There is no record of the Rosenberg argument, and that is a pity.[17] There is no clear record that any of the four lawyers who argued in support of the stay on that Thursday afternoon took the indictment in the Rosenberg case in hand, read it to the Court, or pointed out that it charged the Rosenbergs with a continuing conspiracy from June of 1944 to June of 1950. That would have taken sixty seconds; it would have dispatched Stern's thesis with utter finality.

Frankfurter did go after Stern. What would happen if the Court simply decided that a jury recommendation was necessary because of the 1946 act? Could the Rosenberg jury be reconvened to make its recommendation? Stern replied that there was no question in his mind that, under the 1946 act, *some* jury would have to make a recommendation. Frankfurter then volunteered that it seemed very doubtful to him that the Rosenberg jury could be reconvened for this purpose alone.[18]

Stern spent the greater part of his time arguing that the 1946 act could not lawfully apply to the Rosenbergs. As it often is with cases before the Supreme Court, the intensity of the justices' questions falsely implied apparent misgivings inside the Court. A majority of the Court actually had no misgivings at all; they were twenty-four hours away from deciding that all of the Rosenberg arguments were frivolous.

The government brought little light to the murky new question. Plagued by the policies of the situation, impelled by the burning urgency that now obsessed his nominal superior, Attorney General Brownell, to bring the case to a close, Stern troubled the Court more than he helped it. Looking back with the hindsight of thirty-five years, it now seems clear that the Rosenberg-Edelman forces might have swayed five justices if they had organized more and fought less. But that speculation fails to include a telling emotional fact: the deep bitterness of the justices over what Douglas had done. Some of the majority might have accepted the need for study, thought, and delay had they not, every one of them, agreed just five days before *not* to delay execution—for anyone, or for any reason. The Court's majority kept the faith. Douglas had gone astray. To join Douglas would be to dignify his bad faith, and it would keep this case in the world headlines for God knew how long.

Bloch followed Stern.

The Rosenberg lawyers had not met to discuss tactics or strategy. It was free-form. Justice Jackson took up the same point. What did Bloch think about the 1946 act? Bloch openly admitted that he was not prepared to offer any technical arguments on this point.[19] He urged the court to accede to Douglas's stay and to return the case to Judge Kaufman in New York for full briefing and argument on the 1946 act. But that did not satisfy Jackson. In response to his question, if the act did apply to his clients, Bloch said, then the entire prosecution would have to be thrown out: the Rosenbergs would have to be reindicted and retried under the 1946 act. When Bloch spoke these words, silence fell across the marble and oak room.[20] The impact of Bloch's words seemed to stun everyone in the chamber—justices, lawyers, and observers alike.

There were moments of pathos.

Bloch, ever the honest, faithful soul, ate humble pie for all to see. He had been wrong, utterly wrong, in rejecting Marshall and Farmer. The Court was given the most abject admission of error by this earnest, decent lawyer, plainly out of his depth. The spectacle moved nine justices, already full of sympathy for this gallant but outclassed warrior. When one of the justices gently nudged Bloch toward an explanation of his views of the 1946 act, Bloch answered that he simply had not had the time to prepare himself in the few hours since word of the Court's special term.[21] It was the best possible answer, and it carried the essence of Justice Douglas's point home. Human lives were at stake. Out of respect for itself, the Court had to allow decent time for briefing, for argument, for lawyers to ply their skills on both sides of this new controversy.

It may have been the best answer, but it wasn't Finerty's answer. He rose next, prepared to give the Court chapter and verse. He had the 1946 act at the tip of his tongue and there was no point in keeping the truth from the nonbelievers. He strode to the podium, town-meeting style, ready to tell the Court that the acting solicitor general was a knave and a fool, and the Rosenberg prosecutors dishonest charlatans for keeping this point buried. At the lectern, he bumped straight into the bulk of a very determined Bloch, as unwilling to have that argument made that day—and in those terms—as Finerty was intent upon making it. It was a rare example of Bloch's having the better tactical sense.

The Supreme Court and the packed chamber of observers were treated to the spectacle of the first shouting match in history at the High Court's lectern. Bloch, the much bigger man, held his ground. But Finerty kept talking, and he had a louder voice. He literally outshouted Bloch, another spectacle the Supreme Court had been spared during its 164-year history. Finerty, ignoring Bloch, then took off on the Court itself, arguing that the reconvening of it was a reflection on the integrity of Justice Douglas; further, it was wholly improper for Attorney General Brownell to seek the reconvening of the Court. Justice Jackson stopped Finerty.[22] What was improper about Brownell's conduct?

Justice Jackson told Finerty that the only thing he saw in all of the papers that was unusual was Brownell's statement that reconvening the Court for the special term was "unprecedented." The excitable Finerty flared up even more. He attacked Brownell and the Department of Justice for their handling of the Rosenberg case from the start. Finerty told the Court that the Department of Justice had "permitted a fraud on this Court to happen" by initiating a prosecution that the prosecutors knew to be perjured.[23] That wasn't all. Finerty unloaded all of the frustration felt by the Rosenberg team now that one judge was openly willing to interfere on behalf of the Rosenbergs. Finerty cannonaded the Department of Justice and prosecuting attorney Irving Saypol. He told the startled Court: "There never was a more crooked District Attorney in New York than the one who tried the Rosenbergs."[24]

Then Finerty identified Saypol by name, adding that Saypol was now a judge of the New York Supreme Court. Justice Clark shook his head at this outburst and told Finerty that he would be more helpful to the Court if he stuck to the legal issues. Justice Minton was less constrained; he informed Finerty that he had no right to abuse Saypol personally.

Finerty sat down. Marshall had been given fifteen minutes of the Rosenberg team's arguing time, and he then rose. Quickly the tension in the vast chamber reached a crescendo. Justice Jackson, who had led the Court's praise of Bloch, greeted Marshall as he reached the podium with an immediate thrust: Whom did Marshall represent? Marshall said that he "spoke" for Irwin Edelman of Los Angeles. Jackson's next question hit Marshall before Marshall's words were out of his mouth: "Was he the Edelman who was before this Court last year in a vagrancy case?"[25]

Marshall answered the patrician Jackson angrily, as the justice sat in his chair apparently satisfied that he had made this identification for all of his robed brethren. Marshall shook his finger at Jackson and shouted in Jackson's direction: "It was a free speech case. It is improper to call it vagrancy. I think that this is shocking in a capital case where human lives are at stake."[26]

For the first time in recent memory, the somnolent marshals of the Supreme Court, blinking and aroused, were on their feet during an argument to bring order out of this shouting match. But they had not reckoned with the chief justice. Fred Vinson was by instinct a peacemaker. Vinson had spent his life making peace between arguing adversaries at various levels of public life, and his owl's face often quieted people even without words. Now the chief justice simply leaned forward toward Marshall and with a calm smile told the angry Californian: "Don't let your temperature rise."[27] This homely touch quieted Marshall. He quickly gave way to his colleague, Fyke Farmer.

Farmer was the only lawyer of the five who told the Court that Thursday afternoon that he was fully prepared to argue then and there the legal significance of the 1946 Atomic Energy Act. Bloch, Finerty, and Marshall had all asked the Court to allow the case to go back to Judge Kaufman for briefs and argument, and then up the long path through the Second Circuit Court of Appeals to the Supreme Court.[28]

Even Stern had been tentative about the 1946 act's meaning: indeed, during Stern's argument, another precedent was set. At Stern's suggestion, a young lawyer, James R. Newman, former counsel to the Senate Special Committee on Atomic Energy, summoned from his vacation on Cape Cod and now sitting at the government's table in a borrowed suit, was asked to answer one of the justice's inquiries about the 1946 act. Newman had written the only learned commentary on the act, and had therefore been summoned from the Massachusetts beaches by the government when the Supreme Court had been reconvened. For the first time before or since, the Supreme Court listened as a total outsider to a case answered the Court's inquiries.[29] It was symbolic of the new world that the Supreme Court was struggling into.

But this new world held no peril for Farmer. He was prepared to argue all of the points raised by the 1946 act, and he proceeded to do so, finishing the argument before the Court by telling it that the 1946 act required the Court to vacate the Rosenbergs' death sentences, vacate the indictment against the spies, and send the case back to the New York grand jury for another indictment.[30]

Shortly after 4:00 P.M. on the sunny Thursday afternoon, the Supreme Court disappeared behind the panels whence they had appeared two hours earlier. The case was in their hands.

Judicial Conference, U.S. Supreme Court

The clearest record of that emotion-packed conference of justices after argument on Douglas's stay is found in the papers of apparently the only justice who took careful notes of that painful proceeding: Felix Frankfurter. Frankfurter's notes make three points:

First, whereas the chief justice's opinion stated that the Court had "deliberated in conference for several hours," Justice Frankfurter questioned "who deliberated on what?" He adds that "the fact is that all minds were made up as soon as we left the bench—indeed, I have no doubts from some remarks made to me, before we went [in] on it."[31]

Frankfurter added that the prime concern of the majority was that the announcement of the decision be delayed until the following morning so as to provide the illusion of minimal consideration.[32] Frankfurter added that the Friday session added absolutely no additional consideration whatever of the merits of the matter before the Court.

Second, Burton's own notes indicate that he was willing to

provide a decent period of briefing and argument on the points raised by Douglas's stay before the Supreme Court, perhaps allowing two to three months for briefing and the oral argument.[33] But as Frankfurter noted: "Burton said in effect that he would make a fifth if there were four votes either for upholding Douglas' action or for vacating and making some other arrangement for hearing full arguments on the Atomic Energy Act point."[34] Frankfurter sadly added: "There were only three— Black, Douglas and I." Thus, on the very last day, Supreme Court review was so close and yet so far away.

Sing Sing Penitentiary

Thursday, June 18, was Julius and Ethel Rosenberg's fourteenth wedding anniversary. Having been told just twenty-four hours earlier that they were not to die that week (and knowing no more), the pair was still riding the euphoria of Douglas's stay. During the Sing Sing morning, after the prison breakfast and the morning work detail (which, as prisoners under death sentence, they did not share), the couple met in the conference room. They were separated by a wire screen that extended from the ceiling to the floor between them while they talked for ninety minutes. This was longer than usual; Warden Denno seemed to recognize the unusual turn of events by allowing the pair almost double the time normally given them in the conference room.

Later in the morning, Rabbi Koslowe, the Jewish chaplain at the prison, visited each of their cells. The rabbi spent little time with the prisoners. This was a day for the events of this world, not for preparation for the next. Shortly after the noon meal, both prisoners returned to the conference room for the second time. Their sons, Michael (then ten) and Robert (then six), burst through the doors on either side of the screen. The excitement had spread to the boys. It was a joyous reunion, the first one that had brought any joy to the family since the boys had made their first prison visit many months earlier. The little group had its own celebration: while each parent held a child, they congratulated each other in honor of the anniversary. Julius said that the exciting events just one day earlier were a harbinger: next year they would all celebrate June 18 together, free in their own home. When the boys left after their short visit, the good-byes were much less painful than usual. There was hope.

Early in the evening, Warden Denno announced to the press that the Rosenbergs had eaten the regular prison dinner late that afternoon. He added that he took the view that until he was told otherwise, the Douglas stay was in effect. "They ate regular prison fare," Denno said. "We have no execution scheduled."[35]

Newsreel: June 18, 1953 (Morning)

On that Thursday, the Vatican radio broadcast an appeal for clemency for the Rosenbergs in four different languages. In Paris, the city's Roman Catholics were called by hundreds of priests to a special hour of prayer for the Rosenbergs at Notre-Dame. Douglas Dillon, our ambassador in Paris, openly urged commutation of the sentence on President Eisenhower. A convocation was called by the Christian Committee for Revision of the Rosenberg Trial and was approved by Maurice Cardinal Feltin, archbishop of Paris. The archbishop himself sent President Eisenhower a cable urging clemency. Church leaders of six denominations in Sydney, Australia, sent a joint cable to President Eisenhower asking clemency. In London, a throng gathered in the lobbies of the House of Commons buttonholing members of Parliament to sign a petition to be presented to Prime Minister Churchill requesting him to ask for clemency. The Belgian Socialist General Trade Council cabled from Brussels urging a reprieve for the spies. Tugmen in Melbourne met to organize a boycott of American shipping in the port if the Rosenbergs were put to death. The Polish press repeated its government's earlier offer of political asylum for the Rosenbergs: a State Department spokesman frostily termed the offer "an impertinence." In Ottawa, pickets marched in front of the U.S. embassy with placards stating that "thousands" of Canadians favored clemency.

The controversy had become a fire storm.

Sunset over Washington

As the broiling sun set over Washington on Thursday, June 18, the massed Rosenberg supporters on the Mall sang labor songs and chanted various of their slogans. They were convinced that no matter what the Court did on the following day, their heroes had been given a lease on life that could be measured in months, perhaps years. The Rosenberg supporters felt that the worst that could happen would be a Supreme Court order to brief and argue the new point. And that would mean briefs over the summer and argument at the beginning of the fall term in October. The more that Bloch and his conferees studied the Farmer-Marshall papers, the more they, too, became convinced that their clients would have to be recharged and retried. That would mean years, not months.

And in the midst of all this euphoria there were those optimists who openly declared that if it were necessary for the Rosenbergs to be reindicted, the second trial would never even take place. The virulent toxin of McCarthyism, at its peak during that June, would surely trail off in 1954 and 1955. The virus spawned by the Wisconsin senator would not be strong enough to bring the Rosenbergs to trial again; those who had maintained that the original prosecution was political now had hope that the political mood would change.

The Rosenbergs themselves felt that the Douglas stay marked a turning point in their luck. Nothing, absolutely nothing, had gone their way since the first day thirty-five months ago when Julius was arrested. Now, they felt, the falseness of the whole charge was being disclosed. Neither of the prisoners now had any doubt that he (or she) would eventually be freed. It was just a matter of time until the entire judicial system joined the one wise justice within the Supreme Court in deploring what had happened to them. No one had explained to the Rosenbergs that Douglas's stay had nothing to do with their guilt under either statute. No one, not one soul anywhere among the thousands of lay Rosenberg supporters, had any idea that the convicted spies were within twenty-four hours of death. The euphoria of a single victory had blinded them all to the realities of that June evening: the Department of Justice was totally determined to bring this hideous controversy to an end within hours, not months or years; and the Supreme Court (as was clear to anyone who had listened closely) was divided, with insufficient votes to stop the government. But not one Rosenberg adherent faced up to these realities, and no one said a word about them.

Newsreel: June 18, 1953 (Evening)

On the night of Thursday, June 18, 1953, there were Communist fire storms elsewhere.

Inside the United States, the Red scare was in full bloom. All of the newspapers in the East printed a Washington story that the FBI was investigating a plot to assassinate Senator McCarthy. The New York teacher William Frauenglass, advised by Albert Einstein to shun the congressional investigation of his political beliefs, did so, and was fired by the school system for refusing to testify. Professor Naphtali Lewis of Brooklyn College, the recipient of a Fulbright fellowship, had it revoked by federal authorities on June 18, for leftist affiliations. A famous name, Franklin Roosevelt, backed into the McCarthy fray. Franklin, Jr., a New York congressman, urged that all congressional investigations into Communist beliefs be consolidated into one committee's responsibility. His urging was wholly ignored by the five or six separate committees (or subcommittees), each of which was making glorious political hay of the nationwide hysteria. Seven residents of Hawaii were found guilty of Red conspiracies amidst comments that the island's shipping lanes were endangered.

Beyond American borders, the world was stunned by the Berlin revolt. It had become just that, a revolt, by June 18. June 15, 1953, the day the uprising began, is celebrated to this day as a national holiday in West Berlin and in West Germany. International resentment over the use of Soviet tanks to put down the Berliners with massive bloodshed made Thursday the eighteenth of June (the day the revolt was crushed) a day of glory and tragedy in free Western Germany. In Korea, negotiations with the Chinese and the North Koreans continued in an atmosphere further polarized by what had happened that week in Europe.

Former American commander General Van Fleet declared on Thursday, June 18, that American terms for a peace were deplorable and a sellout to the Reds. Korea and Berlin were the flash points for public focus on that Thursday, a focus on the international Red conspiracy that dominated the news.[36]

Washington–New York, Wednesday–Thursday, June 17–18, 1953

Bloch had contingency plans of his own, meager as they were. When he learned on Wednesday afternoon that Vinson was to reconvene the Court, he telephoned colleagues in New York to stand by. Bloch had no illusions where the votes on the Supreme Court were. But in the frenetic last week there could always be some move, somewhere, that might be as surprising as Douglas's. Bloch's telephone call on Wednesday evening was to Marshall Perlin, a New York lawyer who had kept close to the case. Perlin, for one, understood what Farmer was talking about and had tried to convince Bloch of the position's rectitude weeks earlier with no success.

Late Wednesday afternoon, Bloch told Perlin to stand by in New York against events in Washington. While the Supreme Court reassembled, Perlin prepared papers (based on the 1946 act) for filing before Kaufman on the very moment that the Supreme Court vacated the Douglas stay. The scenario was that Kaufman would immediately deny anything that Perlin would file. But then Perlin could take an immediate appeal to the Second Circuit. What might happen before Judge Jerome Frank, Thomas Swan, and company might be a very different thing.

Bloch called Perlin again late on Thursday afternoon, June 18, after the argument. Bloch told Perlin there was no question: the Court would vacate the stay. Perlin prepared his papers for the dry run before Kaufman. Keyed to telephone calls from Washington, two lawyers from Perlin's office were to be dispatched immediately to Kaufman's office after the Supreme Court vacated the stay. Meanwhile, Perlin, Arthur Kinoy, and Sam Gruber—

colleagues of Perlin's—took the train to New Haven on Thursday night, where the only chance, the last chance, remained. The Second Circuit, a court of conscience and justice, might do something.[37]

CHAPTER EIGHT

✦

FRIDAY, JUNE 19, 1953

The Statler Hotel, Washington, D.C., and the White House

SOPHIE ROSENBERG, Julius's mother, waited in Washington on Friday morning. The elderly lady had flown down on Wednesday, the day before the Court's reconvening, to seek a personal audience with President Eisenhower. On Thursday, all through the day of the argument before the Supreme Court, she sat in her hotel room while emissaries tried a dozen or more different ways to arrange a meeting with the president. She was still waiting on Friday morning.

The emissaries were wasting their time. The president had told his staff weeks before that he would never meet with any representative of the convicted spies. The soldier-politician had no sympathy for the Rosenbergs, whom he looked upon as traitors to the cause for which so many soldiers under his command had given their lives. More than that, he was appalled by the length and complexity of the judicial process that had led to what was now going on before him. Eisenhower, like so many men trained in the military, neither understood nor had any patience with the interminable checks and balances of the capital's political and judicial systems. He was fed up with the delay that kept this nagging controversy alive to annoy him with its daily repercussions around the world.

Supreme Court Courtroom

Disaster struck quickly.

The Supreme Court stepped out from behind the partitions precisely at noon. Each of the nine men looked as if the past twenty-four hours had been a personal trial. It had. The argument had been long and bitter. Black, ill and disturbed, viewed his colleagues with open contempt. Frankfurter, the busy gadfly, sat stock-still as if censured by a maiden aunt. Vinson, the first to speak, delivered the majority opinion with a visible shaking of his head, as if to admit to the world that the agonies of the damned had been visited on him and that what he was about to do was his best, but not necessarily right.

Within thirty seconds after he began reading, Vinson's point was clear. The Supreme Court had decided to vacate Douglas's stay. The death sentences were reinstated. Vinson ended by announcing that his own opinion was joined in by justices Reed, Jackson, Burton, Minton, and Clark.[1]

When Vinson was finished, the throng of reporters trampled over each other toward the back of the chamber and raced for the telephones that had been placed on tables stretching from the clerk's office. It was all over. By fifteen minutes after noon on that Friday, the world was to know it.

Back in the Court chamber, Justice Clark read his concurring opinion,[2] in which he was joined by the chief justice and the other five justices. It added little to what the chief justice had said in the first thirty seconds. Justice Jackson then read his own concurring opinion in which he renewed his attack on Marshall and Farmer as interlopers.[2a]

No one was left in the chamber except the lawyers and a hard core of followers. All the reporters were gone. Three of the justices, Frankfurter, Douglas, and Black, had dissented and were still to be heard from. Justice Frankfurter, speaking first for the dissenters, spoke in scholarly terms, but his point was unclear. He stated first that his position was neither an affirmation nor a dissent. He had decided that the new questions were "complicated and novel"; what was required, Frankfurter stated, was more time for careful study and argument. For this reason, he opposed vacating the Douglas stay.[3]

Black had no time for such sophistries. He opened by stating that there had never been an occasion in the history of the Supreme Court when a stay entered by a single justice during the Court's vacation had been vacated by the full Court before the Court had reassembled in the fall for the beginning of the regular term. The reconvening was hasty, precipitous action, Black felt, and probably illegal. Even more than Douglas, Black appeared moved by what was happening. In a voice breaking with anger and in words that leaped out at double the rate of Black's normal slow and careful drawl, he threw down the gauntlet: "I find no statute or rule of Court which permits the full court to set aside a mere temporary stay entered by a justice in obedience to his statutory obligations."[4]

Black was not finished there. He went on to state that he agreed with Justice Douglas that the 1946 act applied in this case, and that no death sentence could be meted out without the jury recommendation. But his harshest words were reserved for the speed of the Court's decision. Voicing again the theme that he had stated for the public record earlier, Black said that the trial record before Judge Kaufman had never been reviewed by the Supreme Court. As he measured each word and pounded the lectern before him, the Alabaman stated that the Court should have taken more time to review the new questions before it. To refuse to do so would compound the error of the Court's refusal to review the trial record. The end result was that the executions of these individuals would remain under a question "as to whether [they] were legally and rightfully carried out."

Douglas was the last to speak. His opinion was long. Earlier, he said, he had felt that the new point raised concerning the 1946 act was a novel one requiring the Court's study. But now Douglas was clear: "Now I am sure of the answer. I know deep in my heart that I am right on the law. Knowing that, my duty is clear. . . . The cold truth is that the death sentence may not be imposed for what the Rosenbergs did unless the jury so recommends."[5]

When all of the opinions were read, Bloch, his face ashen, struggled to the lectern. Speaking in a shaking voice that cracked with tears, Bloch asked the Court to stay the execution of the Rosenbergs so that he could make still another attempt to secure clemency from President Eisenhower. While Bloch was on his feet at the lectern, he was joined by Marshall, who waited until Bloch had finished his short statement. Marshall then asked the Court to stay the execution of the Rosenbergs until he could brief and argue the question of the Court's power to override a stay imposed by one of its justices. Vinson looked to his right and to his left. The careful and totally unhappy chief justice whispered for a moment to Jackson, sitting at his side. Then he rose and adjourned the Court, telling the few remaining observers that the Court would return that afternoon with its decision on Bloch's motion and on Marshall's. The justices disappeared behind the partitions.

As the last black robe disappeared, Bloch collapsed into a chair next to the lectern, put his head in his hands and sobbed uncontrollably. While his colleagues tried to comfort the beaten lawyer, Marshall stood aside with Farmer. The two looked like consultants called into an operating room at the moment of the patient's death. It was all over and they knew it. But the despair was Bloch's. He had lived and died with his clients for three years. Marshall and Farmer could only shake their heads in disbelief; they understood neither then nor thereafter how the Supreme Court of the land could act so irrationally.

Within ten minutes, the justices reappeared. Vinson now looked as if he were succumbing to Black's illness. His normally resonant voice was hollow and weak. Before his brethren had even seated themselves, Vinson announced that both motions had been denied.[6] He added that Justice Black had dissented from both denials. With a near-violent shake of his head, Vinson then looked at the tuxedo-clad court clerk with a look that seemed a plea. In response, the clerk rose and intoned the archaic phrases that closed the Court's special session. Even the words within it seemed to cause pain to Vinson as the chief justice stood listening. The clerk stated that the special term called on the application of Attorney

General Herbert Brownell was now adjourned. The justices silently turned away and slipped through the partitions behind them.

The legal battle in the Supreme Court was over.

It is appropriate to examine the thoughts of two justices as they ruled that day.

One is Jackson, the elegant Jackson, not one of the stalwarts who reacted automatically, negatively, to every claim of wrongdoing at trial. Who, indeed, had urged Frankfurter to spare no words in criticizing Saypol for Saypol's conduct in running his press conference starring Perl during the Rosenberg trial. Where was Jackson on June 18 and 19? Jackson was preoccupied, persisting in his scholastic endeavor to establish that Farmer did not represent the Rosenbergs. As two human beings were to die, here are Jackson's concerns:

The lawyers who have ably and courageously fought the Rosenbergs' battle throughout then listened at this bar to the newly imported counsel make an argument which plainly implied lack of understanding or zeal on the part of retained counsel. They simply had been elbowed out of the case.

Every lawyer familiar with the workings of our criminal courts and the habits of the bar will agree that this precedent presents a threat to orderly and responsible representation of accused persons and the right of themselves and their counsel to control their own cases. The lower court refused to accept Edelman's intrusion but by the order in question [the Douglas stay] must accept him as having standing to take part in, or to take over, the Rosenbergs' case. That such disorderly intervention is more likely to prejudice than to help the representation of accused persons in highly publicized cases is self-evident. We discountenance this practice.[6a]

Jackson could never swallow allowing Farmer and Marshall to argue for the Rosenbergs. If Jackson had been less concerned with the fitness of things in the Supreme Court of the United States and more concerned with what the Rosenberg lawyers did not themselves argue for their clients, Jackson's words would be far less calloused. Anyone reading Jackson gets the strong feeling that he would say the same thing in a routine antitrust case, not a case where two lives were within eight hours of extinction when he wrote those words. The cruelty of the law is the protection it gives to the cruel. That is the best that can be said about Jackson.*

The legal battle in the Supreme Court may have been over but not the concerns of the deeply disturbed Frankfurter. His concerns were in sharp contrast to Jackson's. This is what Frankfurter wrote and filed early on that Friday afternoon:

On the assumption that the sentences against the Rosenbergs are to be carried out at 11 o'clock tonight, their counsel ask this Court to stay their execution until opportunity has been afforded to them to invoke the constitutional prerogative of clemency. The action of this Court, and the division of opinion in vacating the stay granted by Mr. Justice Douglas, are, of course, a factor in the situation, which arose within the last hour. It is not for this Court even remotely to enter into the domain of clemency reserved by the Constitution exclusively to the President. But the Court must properly take into account the possible consequences of a stay or of a denial of a stay of execution of death sentences upon making an appeal for executive clemency. Were it established that counsel are correct in their assumption that the sentences of death are to be carried out at 11 p.m. tonight, I believe that it would be right and proper for this Court formally to grant a stay with a proper time-limit to give appropriate opportunity for the process of executive clemency to operate. I justifiably assume, however, that the time for the execution has not been fixed as of 11 o'clock tonight. Of course I respectfully assume that appropriate consideration will be given to a clemency application by the authority constitutionally charged with the clemency function.[7]

---

* In an interesting footnote to Justice Jackson's role in the Rosenberg case, a memorandum from his then law clerk, written in 1953, surfaced thirty-three years later. The law clerk had definite views. He wrote to the justice in 1953 that Julius and Ethel Rosenberg were "fitting candidates" for execution. The law clerk wanted to be absolutely clear. He added: "It is too bad that drawing and quartering has been abolished." That law clerk has gone on to prominence of his own: his name is William Rehnquist and he is the chief justice of the United States. (See quotes from the Jackson Papers in the *New York Times* article by Stuart Taylor, Jr., July 27, 1986.)

There is evidence that Frankfurter was sufficiently disturbed to inquire himself on that Friday, June 19, to see if the executions were to be held late that evening. He was told quite accurately (if not fully) that there were no plans to execute the Rosenbergs on the Jewish Sabbath. What was not told to Frankfurter, who was livid when he learned the truth, was that the executions had been moved forward to eight o'clock that evening, *before* the Sabbath, before there was any chance for the White House to examine in detail Justice Frankfurter's clear call for executive clemency. The rush to execution in the Rosenberg case sickened Frankfurter more than anything he had faced in fourteen years on the high bench.

The Frankfurter order addressed to clemency (and the telephone call that appears to have been made seeking assurances that the Rosenbergs would not be executed that day) were appeals to executive reason by Felix Frankfurter, as deeply disturbed as he had ever been. But the Justice Department had no intention of reasoning with anyone or analyzing anything. And the president was of no mind to listen to any message from men in black robes who had immeasurably complicated presidential tasks during the past months. Justice Department officials were as good as their word. The Rosenbergs would not die on the Jewish Sabbath. Even though it was already midafternoon on Friday, the Rosenbergs would be executed by nightfall, within five hours. The agony would end even more quickly than the attorney general had originally planned. Brownell wasted no time to get on the telephone to Warden Wilfred Denno. The time of the execution was changed to 8:00 P.M. on that Friday evening. No one could argue about that—or so Brownell surmised.

Chambers of Judge Kaufman, New York City

The word from Washington quickly spread to Judge Kaufman's chambers. The two men standing by from Perlin's office presented their papers to Kaufman. Without a word, Kaufman wrote across them "Denied." Racing upstairs to the clerk's office in the Foley Square building, Perlin's colleagues filed an immediate notice of appeal to the Second Circuit Court of Appeals.[8]

Federal Courthouse, New Haven, Connecticut

Perlin, Gruber, and Kinoy went directly from the train depot to the federal courthouse in New Haven, where the Second Circuit was sitting. They were looking for judges.[9] Their first choice was Learned Hand, who had granted the Rosenbergs a stay of execution pending an appeal to the Supreme Court—it now seemed years ago. Hand could not be found.

But the three men found Judge Swan, who received them and listened to them for over an hour. It was now midafternoon on Friday. Perlin, Kinoy, and Gruber argued one point and one point only: all they wanted was a panel of three judges who would listen to the new arguments on the 1946 act that had been brushed aside so cavalierly by the Supreme Court. The three men were prepared to argue that afternoon, they were prepared to argue that evening, they were prepared to argue the next day—anytime, anywhere. Just give us three judges who will listen to us, they repeated many times. Just give us three judges who will listen to us argue the substantiality of the new point, they pleaded. All we want is to convince three judges that there is a major question before them, not, necessarily, that we, Perlin, Kinoy, and Gruber are right.

The three lawyers got a chance. Swan told the three lawyers that if they could find two other judges, Swan would convene a panel to hear them on that point. But that was the rub: where were the two other judges? Regardless of where and who they were, Judge Swan exhibited extraordinary courage in agreeing to convene a panel. He was prepared to convene a panel of appellate judges to hear argument on the very point that the Supreme Court had rejected no less than three hours earlier. It was an act of pure judicial courage. Swan then called Judge Jerome Frank on the other side of New Haven and found that Frank was home.

Swan then volunteered to take Perlin, Gruber, and Kinoy in Swan's limousine across town to Frank's house. It was a singular carload. Three lawyers obsessed with the imminent execution of their clients, a judge who was not convinced but who would listen, all in the judge's limousine, driven by the judge's chauffeur, to see another judge whose views on what was to come before him could not be predicted.

Home of Judge Jerome Frank,
New Haven, Connecticut

When Swan's limousine reached Frank's house, Swan asked the three lawyers to wait while he spoke with Frank alone. The lawyers waited outside the house. Then Swan came out, said nothing, did nothing, got back into his limousine and left. The three lawyers were then ushered into Frank's presence. Frank had been gardening. He had his spade and trowel in his hand. Frank opened the conversation with an unusual comment. He told Perlin, Kinoy, and Gruber that if he, Frank, were their age, he would be doing precisely what the three young lawyers were doing, attempting to save their clients. Frank told the lawyers that they should be proud of what they were doing; it was a professional act of worthiness and he, Frank, wished to acknowledge it.

Then they got to business. Frank said that it was a terrible mistake that the 1946 act had not been raised before. Frank said that if it had come up earlier on, he could have secured at least one other vote in favor of the 1946 act's application to the Rosenbergs. Frank was categoric: You are absolutely right on the point you are raising with me, not only was it a substantial point, but the point was right, the 1946 act *did* apply. Perlin saw his chance: he asked Frank to grant a stay so that they could argue this point to a panel of three judges.

Frank then broke down. He sobbed audibly and shook his head. He said, "I know you are right, but when the bosses have acted, what can you do?" Frank then added, through a voice choked with sobs, that the "bosses" were more than just the Supreme Court—there were other elements involved in controlling this tragic situation. He said, "There has been such touch and go; perhaps it would be better to get it over with."

Frank then composed himself. He told Perlin that he, personally, could not grant a stay. But he did say that if the lawyers could find a third judge, he would sit with Swan and the third judge on the panel to hear the lawyers. There was simply nothing more that Frank could do.

Perlin, Gruber, and Kinoy made up their minds to find Charles Clark, a third member of the court who, they had been told, was in New Haven. Going back down to the federal courthouse in a taxicab, they found where Clark lived. Back in Gruber's car, they drove out to Clark's house. There was no answer to knocks, either at Clark's front door or at his back door. They then called the clerk of the U.S. court downtown to see if he knew where Clark was. The clerk guessed that Clark might have been at Clark's golf club that Friday afternoon.

A Gas Station in New Haven

Then a frightening piece of news intervened. Over the radio in Gruber's car, the three lawyers found out that the Rosenbergs were to be executed that evening, now no more than four hours away. Perlin, Gruber, and Kinoy went to a public telephone in a gas station to call Clark's country club to try and locate him. After a long wait, Clark himself came to the telephone. Perlin explained to Clark what the quest was: that two judges of his court had agreed to sit on a panel to hear arguments on a stay on the merits of the 1946 act argument. What the lawyers desperately required was a third judge to sit on that panel.

Clark told Perlin that he had had nothing to do with the Rosenberg case: had never sat on a panel reviewing it, had never looked at it—had had no part of it. Clark said that he was glad that this was so. But Clark agreed to telephone Judge Swan and Frank and call Perlin back at the telephone booth at the gas station. It was now 5:45 P.M. on the day that the Rosenbergs were to be executed at 8:00.

Minutes later, the telephone rang in the booth. It was Clark. He told Perlin that he had spoken with Swan and Frank. They had decided to deny a stay; they had also decided not to convene a panel to hear the lawyers. It was now 6:00 P.M.

It was entirely appropriate that the first argument that the 1946 Atomic Energy Act applied to Julius and Ethel Rosenberg took place between Fyke Farmer and a doorman on Park Avenue in New York City; the last argument on whether the 1946 act applied took place in a pay booth at a gasoline station in New Haven. Two high moments in the law.

It was now 6:10 P.M. on Friday, June 19, 1953, in New Haven.

Statler Hotel, Washington, D.C.

Bloch had his own desperate plan miles to the south.

Bloch shared the justices' anxieties about time. Hearing the majority's opinion at 12:30 in the afternoon, Bloch handed his formal petition for clemency to his adversary, Acting Solicitor General Robert Stern, and went back to his hotel.

The radio was on in his room, and over the noise of the hangers-on who had gathered, Bloch got his second jolt of bad news within an hour. The White House announced that President Eisenhower would not grant clemency. The president's statement was read by a spokesman:

When in their own solemn judgment the Tribunals of the United States have adjudged them guilty and their sentence just, I will not intervene in this matter. The executions of two human beings is a grave matter. But even graver is the thought of the millions of dead whose death may be directly attributable to what these spies have done. I deny the petition.[10]

Paled, but undaunted, Bloch became obsessed with the passage of time. He tried to telephone Stern to ask him to relay a request for a stay of execution—based on the same religious ground raised by a justice of the Supreme Court—to Attorney General Brownell. Finally, late in the afternoon, Bloch got Stern on the other end of the line. Bloch explained his request. "It is only one day that I ask," Bloch pleaded.

Stern said that he would talk to the attorney general immediately. True to his pattern of courtesy, Bloch thanked Stern "with all my heart."

Bloch then took Ethel Rosenberg's own handwritten letter pleading for clemency and with Finerty walked down Sixteenth Street to the White House. The two men pushed their way through hundreds of pickets representing both sides of the case, asked the guard if they could arrange for delivery of the letter to the president, and asked for a personal interview with Eisenhower.

It was a pathetic performance. The guard took the letter, but told Bloch and Finerty that they could not be admitted to the White House without an appointment. There was no telephone in the guard's little booth. Bloch and Finerty decided to return to the Statler four blocks away to try and call either James Hagerty, the president's press secretary, or Sherman Adams, his executive assistant. Accompanied by over a hundred pro-Rosenberg pickets, the two lawyers marched back to the hotel.

At the hotel, they rang up the White House and were told that neither Haggerty nor Adams was available. Bloch waited for twenty minutes while the White House operator found someone willing to talk with him. Finally, Assistant White House Press Secretary Murray Snyder got on the line. Bloch asked Snyder if the president had read either the Court's decision or Ethel Rosenberg's letter, delivered to the White House an hour earlier. Snyder answered that it was not his job to find out what the president had or had not read. It was now after 5:00 P.M. Understandably, Bloch lost his temper. He told Snyder, "Damn it! People are going to die; make it your function." Bloch asked Snyder to make an immediate appointment with Eisenhower for himself and for Sophie Rosenberg, Julius's mother. Snyder told an agitated Bloch that he would put the request into the "proper channels."

At the Statler, Bloch was not only living out events on that crucial afternoon but also listening for them on the radio. While he was talking with Snyder, the radio announced another special bulletin from the White House. The president issued a statement that he had "read the letter of the defendant Ethel Rosenberg. He states that in his conviction it adds nothing to the issues covered in his statement of the afternoon." The flash ended with the president's refusal to see Sophie Rosenberg.

Another bulletin, this time from the Department of Justice, rekindled a spark of hope. The attorney general had announced that the executions would not violate the Jewish Sabbath. Bloch immediately concluded that he had another twenty-four hours, at the very least. He pounded the phone down on the rack. There had to be a way to reach the president. Bloch paced the little room, crowded with partisans as the afternoon gave way to early summer dusk.

Then still another anxiety beset Bloch. Would word get to Denno in time? He decided to call Sing Sing. Within seconds, he had the warden on the phone. Bloch told Denno that he wanted to confirm that the executions had been postponed until Saturday night. What happened next stunned the crowd in Bloch's room. The distracted lawyer literally screamed into the telephone; the instrument was waved back and forth like a club in the hands of the frantic lawyer. Finally, without expecting an answer, Bloch bellowed into the telephone: "What? Moved ahead? By God, eight o'clock! It's seven-thirty now. My God, no!"

Bloch sat on the bed continuing his tirade into the telephone. "What kind of animals am I dealing with? This is barbaric. Eisenhower rejects our position without even hearing us. He acts like a military dictator. They are all without feeling, like Nazis. I want the whole world to know what animals they are. I am ashamed to be an American."

Finally, without a word to Denno on the other end of the line, Bloch's colleagues gently took the telephone out of his hands and pushed him into an armchair next to his bed. They brought him water. Bloch's face was covered in tears. He was still talking, but the words had lost all meaning.

Then another thought brought Bloch out of his agitation. He straightened up and pushed his friends away. Bloch asked them to get Denno back. Sing Sing said that Denno had left the line and was unavailable. Bloch asked that U.S. marshal William Carroll, in charge of the arrangements at Sing Sing for the federal authorities, be called. Carroll was reached. Bloch was again aroused. He said to Carroll, "This is Manny Bloch. Please tell Julie and Ethel I did the best I could for them. Tell them I will take care of the children. Tell them I love them. Tell them . . ."

Bloch broke. He could get nothing more out of his tortured mind and body. He bent over in his chair, put his head between his knees and sobbed uncontrollably.

It was 7:50 P.M.

Judge Kaufman's Chambers

It was the second appearance of a Rosenberg team before Kaufman that Friday afternoon. Perlin's lawyers had succeeded in getting but one word, "Denied," written on their papers. That was all that they wanted. But Milton Friedman and Frank Scheiner—the second platoon of the defense team—had more to say and do. Friedman and Scheiner were old-timers in the cause. They had been stationed in New York by Bloch weeks earlier. It was good planning: the agitated Bloch would have had difficulty in getting through to Judge Kaufman, his nemesis. Not Friedman and Scheiner; they knew exactly where to find him. They had known for days that if things really hit rock bottom, if the Supreme Court said a final nay, if death for the Rosenbergs was in a matter of hours and Bloch was still in Washington, the two of them would have to face Irving Kaufman on behalf of the doomed prisoners. And Kaufman was waiting for them in his courtroom. No friends to answer phone calls. No deadlines. No bureaucracy. Judge Irving Kaufman was in his courtroom waiting for the Rosenberg lawyers. His docket was clear. He could see the lawyers without delay that Friday afternoon. It was as if Kaufman had known it would come to this in the final hours, the judge facing a group of distraught lawyers while the clock ticked down.

Friedman and Scheiner had a slightly different message. Friedman's message was brief. He asked Kaufman to stay the executions—because "it would be an outrageous insult to World Jewry to permit the execution to go forward after the Sabbath had begun." Kaufman started to speak, but Friedman was not finished. He asked the judge for a stay of at least twenty-four hours because any attempt to execute the Rosenbergs that evening would risk encroachment on the Sabbath. Friedman went on in a learned vein, outlining to Kaufman the different views within Judaism as to when the Sabbath began. Some Orthodox Jews, he said, saw the Sabbath as starting at sundown; others argued that it began with sight of the first star. Better, Friedman said almost conversationally, to avoid all possibilities of the sacrilege of bloodshed on the Sabbath by staying the execution for twenty-four hours.

Kaufman listened until Friedman was finished. Then, just as conversationally, he cut through the argument. He spoke as if the folklore of the Jewish Sabbath were nothing new to him. Dispassionately, in a low but edged voice, Kaufman told Friedman that the possibility that the execution would occur on the Sabbath had also concerned him, so much so that he had personally called the attorney general. The judge told Friedman that Brownell had just assured "this Court that the execution would not be carried out through the sabbath. Accordingly, there is no need for the stay argued here."*[11]

Before Friedman sat down, he looked at Scheiner, his colleague. There was a smile of satisfaction. Friedman assumed that no matter what happened anywhere on that awful day, the Rosenbergs would not die. Both he and Scheiner left Kaufman's courtroom fully convinced that the executions would be delayed at least twenty-four hours. Despite the appearance of a cruel deception, there is every reason to believe that Kaufman knew no more than the two lawyers; Brownell was keeping to himself the rush to execution on that very day, only five hours later.

Scheiner and Friedman left Kaufman's court at 3:30 with a sense of terrible desperation tempered only slightly by the twenty-four hours that they assumed still lay before them for further moves.

National Airport, Washington, D.C.

For Marshall, it was a voyage all his own.[12] The California lawyer had flown off from Washington to New York on the first plane after the disastrous decision came from Vinson. Marshall had a copy of the Supreme Court's order and thought he saw a chink of light, just a glimmering amidst all the dreadful words.

In any event, with just over twenty-four hours of life remaining for his new clients, there was nothing to be lost by the try. As Marshall boarded his plane at National Airport at 4:00 on Friday afternoon, he and the rest of the world believed that the Rosen-

* There is no evidence that Kaufman himself knew that the execution had been moved forward to 8:00 P.M. That announcement was not made until after 5:00 P.M. on Friday, June 19.

bergs would live through the next day. Marshall also knew that his was an act of pure desperation: he had made up his mind to present personally an argument drawn from a faint glimmering that he saw in the Supreme Court's opinion, to Kaufman, or to any federal judge in New York who would listen.

Marshall's point was a minor one. He had read the Supreme Court's order simply vacating Justice Douglas's stay of the Rosenberg executions. But nothing in the final opinion said anything or did anything about that part of Douglas's stay that had sent the issue of the 1946 act back to Kaufman for briefing. Logically, realistically, it was an argument that went nowhere because of the clear intent of the majority of the Supreme Court. Because there were human lives at stake here, it was not inconceivable that a judge in New York might see the same distinction Marshall did, and read the Supreme Court's order as sufficiently vague to require the Supreme Court—again—to clarify what it wanted done. But that would surely be in October. Marshall was certain that there was no chance that the Supreme Court would reconvene for a second time. Marshall's point was so narrow, so technical, that he kept it to himself and went off on his desperate trip to New York alone.

By the time he landed at LaGuardia at 5:00 on Friday afternoon, the desperation of Marshall's mission had been com-pounded a hundredfold. The radios at the airport carried Brownell's announcement that the Rosenbergs were to be exe-cuted at 8:00 that very evening. Marshall felt as though he were on his way to visit a dying relative, as he taxied toward Foley Square in Lower Manhattan.

His first step when he arrived at the courthouse was to see who the emergency judge was. All federal courts have a judge standing by for emergency duty on weekends. Marshall reasoned that if he could get before the emergency judge, he would clearly have a better chance than he would before Kaufman. Kaufman's threat of contempt against him and Farmer just four days earlier was still fresh in Marshall's mind. It was Judge Edward Dimock, however, who was covering at the courthouse, and Marshall explained to Dimock's secretary what he wanted. Formally, he was seeking a writ of habeas corpus staying the execution so that the unrevoked portion of Justice Douglas's order, remanding the new issue to Kaufman, could be put in effect. Dimock's secretary remained in Dimock's inner office for less than thirty seconds. Dimock would have nothing to do with Marshall's petition. He referred him to Kaufman, who, Marshall was informed, was still in the building.

The trip to Foley Square had taken over an hour. Finding Dimock and being rebuffed by him had taken Marshall the better part of another hour. To Marshall, it seemed that each word was taking up precious seconds. Kaufman, to Marshall's surprise, agreed to see him immediately and to hear Marshall's argument in chambers. This was a shot in the arm to Marshall. One of his fears on the plane had been that Kaufman might continue to deal with him as an interloper and simply refuse to see him.

At 7:15 P.M., Marshall began arguing before Kaufman. He reviewed the tangled recent history of moves in the case. Kaufman seemed terribly annoyed but did not interrupt. Within minutes, the judge began looking at his watch. While Marshall argued, another lawyer joined the small group in Kaufman's chamber. It was J. Edward Lumbard, U.S. attorney for the Southern District of New York and chief federal lawyer in New York City.

Marshall stopped briefly to look at his notes. Kaufman nodded toward Lumbard. The U.S. attorney then told Kaufman that Justice Jackson, in his concurring opinion, which was just five hours old, had ruled that Marshall had no standing in the Rosenberg case. Marshall looked furiously at Lumbard. With the execution of two human beings thirty-four minutes away, the government was still hiding behind legal niceties. Kaufman, surprising Marshall again, ignored Lumbard's intervention. The judge turned toward Marshall.

"Mr. Marshall, I remind you that the executions in this case are set for eight P.M." Kaufman looked at his watch again. "You had better get along with your argument."[13] Kaufman looked down, fingered his wristwatch and then stared right at Marshall. Marshall shook his head violently. It seemed clear that Kaufman was not going to let him finish his argument. Marshall then pleaded with Kaufman to call Warden Denno at Sing Sing.

"Your Honor, just stay the execution long enough for me to finish my argument."

Kaufman was in a bind and Marshall knew it. The beginning of the Jewish Sabbath was indeed on Kaufman's mind; so was the impropriety of a Jewish judge permitting the sacrilege of executing Jewish prisoners on the Sabbath. But when did the Sabbath start? Kaufman plainly had no intention of touching the determinations made by the Department of Justice that 8:00 P.M. was a safe hour. So while Marshall pleaded with Kaufman to call Denno, Kaufman steadfastly refused to touch his telephone. Kaufman reached over his desk and told Marshall that he had read all of Marshall's arguments when he had first received them and understood all of Marshall's points.

By 7:30 P.M., Marshall was still deeply enmeshed in a technical analysis of what the Supreme Court had done and what it had not done. He had spoken for less than fifteen minutes about a Supreme Court ruling that filled six pages and thousands of words. Narrow or not, Marshall had a sticky point and he was determined to make it. But at 7:30 P.M., Kaufman stopped Marshall with a wave of his hand. How much longer did Marshall intend to argue? Kaufman's edginess bit into his voice. Marshall said it would take at least twenty minutes to present the various individual opinions of the justices and what they added up to—the guts of his argument. Kaufman sat back in his chair. Pounding his desk front for emphasis and cutting each word off with a bite, Kaufman said, "I will not call Sing Sing prison unless you convince me that there is merit in your application. I am not inclined to issue a stay from what I have read in your papers and what you have said thus far."[14]

Marshall labored on. It seemed like hours to the lawyer as Kaufman fretted before him. Marshall concluded by saying that the Douglas order for remand was still in effect; it was necessary for Judge Kaufman to stay the execution of the Rosenbergs so that the briefing and argument on the 1946 act would not be rendered meaningless by execution of the defendants. Lumbard, for his part, simply waved his hands. He had nothing more to say. Kaufman looked at Marshall. "Your petition is denied," Kaufman said. It was all he needed to say. It was all over. It was 7:45 P.M.

Sing Sing: The Death House

Julius Rosenberg shuffled trancelike the hundred yards from his cell to the electric chair. He had to have help from Rabbi Koslowe, Sing Sing's Jewish chaplain. It was a slow procession of guards, the chaplain, and the numbed prisoner. Without a word to anyone, Julius Rosenberg died in the electric chair at 8:05.

Ethel Rosenberg died courageously. Her head was high as she marched into the death chamber. Briefly, she turned to a matron and embraced her. The matron was in tears, but Ethel Rosenberg was dry-eyed. In the chair, she helped the attendant fasten the mask that was placed on her face. She said nothing as the straps were fastened and then the mask locked into place.

To her final minutes, Ethel Rosenberg was composed. The executioner threw the switch that sent deadly voltage through her body. The charge was repeated once and then again. The prison doctor then went to the chair and examined the slumped body with his stethoscope.

"This woman is still alive."

The executioner was notified by the guards, and the little assembly of witnesses, the rabbi, and the doctor watched as three more shocks were sent through Ethel Rosenberg's body. There was the unmistakable smell of cooking flesh in the hot room. After the second series of shocks, the prison doctor again examined the body.

"This woman is dead." The doctor stepped back from the chair.

It had taken the United States government until 8:16 P.M. on Friday, June 19, to execute Ethel Rosenberg.

The New York Weather Bureau recorded that sundown had occurred that evening at 8:13.[15]

Chambers of Judge Irving Kaufman, New York City

Irving Kaufman passed his vigil in his chambers in the federal courthouse on Foley Square. At 8:30 P.M., he received a phone call from Sing Sing. The judge listened impassively, said nothing.

Then he rose, went through his chambers, and closed the door behind him. FBI men were standing outside the door. They had been there for a week, ever since the judge had begun receiving letters threatening his life. With his bodyguards, Judge Kaufman took the elevator to the ground floor. As he did, it ceased being zero hour and became just another summer evening. The judge and his companions got in Kaufman's car for a drive to the judge's summer home in the Adirondacks for the weekend.[16]

Chambers of State Supreme Court Judge Irving Saypol

Three blocks away, another vigil ended. Irving Saypol, now a judge of the New York Supreme Court, New York's name for its lowest court of general jurisdiction, got his phone call from Sing Sing. Saypol looked straight ahead for a long time, sighed, and left his new chambers. Below on the street, he turned his car west toward his summer home at Long Branch, New Jersey, for the weekend.[17]

Bach Family, Tom's River, New Jersey

At Tom's River, New Jersey, the ten-year-old son of the Rosenbergs, Michael, had been kept away from the radio by the Bach family, where Michael and Bobbie, age six, were staying. Bobbie was in bed. Michael had been allowed to watch the New York Yankees–Detroit Tigers twi-night doubleheader. But in the middle of the second game the announcer interrupted the play-by-play to announce President Eisenhower's denial of clemency. Michael started crying, mumbling almost inaudibly, "Good-bye."[18]

Pershing Square, Los Angeles

In Pershing Square in downtown Los Angeles, there was a pro-Rosenberg demonstration and an anti-Rosenberg counter-demonstration. The star of the pro-Rosenberg show was Irwin Edelman, Rosenberg's "next friend" who had figured so prominently in the argument before the Supreme Court. He spoke briefly.

The counterdemonstration became ugly. A mob of three hundred, carrying placards denouncing Edelman, advanced across the block-long park. The Rosenberg demonstration was moribund, milling around Edelman and trying to console each other. Suddenly, the mob from across the square confronted Edelman, and a number of the mob began to shout obscenities at the fifty-four-year-old man. Seeing what was happening, Edelman shouted back, "If you are happy with the execution of the Rosenbergs, you are rotten to the core."

That ignited the mob. They moved menacingly toward Edelman, who backed off and then ran headlong into a coffee shop entrance of the Hotel Biltmore. Part of the crowd pushed its way through the revolving doors and into the coffee shop looking for Edelman. Policeman P. N. Olsen, on duty in the park that evening and watching for trouble, appeared on the scene and rescued Edelman from the crowd in the coffee shop. The policeman's uniform quieted them down.

Edelman was led out of the coffee shop into Olsen's police cruiser. They drove a block away and Edelman got out of the car. Patrolman Olsen warned him to stay away from Pershing Square.[19]

Union Square, New York City

Five thousand people had gathered for a vigil in New York City's Union Square. When news reached them that the Rosenbergs were dead, a wail of grief went through the crowd. For minutes there was no speaker, no program, simply grief. Then one of the leaders went onto the platform and denounced President Eisenhower. The demonstration went on with speakers attacking the president, the Supreme Court, Judge Kaufman, the Department of Justice, and American justice in general.[20]

It was one of fifty such demonstrations across the world. What Brownell had feared took place. Worldwide indignation had come to a boil.

The Supreme Court of the United States in 1953. *Front row, left to right:* Justice William Douglas, Justice Stanley Reed, Chief Justice Fred Vinson, President Dwight D. Eisenhower, Justice Hugo Black, Justice Felix Frankfurter. *Back row, left to right:* Sherman Adams, executive assistant to the president; Attorney General Herbert Brownell; Justice Sherman Minton; Justice Tom Clark; Justice Robert Jackson; Justice Harold Burton. (SUPREME COURT HISTORICAL SOCIETY)

Chief members of the prosecution team in the Rosenberg case. *Left to right:* U.S. attorney Irving Saypol, first assistant Myles Lane, special assistant Roy M. Cohn. (UPI/BETTMANN NEWSPHOTOS)

Co-defendant and witness for the prosecution David Greenglass with federal marshal. (UPI/BETTMANN NEWSPHOTOS)

Daniel Marshall, of Los Angeles, and Fyke Farmer, of Nashville, the lawyers who authored the theory that moved Justice Douglas to stay the execution of Julius and Ethel Rosenberg. (UPI/BETTMANN NEWS-PHOTOS)

Rival sets of defense lawyers celebrating the stay entered by Justice Douglas on June 17, 1953. *Left to right:* Daniel Marshall and Fyke Farmer, of Los Angeles and Nashville, respectively; Emanuel Bloch, of New York, and John Finerty, of Washington, D.C. (UPI/BETTMANN NEWS-PHOTOS)

Lawyers who argued on behalf of the stay of execution of the Rosenbergs, shown leaving the Supreme Court on the afternoon of June 18, 1953, after arguing before the Court. *Left to right:* John Finerty, Emanuel Bloch, Fyke Farmer, and Daniel Marshall. (UPI/BETTMANN NEWSPHOTOS)

Judge Irving R. Kaufman, the trial judge who imposed the death sentence on Julius and Ethel Rosenberg. (UPI/BETTMANN NEWSPHOTOS)

Master atomic spy Klaus Fuchs, after his release from prison in England, on his way to East Germany in 1959. (UPI/BETTMANN NEWSPHOTOS)

Julius and Ethel Rosenberg leaving the U.S. Courthouse after being convicted on March 29, 1951. (UPI/BETTMANN NEWSPHOTOS)

Demonstration in Paris, France, in support of Julius and Ethel Rosenberg on June 18, 1953, the day before they were executed. (UPI/BETTMANN NEWSPHOTOS)

French demonstrators, participating in the Bastille Day Parade in Paris on July 14, 1953, protesting the execution of Julius and Ethel Rosenberg. (UPI/BETTMANN NEWSPHOTOS)

Crowd on East Seventeenth Street, New York City, listening to speeches condemning the imminent execution of the Rosenbergs. Demonstrators were not permitted to enter Union Square, traditional meeting point for protesters; the square had been roped off. (UPI/BETTMANN NEWS-PHOTOS)

CHAPTER NINE

FATAL ERROR

THERE WAS more than one error committed by the Supreme Court in the Rosenberg case on June 19, 1953. There were at least six, and possibly more. For anyone to understand the great tragedy of this case, these errors must be understood.

Very often legal disputes are unintelligible to nonlawyers. This need not be so. The legal arguments about what happened (and what should have happened) to the Rosenbergs are quite simple. No one should be permitted to confuse them; otherwise, the basic injustice of what occurred is obscured.

Did the Supreme Court have the power to vacate Justice Douglas's stay?

Probably not.

No one doubted that Justice Douglas *could* do precisely what he *did* do. The power of a single justice to stay the execution of the Rosenbergs was conceded by the government in all of its briefs and in oral argument by Acting Solicitor General Stern.*

---

* Supreme Court procedure is not complicated, but a word about it is helpful. Five votes (a majority of the Court of nine) were and are required if the Court is to take action, such as sustaining the Douglas stay. Only four votes were and are required in order for the Supreme Court to accept a case for consideration of any kind (known as the grant of a writ of certiorari). Then, in the ordinary course, when the Court takes final action after its consideration, a majority vote of the Court is required. Going to the Supreme Court is, thus, a two-step procedure except when one justice takes it upon himself, as Douglas did, to act alone to achieve a temporary (not final) change in the status of a case. Within these limits, a single justice can circumvent the first step, above. No one (including the government) doubted that Douglas had the legal right to take that step. *Vacating* the Douglas stay was a very different question; the Supreme Court had never done it. That question bears on the legal authority of each individual justice. This section examines the full Court's power to vacate such a stay and joins with the dissenters (Black, Frankfurter, and Douglas himself) in determining that the full Court lacked the power to do so.

The power of the Court to vacate the Douglas stay was something else again. The Court had never done such a thing before. In symbolic terms, the undoing of a single justice's determination—that a case required further study—was tantamount to a calculated insult aimed at the offending justice. And, of course, that is precisely what it was: an insult to the maverick who had offended the justices' private, irregular, "perfectly understood" agreement, that the Rosenbergs were to go unimpeded (by any of the justices, at least) to the electric chair.

Since the Supreme Court had never in history vacated one of its members' stay, it is interesting to examine the Court's justification in the Rosenberg case for doing what it did.

The government cited two statutes as granting it the power to do what it was doing. The first was Section 1651 of Title 28, of the United States Code, known to most lawyers as the All-Writs Section.[1] But the use of that statute has two deep flaws. First, it is used to maintain the jurisdiction of a court when actual events seem to be moving ahead of litigation. For example, the court might be deciding on the environmental impact of a dam already under construction. Section 1651 might be called in to stop construction, to prevent the Supreme Court from facing a *fait accompli*. If the *defense* in the Rosenberg case had invoked this statute, it might have made sense: it was appallingly true that if the Rosenbergs were executed, events would, indeed, have moved some considerable distance ahead of the legal argument. But there was no sense whatever in the government's attempt to haul in Section 1651.

Moreover, Section 1651 is hoary with the incrustation of ancient writs. When it *is* used, its use is limited to the issuance of ancient, extraordinary writs, e.g., writs of mandamus, or prohibition, all of which have very precise functions defined over the centuries. It has never been used by any court, anywhere, to vacate a stay, simply because such an action does not fall within the function of these ancient writs.

The other statute cited by the Court, Section 2106 of Title 28, is even less relevant.[2] That statute deals with the Court's power to modify, reverse, or vacate an order of a *lower court* "lawfully before" it. Obviously, the Douglas stay was not an order of a "lower" court; moreover, action by the Court—even if a lower court's order were involved—is premised on the lower court's being "lawfully before" the Supreme Court. And that premise could not be met here. Douglas was a colleague on the highest court, there were no "lower courts" present—even though it is conceivable that Justice Jackson viewed Justice Douglas as an inferior species of judge.

Indeed, in contrast to the void offered by the government on this point, Justice Black (346 U.S. 298) pointed directly to *Lambert* v. *Barrett* (157 U.S. 697), decided, as Justice Black wrote,

in 1895 and never overruled, [in which] this Court held that it has no jurisdiction over an appeal from a habeas corpus order of a circuit judge entered in chambers. The stay order in this case derived from petitions for habeas corpus and was entered by Mr. Justice Douglas in chambers.[3]

The Supreme Court had never behaved in this fashion before; it relied on statutes that had nothing to do with the case and failed to cite a single statute that could support its ruling. The powers of federal courts under our system of law are carefully etched out by statute. Our courts are not free-roaming purveyors of the private conscience of each judge; they are creatures of statute and must act within them. The reason why the Supreme Court was reduced to stating that it had power to vacate the Douglas stay because of statutes that gave it no such power is because there is no such power. No statute anywhere gave the Supreme Court the power to undo what Justice Douglas had done.

Did the Court have any inherent power as a court to do what it did, wholly apart from any statute? The Supreme Court itself is the greatest skeptic of its own "implied" powers. If the Supreme Court had any such implied powers, they could be exercised only as emergency measures to prevent obstruction of justice or wholly arbitrary acts by a single justice. An example would be the arbitrary release of a prisoner from a federal jail for no reason whatever. It defies elementary logic (legal or nonlegal) to characterize Douglas's requirement—that careful judicial attention be given a new argument—as an obstruction of justice. And all parties agreed that Douglas had the power to do what he did; it was not an arbitrary abuse of *his* power (e.g., the peremptory freeing of a prisoner) that the majority objected to, but rather that Douglas was wrong on the law of this new and abstruse point. Assuming that there exists an uncharted domain of the Supreme Court's implied power, the majority could find no refuge there under the facts of the Rosenberg case. And, of course, the rationale that the Court stated in its opinion for acting in its totally unprecedented way had nothing to do with the case and was totally erroneous.

Would it have been constitutional to apply the 1946 act to the conduct of the Rosenbergs?

Yes, it would have.

In all, a very great part of the testimony in the Rosenberg trial concerned events after August 1, 1946. Most of the Elitcher testimony dealt with this later period. All of the Sobell flight testimony dealt with this later period. Whether this was the most important testimony against the Rosenbergs (and Sobell) is irrelevant. The indictment charged a conspiracy "up to and including June 16, 1950." The proof went to that conspiracy, in very substantial part dealing with its later stages. Considering all the nonsense that the Supreme Court was forced to listen to in the third week of June 1953, those basic facts should never be forgotten.

Both the government in argument and the Supreme Court in ruling made a great deal of the fact that the "overt acts" listed in the indictment all occurred before August 1, 1946. And, indeed, they did. But no one bothered to read the indictment to the Supreme Court in its exact words. One need not be a Brandeis or Cardozo to understand that the criminal conduct alleged and proved in a conspiracy case is the agreement to perform criminal acts. The law has imposed certain requirements of proof in a conspiracy trial; one of these is the requirement that the prosecution prove that the conspirators did more than just agree—that they did something (performed "overt acts") in aid of their agreement. But the "overt acts" are not the crime. The crime of conspiracy is the agreement itself. It is a continuing crime, continuing until the parties break the agreement. There was no evidence that the Rosenberg conspiracy was ever broken. It went on until trial; and there was evidence in open court to that effect. Mistaking the rule of proof (that "overt acts" must be proved in a conspiracy) with the definition of the crime of conspiracy itself was error that ran through everything that the government and the Court did and said in that hectic third week of June of 1953.

The majority opinion that vacated the Douglas stay and rushed the Rosenbergs to the electric chair stated its position with total clarity:

> The sole ground stated was that the sentences may be governed by the Atomic Energy Act of 1946 instead of the earlier Espionage Act. The crime here involved was commenced June 6, 1944. This was more than 2 years before the Atomic Energy Act was passed. All overt acts relating to atomic energy on which the Government relies took place as early as January, 1945.[4]

That statement contains the heart of the Supreme Court position.

It is transparently wrong. *When* the overt acts occurred in the Rosenberg conspiracy was entirely irrelevant to the point before the Supreme Court. The beginning and ending of the conspiracy charged in the indictment was the simple, controlling point. As has been pointed out above (but never made sufficiently clear to the justices responsible for this simplistic statement quoted above), the indictment charged the Rosenbergs with a conspiracy beginning in June of 1944 and ending on June 16, 1950.[5]

The speed with which the Supreme Court allowed itself to be swayed is pointedly reflected by the statement quoted above. Any trial court judge sitting in a remote county with rudimentary experience in criminal law would know better. Yet that statement constitutes a major part of the reasoning used by the Supreme Court to rush the Rosenbergs to execution.

One need not go far to find out why it was so important for the Supreme Court to make that kind of erroneous statement. Justice Clark stated (in another opinion the majority concurred in):

In any event, the Government could not have invoked the Atomic Energy Act against these Defendants. The crux of the charge alleged overt acts committed in 1944 and 1945, years before that Act went into effect. While some overt acts did in fact take place as late as 1950, they related principally to Defendants' efforts to avoid detection and prosecution of earlier deeds. Grave doubts as to unconstitutional *ex post facto* criminality would have attended any prosecution under that Statute for transmitting atomic secrets before 1946.[6]

And then Justice Jackson went on to pronounce his "sole ground" dogma quoted above. This second bit of judicial wisdom requires no greater wisdom to shatter. Congress never intended to make transactions that occurred in 1944 or 1945 illegal when it passed the Atomic Energy Act of 1946. What it did was to make certain conduct that occurred after August 1, 1946, criminal and punishable under the act's provisions. And among that conduct was a conspiracy to violate any of the provisions of the act. There can be no doubt that the indictment against the Rosenberg charges was aimed at precisely that: that the Rosenbergs conspired; and *continued* to conspire to violate those provisions long after August 1, 1946.

Of course, the indictment never mentioned the 1946 act. But the legal test is whether the conduct charged against the Rosenbergs fell within the prohibitions of the 1946 act.

The 1946 act is carefully aimed at punishing precisely what the Rosenbergs did, and went on doing, long after the 1946 act went into effect—they conspired to steal atomic secrets for delivery to the USSR. There is no doubt of any kind that the prosecution could have *constitutionally* tried the Rosenbergs under the 1946 act for the very same conduct that it used as a basis for an indictment under the 1917 Espionage Act. We have already seen why.

Did it make any difference that the Rosenbergs' conduct commenced before the effective date of the 1946 act and ended after that date? Certainly, if the spies were charged with spying before August 1, 1946, it would make a great deal of difference. But if the essence of the crime of conspiracy is the agreement to break the law, it makes no difference when the agreement began so long as the agreement continued *past* August 1, 1946. Conspiracy is a continuing offense. Each day of it constitutes an additional indictable act of criminality. Parties to a conspiracy break the law each day they remain in the scheme, until they depart from it—if they ever do.

Thus, it mattered not one whit, constitutionally or otherwise, if the Rosenberg conspiracy began in 1944, or in 1935, or, indeed, in 1917. The key fact is whether the Rosenberg indictment alleged that it continued past August 1, 1946.[7] And the indictment said that it did—until June 16, 1950.

The fact that this indictment began before passage of the 1946 act and went on after the act went into effect was another bit of confusion that the government sowed on a Supreme Court eager to become confused. That fact bore no greater relevance than did the dates of the overt acts, relied on so fulsomely by the Court. The crime was the Rosenberg conspiracy, which endured past August 1, 1946. From a constitutional viewpoint, the argument ended there.

Did Congress intend the 1946 act to apply to conduct such as the Rosenbergs'?

If it can be assumed that the Rosenbergs could be constitutionally prosecuted under the 1946 act for the same conduct that they were actually charged with—under the 1917 act—the inquiry does not end there. What Congress *could* do constitutionally is not always what Congress does. Thus, the next, and far knottier question is whether Congress intended that the 1946 act apply to conduct such as the Rosenbergs', and if it did, what about the 1917 act? What did Congress intend the relationship between the two acts to be with regard to atomic spying (or conspiring to steal and deliver atomic secrets) that occurred after August 1, 1946?

The first question is answered simply. When Congress set August 1, 1946, as the effective date of the Atomic Energy Act of 1946, it meant that all of its provisions went into effect on that date. This has but one meaning: all criminal conduct punishable by the Atomic Energy Act of 1946 was subject to its provisions if it occurred after August 1, 1946. And since the Rosenberg conspiracy went on from day to day from August 1, 1946, until at least June 16, 1950 (the latest date stated by the indictment, but the testimony at trial made it clear that the conspiracy was continuing unabated right up to and through the trial), there is no doubt that Congress intended that the conduct of the Rosenbergs was subject to the provisions of the act.

This was certainly true as to the substance of that conduct. The provisions of the 1946 act all dealt with theft of atomic secrets (and the conspiracy to steal them). That conduct was the essence of the indictment charged against the Rosenbergs. The fact that the government threw in naval spying for tactical purposes does not change the fact that conduct such as the Rosenbergs' was exactly what Congress intended to punish by the 1946 act.

The relationship between the 1946 act and the Espionage Act of 1917 is a more difficult question. One of the most difficult points in the law is to determine what happens to penalty provisions of an earlier, general act of Congress when a later, more specific statute is passed and does not mention the earlier act. That is the case here.

Examination of both statutes gives the observer the clear impression that what happened in the Congress in 1946 was an intensive attempt to fashion a set of controls over the new scientific genie; an effort, which, by all logic, should have superseded the general terms of the 1917 statute that was aimed at spying on ship movements, location of armament dumps, and the development of military weapons that were important national concerns in 1917 (and required the protection of the Espionage Act), but did not have the cataclysmic impact as did atomic weaponry, which brought a different kind of warfare to the world in a clear break from conventional weapons of the past. From any reading of the 1946 act the visceral reaction that Congress, in 1946, devised a new statute to deal with this vast new force, pushing aside all old laws, emerges clearly and with a compelling urgency. But the courts do not deal in visceral reactions. They deal in such esoteric concepts as "repeal by implication," "posi-

tive repugnancy," and other legal jargon that divides and sub-
divides the question until logic seems to be filtered out of the
process.

Nonetheless, this judicial word play and debate over concepts
must be examined to determine what the alternative conclusions
faced by the Supreme Court were (in determining the relationship
between the two acts) and whether it chose the correct one.*

There were three alternatives before the Supreme Court in
deciding what Congress intended to be the relationship between
the Atomic Energy Act of 1946 and the Espionage Act of 1917.
The first alternative was that there was no relationship at all, that
is, both acts stood untouched by the other. A federal prosecutor,
under this view, could pick and choose an indictment under either
act if the conduct of the defendants was punishable under both.
Not only could a prosecutor pick and choose whichever act
seemed more inclined to secure a conviction, but the punishment
available to the sentencing judge after conviction was that of the
act chosen, and was totally unmodified by the existence of
dissimilar punishments (for the same conduct) under the other
act. This is the alternative pressed by the government on the
Supreme Court in the Rosenberg case, and the alternative which
the Supreme Court accepted.

Moreover, if the execution of the Rosenbergs was lawful, it
was the *only* alternative that the Supreme Court could choose in
deciding how these two statutes interacted. Either of the other
alternatives made the death penalty pronounced by Judge Kaufman unlawful.

The second alternative follows the first in the view that the
substantive provisions of the earlier act are totally unmodified by
the enactment of the second statute. Again, the prosecution is free

---

* And Section 10(b)(6) of the 1946 act clearly states: "This section shall not exclude
the applicable provisions of any other laws except that no government agency shall take
any action under such laws inconsistent with the provisions of this section." To many,
this provision explicitly invited .continued use of the Espionage Act of 1917 after 1946.

to pick and choose the statute that it desires to proceed under, so long as the conduct of the defendant is punishable under both. The sole difference between the first and second alternatives is that the "rule of clemency" intervenes under the second alternative.

What is the "rule of clemency"? It is a remote and fleeting doctrine in the law, very often ignored, but very much on the books. What it says is quite simple: If two statutes punish the same conduct, the Court will impose on the defendant the lesser penalty (as between the statutes) upon conviction. Why does the law do this? There are a number of explanations. One deals with the rule of clemency as being a rule of repeal: that a legislature must be presumed to understand that it is punishing the same conduct under two statutes, and that the more severe punishment must be impliedly repealed by the lesser penalty (if the lesser penalty is later enacted into law), or if the lesser penalty is first enacted, that the legislature must have intended to apply it in cases triable under both statutes; legislative silence when the more severe penalty is enacted will be so construed.

This rule applies to our inquiry. The 1917 act carried the more severe penalty (the death penalty without jury recommendation) and the 1946 act the lesser penalty (the requirement of a jury recommendation before the death penalty could be imposed). If the rule of clemency is a rule of repeal, it meant in the Rosenberg case that Congress impliedly repealed the punishment provisions of the 1917 act in all cases that could be tried under both it and the 1946 act.

There is another view of the rule of clemency that is not so convoluted. That view is that the rule is not a repeal rule at all, but rather a rule of due process in the administration of the criminal law. Put simply, this view states that fairness in dealing with criminal defendants requires society to punish them under the lesser of the two penalties if society is to be given the option of proceeding under the two statutes for the same criminal conduct. There is sound sense in this. Giving the prosecution two paths toward conviction is a tremendous advantage in tough criminal trials. In return, the defendant is assured that he will be given the lesser punishment in return for this prosecutorial advantage.

Viewed as either a rule of repeal or as a matter of due process, the intervention of the rule of clemency constituted the second alternative available to the Supreme Court in determining the relationship between the two acts. This view meant that the prosecution was free to proceed against the Rosenbergs under the 1917 act—for conduct equally punishable under its terms and under the provisions of the 1946 act—but Judge Kaufman was restricted to imposing the penalties of the 1946 act in any conviction if its penalties were less severe. Therefore, this also meant that he could not impose the death penalty on his own decision, but had to base it on the recommendation of the jury.

Since there was no jury recommendation in the Rosenberg case, the second view of the interaction between the two statutes would have been fatal to the government in its argument before the Supreme Court.

The third alternative was just as simple as the first. This alternative view would have followed the terms of the 1946 act literally and held that any atomic spying that occurred after August 1, 1946, was punishable solely under the 1946 act. This view follows from the very special provisions of the act that strongly indicate a congressional desire to deal with criminality in the safeguarding of atomic secrets under a special plan carefully designed by Congress to deal with the new and monumentally different force. Acceptance of this view would also have meant defeat to the government before the Supreme Court in the third week of June 1953.

Which of these alternatives did Congress intend?
It is not easy to say today. There exists, however, unmistakable evidence on this point. The Supreme Court of the United States makes these judgments a dozen times during each term. The judgment it made in June 1953 concerning the relationship between the two acts appears to be wrong. Why was this so?

What the Department of Justice sought to convey as Congress's intent was to give both the prosecution and the sentencing judge complete freedom to choose the statute and the penalty in the Rosenberg case. That choice inevitably meant that any federal prosecutor could ignore the penal provisions of the Atomic Energy Act of 1946 in any theft of atomic secrets that occurred after July 31, 1946. There is no other view possible: if the prosecutors' option to try the Rosenbergs under the 1917 act was lawfully available to the prosecution, it must follow that the prosecution could simply ignore the 1946 act in dealing with the Rosenbergs' conduct; and it also followed that Congress had intended this to be the case. Whatever else this view meant at the time, it rendered wholly without meaning all of the Congress's work in creating the carefully balanced, hotly battled, and craftily compromised Atomic Energy Act of 1946.

One other fact is just as clear: The scientists involved in the fight that ended in civilian control of atomic energy never dreamed that their handiwork would be totally ignored at the whim of any federal prosecutor.

There are at least four reasons why Congress never intended alternative one, the alternative chosen by the Supreme Court.

First, the breadth of the prohibitions under the 1946 act was far wider than that under the 1917 act. The 1946 act prohibited the unauthorized transmission of any "restricted data." Restricted data were, under the sweeping definition found in the 1946 act, "all data concerning the manufacture or utilization of atomic weapons, the production of fissionable material, or the use of fissionable material in the production of power."[8]

Thus, the penalties of the 1946 act extended to unauthorized release of atomic information far removed from weaponry. The 1946 act's penalties, to be sure, were severe only when an "intent to injure the United States" was present, but the prosecutors' option to ignore this act (if the option existed at all) existed with regard to *all* violations of the 1946 act and not solely to minor ones. Thus, federal prosecutors were free to ignore unauthorized transmittal of restricted atomic information of major importance if the Supreme Court was right as to what Congress intended. To be sure, most of such information would possibly also be "information relating to the national defense" and thus punishable under the 1917 act. The prohibitions under the Espionage Act are, however, far narrower. The 1917 act prohibits unauthorized transmittal only of "information relating to the national defense."[9] The legislative history of *that* act makes it clear that only trafficking in "official secrets" that bore directly on national defense were punishable under it. And, indeed, if the prosecution sought the death penalty under the 1917 act, such violations had to occur during wartime. Thus, a violation of the 1917 act for which death was sought had to involve a wartime theft or betrayal of an "official secret" concerning national defense.

By contrast, the 1946 act provided that "mutilating"[10] a "sketch" (so long as the multilated effort was partially financed by federal funds), which occurred either in peacetime or in war, could invoke the death penalty. That the violation under the 1946 act had to be done with "intent to injure the United States" in no way bridges this awesome gap between the two acts because "injury to the United States" is a broad and indefinite phrase hardly calculated to protect atomic thieves. Clearly, the prohibitions under the 1946 act were draconian. The leading commentator on the act, James Newman, stated flatly that they revealed Congress's obsession with the safeguarding of atomic secrets of any kind. Yet Congress's concern for atomic secrecy could be totally ignored by any federal prosecutor confronted with a theft of atomic secrets if the Supreme Court's view taken in the Rosenberg case was correct.

A hypothetical violation occurring after August 1, 1946, is a useful illustration of the distortion of Congress's intent inherent in the Rosenberg decision. If the Rosenberg facts are altered so that the leakage of secrets was made wholly after World War II ended and the Cold War began, and had to do with improving the generation of power from nuclear plants rather than with the bomb, the gravity of the violation might, to most laymen, become very much more moderate. But such a leakage of atomic secrets is specifically punishable by the provisions of the 1946 act. And if the intent of leaking the secrets was made by leftists whose antigovernment pronouncements were very little different from the sentiments of the Rosenbergs, the death penalty under the

1946 act very much covered this conduct, so long as a jury approved. The law carefully made this kind of activity punishable, under the above hypothesis, by death. What the Supreme Court said in the Rosenberg case was that a federal prosecutor could ignore all of this, the entire congressional mandate, and choose *not* to prosecute these hypothetical defendants if—for any of the hundreds of tactical or political reasons that weigh on prosecutors when they have such discretion—the prosecutor decided not to.

Not for a moment did Congress intend such a result.

Perhaps Congress intended a variant of this undesired result: If the unauthorized disclosure could not be prosecuted under the Espionage Act of 1917, Congress might have intended it to be mandatory upon federal prosecutors to prosecute the disclosure under the 1946 act. This formulation has a certain innate sense in it, but it is found nowhere in the legislative history of the 1946 act. The Supreme Court's view of that act is inconsistent with it.

But, most plainly, the Rosenberg Court could not have reached its conclusion unless it was implicitly holding that prosecutors could ignore the 1946 act under any circumstances and for whatever reason they wished, including the circumstance that atomic spies remain unprosecuted under any statute. Clearly, Congress never intended that.

Not one word concerning this point was argued to the Supreme Court in its deliberations in the final week of the Rosenberg case.

There is a second objection to the view that prosecutors could freely choose to ignore the 1946 act. Among the various provisions that Congress brought forth out of the compromise between the scientists and the military was the notion that major prosecutions for leakage of atomic information were restricted to leakage that involved an "intent to injure the United States."[11] This concept may have been loosely worded and formulated, but the language is in the 1946 act and applies to every case in which the prosecution for atomic theft seeks the death penalty. Plainly, Congress felt that the punishment of death for atomic spying had to be restricted to fewer and narrower situations than those in which theft of "official secrets" (under the 1917 act) occurred.* It is absolutely clear from what little legislative history is available on these matters that Congress, in 1946, did not consider "advantage to a foreign power" to be reciprocal of injury to the United States. They were separate concepts, joined by Congress in the 1917 act and rejected by Congress in the 1946 statute.[12] Thus, in addition to the highly questionable power of federal prosecutors to ignore the 1946 act entirely, there is the separate problem of ignoring the tie imposed by Congress (in the 1946 act) between atomic theft and injury to the United States. Congress made it quite clear that when atomic thievery was involved, the prosecution had to establish an intent to injure the United States and had to secure a jury recommendation if it sought the death penalty. Ignoring both requirements—as the Rosenberg Court did—was as clear a violation of congressional intent as the implicit license (granted by the Rosenberg Court) to prosecutors to ignore the entirety of the 1946 act.

The Court's casual view of congressional intent makes even less sense in light of the struggle out of which the 1946 act was born. The fight between the scientists and the military over first the May-Johnson Bill, and then the McMahon Bill, went on over these precise provisions. It is singular that what were alternative grounds for imposition of the death penalty under the 1917 act (that is, if either injury to the United States or advantage to a foreign power was intended) became very separate provisions under the 1946 act. If injury to the United States was intended, maximum penalties (including death upon recommendation of the jury) could be meted out. But if advantage to a foreign power (rather than injury to the United States) was found to be the violator's intent, the maximum penalty under the 1946 act was a prison sentence of up to twenty years or a fine of $20,000, or

---

* If a jury found either advantage to a foreign power *or* injury to the United States, it could convict under the 1917 act and the judge was free (if the offense occurred in wartime) to impose the death penalty.

both.[13] It is folly to believe that Congress intended this contrast in penalties to be ignored.

Those provisions are very much part of the compromise leading to the passage of the 1946 act. The Senate Special Committee spent a good deal of time and energy on the gradation of punishments it would include in the act. It specifically rejected an attempt to insert the word "military" as a modifier of "advantage to a foreign power."[14] This action was evidence of the care with which the congressional committee approached the structuring of penalties under the 1946 act. The hand of the scientists was much in evidence in turning Congress away from the broad discretionary penalties under the 1917 act, and in their place enacting the careful alignment of punishments that are found in Section 10 (the penalty section) of the 1946 act. Reading the Rosenberg opinion, one would never guess that this had taken place.

Not one word concerning this point was argued to the Supreme Court in its deliberations in the final week of the Rosenberg case.

A third reason why the Supreme Court's view of the matter was wholly in error arises from a novel provision in the 1946 act, inserted at the insistence of the scientists. Section 10(b)(5)(A) of the act directed that no prosecution under it could be begun except upon the direction of the attorney general, and then only after the "attorney general has advised the Commission [the Atomic Energy Commission] with respect to the prosecution."[15] The Senate report on this provision explains it as

an assurance to scientists working in atomic energy fields that prosecutions would not be initiated without review by persons having the technical and scientific background necessary to determine the significance of the acts complained of.[16]

This, too, was a limitation placed on the prosecutors by the scientific community in the compromise that led to passage of the 1946 act. Again, it defies logic for Congress to have imposed this procedural precondition on prosecutions for atomic spying and then to allow individual prosecutors to ignore it. Dialogue between the Atomic Energy Commission and the Department of Justice as to the severity of the violation was obviously contemplated by this provision. It was the essence of what the scientists insisted on. The power of the government to ignore this procedure if it chose to was in defiance of the essence of the scientific-military compromise leading to passage of the 1946 act.

Not one word concerning this point was argued to the Supreme Court in its deliberations in the final week of the Rosenberg case.

Finally, the theory of the Supreme Court in the Rosenberg decision was that government prosecutors were given two alternatives for unfettered use in cases of leakage of atomic information. No one in Congress seriously believed this in the summer of 1946. No one seriously believed this in June of 1953 except for six members of the Supreme Court of the United States. They did so without any careful briefing on any of the points discussed in the last pages. Quite literally, the Supreme Court acted out of an abundance of ignorance on matters of which they could have and should have been well informed. But to be well informed meant that they had to be fully briefed and that careful, planned oral argument had to take place on the points that had been briefed. That took time, and time meant delay of the execution of the Rosenbergs. Thus, the Supreme Court permitted itself to act on nothing more than its own ignorance.

The second alternative of the three available to the Supreme Court in determining the relationship between the 1917 Espionage Act and the Atomic Energy Act of 1946 was the "rule of clemency." To define that rule requires examination of how it has been applied.

In 1917, shortly after Congress passed the Volstead Act, the noble experiment abolishing the lawful production and consumption of alcoholic beverages, one Yuginovich was indicted for running an illicit still in Oregon.[17] Yuginovich was, however, not indicted under the Volstead Act, but rather under an ancient statute passed by Congress long before, that made it a criminal act to manufacture distilled spirits without paying a proper federal tax on the spirits and simultaneously depositing the liquor in a bonded warehouse. The reason that the Oregon authorities used the old law was that it carried a penalty requiring the distiller to forfeit his distillery, the distilling apparatus, and all of the whiskey plus a fine and imprisonment of up to three years.

Under the Volstead Act, the penalty for all this was much lighter: a first offender could be fined only $1,000, be imprisoned for no more than six months and no forfeiture was involved. The later act also contained a provision not unlike Section 10(b)(6) of the Atomic Energy Act of 1946. It said that passage of the Volstead Act did not "relieve any person from liability under laws in existence when it was passed," ostensibly keeping in effect the strictest provisions of the older statute. That clause was very much like Section 10(b)(6) of the 1946 Atomic Energy Act, which preserved relevant laws in existence when the 1946 act was passed. But in the Oregon liquor case, the Supreme Court disregarded the government's contention that the old penalties were kept alive by the provision that seemed to say so, and the Court ruled: "In construing penal statutes, it is the rule that later enactments repeal former ones practically covering the same acts but fixing a lesser penalty."[18]

The Supreme Court said so notwithstanding the language of the provisions of the Volstead Act that seemed to keep the harsher penalty alive. The federal court in Oregon then quashed the indictment against Yuginovich under the old act. In June of 1921, the Supreme Court affirmed. Yuginovich was released, either to go on making his moonshine unabated or to be tried under the milder penalties of the Volstead Act.

This is settled law in federal courts. Its earliest pronouncement came in 1851, when a later, lesser penalty for theft of slaves was held to supersede an earlier one.[19] The states follow the principle: in 1937, a California court reduced a $50 fine for the sale of moldy eggs to $35 proposed under an earlier statute when this conduct was punishable both under the earlier statute and the California Pure Food and Drug Act (which imposed the $50 fine).[20]

It is just as clear that the courts regard imposition of the death penalty without the requirement of a jury recommendation as a more severe penalty than requiring such a recommendation. At least two states have made that plausible rule explicit and there is no reason to doubt it.[20a] Thus, there is a substantial body of law that the "rule of clemency" was alive and well when Judge Douglas articulated it in his stay on Tuesday, June 16, 1953, in the Rosenberg case.

The majority of the Supreme Court thought it had an answer to the rule of clemency. It was hasty and not very precise, but it was an answer. Justice Clark wrote:

Where Congress by more than one statute proscribes a private course of conduct, the Government may choose to invoke either applicable law: "At least where different proof is required for each offense, a single act or transaction may violate more than one criminal statute."[21]

This principle has substantial use in drug cases. The courts have little trouble with multiple penalties for essentially the same criminal act because they recognize what it is all about: to deter drug abuse.

Somehow, somewhere, Justice Clark found a substantial difference between what had to be proved under the 1917 Espionage Act and what had to be proved under the 1946 Atomic Energy Act. Accordingly, the Supreme Court said that the prosecution could proceed under either statute.

What the Court overlooked is that the 1946 act also contained a provision in it that it is a violation of law to steal atomic secrets with the intent to benefit a foreign power.[22] *That* offense was identical to the offense charged (and proved) against the Rosenbergs under the 1917 act. There was no requirement of "different proof," as Justice Clark prescribed. The only difference was that the penalty under the 1946 act could not exceed twenty years' imprisonment. The ingredient that gave (and gives) prosecutors multiple convictions out of a single act—an additional fact to be proved under one statute—did not exist. And the rule was very clear: if, indeed, two statutes have identical proof, then one or two statutory offenses may have occurred. The technical business of proceeding under one statute (or both) may go on. But when it comes to sentencing, the rule of clemency applies. The lesser penalty as between the two statutes must be imposed.

One need only look at the times to understand this. No one in Congress in 1946 had the faintest idea that the new atomic energy legislation was simply another prosecutorial weapon in the federal arsenal against spying. No one in Congress ever said that, or anything like that. Justice Clark's rule had its greatest use in antidrug enforcement. Multiple penalties for single acts were considered to be a major deterrent against drug sales. And it has been that deterrent. Congress intended two very different results in these situations. But the *Rosenberg* Court was not at all interested nor had it the time to probe the difference.

There is one interesting quirk, however. If the rule of clemency did apply because the provisions of both laws (regarding the intent to benefit a foreign power) were identical, as were all of the other provisions of both laws, the rule of clemency would not have required a jury recommendation before sentencing. The lesser provision of the 1946 act dealing with that form of violation (intention to benefit a foreign power, not injury to the United States) required no jury recommendation, but was simply limited to a sentence of twenty years. *That* sentence should have been meted out by Judge Kaufman without reconvening the *Rosenberg* jury, a complication that bothered many of the justices considerably. But this required the Supreme Court to follow the rule of clemency, to vacate the death sentence and return the case to Judge Kaufman with instructions to impose no greater sentence than twenty years on the Rosenbergs.

In all likelihood, that course was the closest to the correct one for the Supreme Court to follow. But the Supreme Court clearly would have no part of it. As noted, the rule of clemency was never mentioned by a single justice except Douglas.

The rule of clemency applied for three reasons: first, because there were indeed identical penal provisions in the 1917 and 1946 acts, both requiring only proof of intent to benefit a foreign power. Second, there was no additional element of proof required under either the 1917 or 1946 act that gave prosecutors the free choice of either statute if the facts fitted both. Finally, there was another example of legislative intent. The 1946 act was never intended to be simply another prosecutorial weapon in the federal war against espionage, as were the multiple narcotics provisions. The 1946 act was specially tailored to cover a particular new offense, which was unknown to man before the atom was unlocked at Los Alamos in 1945.

None of these arguments were made to the Supreme Court during the two days that the rule of clemency was before it. Justice Douglas was the only justice to mention it. The majority buried the point with the language permitting federal prosecutors to use—or not use—the Atomic Energy Act of 1946 if another statute was violated in the case being prosecuted. No one pointed out to the Court that this was error, plain error. And error it was.

The majority plainly was troubled by the rule of clemency, even though the unhappiness of the six justices was readily and superficially resolved. The majority had Justice Clark's point, mentioned above, as one refuge. But it used a second refuge. The second was much used, resorted to when concurrent coverage of two statutes created problems for judges, as it often did. The refuge was called "repeal by implication," and judges use it often because it saves them a good deal of time and effort.

Repeal by implication means simply that a legislature, such as Congress, impliedly repeals an earlier law (without saying so) when it enacts a later one that appears to cover the same area. With uniformity, judges view such repeals with horror, and with some reason. Care should be taken to determine what the later act really means, and whether it actually is intended to supplant the earlier one. But the judicial habit has been simpler: unless the later law specifically repeals the earlier one, such repeals by implication are universally rejected. A result of this broad-brush treatment of the interaction of two statutes—one earlier and the other later— dealing with the same subject is to save judges an immense amount of labor in attempting to ferret out the nub of what the legislature intended the second time around.

Often, the second act is indeed intended to supplant the earlier one, in whole or in part; but the legislators simply neglect to say this in so many words.

Repeal by implication got considerable currency from the majority of the Supreme Court in the last days of the Rosenberg case. The majority held:

It is a cardinal principle of construction that repeals by implication are not favored. When there are two acts upon the same subject, the rule is to give effect to both if possible. . . .[23]

The majority of the Supreme Court was quoting from one of its own 1939 decisions, entitled *United States* v. *Borden* (308 U.S. 188). *Borden* tells a story interesting in itself, illuminating the haste and imprecision in everything the majority did in its last two days on the Rosenberg decision.

Borden was an antitrust case. A group of midwestern milk distributors arranged among themselves to fix the prices of raw milk to be paid to the farmers in parts of Illinois, Indiana, Michigan, and Wisconsin. They did so in the belief that a recent statute, the Agricultural Marketing Agreement Act of 1937, gave them the legal right to do this; such price-fixing was clearly illegal under the antitrust provisions of the Sherman Act of 1891. The Justice Department disagreed with the milk producers. It filed criminal indictments under the Sherman Act against the distributors, their trade association, and just about everyone connected with the price-fixing scheme. Predictably, the distributors defended what they had done by pointing to the 1937 act, and the federal trial court in Chicago ruled for them. The government took it straight to the Supreme Court, as can be done in antitrust cases. The Supreme Court reversed, ruling for the Justice Department. But it is vital to see why it so ruled. The one thing that the milk distributors did not do was get prior approval from anyone for their price-fixing scheme. The Supreme Court ruled that they could find no basis for exempting this price-fixing arrangement from the Sherman Act unless the terms of the 1937 Marketing Act were strictly observed; one such requirement was the prior approval of the Secretary of Agriculture for every price-fixing arrangement; and the milk producers' failure to seek approval from the Secretary of Agriculture removed any possible claim of exemption.

It is certainly true that the Court went on to say that the mere passage of the 1937 act did not repeal the Sherman Act insofar as milk was concerned. But the Court went to great pains to point out that the statutory plan of the 1937 act required hearings before the Secretary of Agriculture, and intensive participation and approval by him in the price-fixing arrangement for milk before any exemption would be countenanced. And this participation by the Secretary of Agriculture simply did not occur in *Borden*.

If that is what the *Borden* decision really means—and its language makes it quite clear that it is—then all of what the *Rosenberg* Court said about the 1937 Agricultural Marketing Agreement Act repealing the Sherman Act for price-fixing in milk production was wholly irrelevant to the result. The language is what the law calls "dictum," gratuitous language from a court that is not part of its holding.

The language in *Borden* on which the Supreme Court leaned so heavily in 1953 is significant.[24] From this language, the 1953 Court divined that the Atomic Energy Act did not repeal the provisions of the Espionage Act of 1917 under which the Rosenbergs were convicted. As was noted, however, this quoted language was wholly gratuitous; *Borden* as a case simply does not stand for any such rule. It was decided on another ground. But the *Rosenberg* Court's reliance on *Borden* is singular for other reasons. The *Borden* Court went on to say:

> "[There must be] positive repugnancy between the provisions of the new law, and those of the old" if the new is to take the place of the old, "[and] even then the old law is repealed by implication only pro tanto to the extent of the repugnancy."[25]

In at least two respects there was such "positive repugnancy" between the penal provisions of the 1917 act and the 1946 act. The 1917 act required either proof of intent to injure the United States *or* intent to secure an advantage for a foreign power in order for the death penalty to be imposed. In contrast, the 1946 act limited the death penalty to cases where proof of an intent to injure the United States was established. That is a repugnancy that is written

into the language of the later act, language that clearly conflicts
with the early statute. The requirement of a jury recommendation
before the imposition of the death penalty was a manifestation of a
vastly different congressional policy in 1946 than that declared by
Congress twenty-nine years earlier. Finally, the prohibitions of
the 1946 act reflect a congressional anxiety over atomic spying
that goes far beyond anything found in the 1917 act.

There is "positive repugnancy" in the narrowness of the
1917 act's prohibition of trafficking in "official secrets," while
protection of the immensely broader area of "restricted data" is
the heart of the 1946 act. This is not simply overlap. It is "positive
repugnancy" because Congress made it clear that it did not wish
atomic secrets to be protected only if they were also "official
secrets," limited by legal definition to national defense. In details
carefully put in the 1946 act, Congress manifested an intention
that it was punishing disclosures that are far broader, concerning a
new national resource not known or even dreamed of in 1917.
Carefully examined, that is "positive repugnancy" if those words
are to be given any thoughtful meaning.

Finally, nothing in *Borden* addresses the rule of clemency. The
Rosenberg Court could have been absolutely correct in holding
that *Borden* meant that the 1946 act did not substantively repeal the
penal provisions of the 1917 act. The rule of clemency would still
apply. The rule of clemency is not generally viewed as a "repeal"
rule, but rather a rule of fairness. If it applied, both the 1917 and
1946 acts would cover the conduct of the Rosenbergs, and it is
beyond argument that federal law would then require a jury
recommendation (the lesser penalty) before a death sentence could
be imposed, rather than permitting the trial judge to impose
execution on his own discretion. Indeed, it is equally clear that the
rule of clemency would also impose the limit of twenty years on
any sentence given the Rosenbergs.

Not one word concerning the meaning of *Borden* and *Borden*'s
failure to undercut or even address the rule of clemency was
argued to the Supreme Court in its deliberations in the final week
of the Rosenberg case. And it is fair to say that the majority of the
Supreme Court wholly ignored the rule of clemency in its last

decision in the Rosenberg case on the day of the Rosenbergs' execution.

Right or wrong, that rule was terribly relevant. The Court's ignoring that rule was inexcusable.

Did Congress intend the penal provisions of the 1946 act to cover all cases of atomic spying, to the exclusion of the 1917 act?

A close look at the deliberations before Congress prior to passage of the 1946 act makes the third alternative (as to the relationship between the two acts) the most valid one by far: that Congress intended that insofar as illegal disclosure of atomic information was concerned (e.g., conduct such as that of the Rosenbergs), *only* the 1946 act should apply. Much of what was said above in outlining the flaws of the first alternative—that Congress intended both acts to apply—can be said with equal force here. The logic that makes the prosecutors' free choice of one statute or the other a mockery of the spirit and words of the scientific-military compromise that spawned the 1946 penalties points strongly to a congressional decision that *only* the 1946 penalties should apply to future atomic spying.

It is not the function of this book to outline in detail the specifics of drafting, of testimony, and of committee reports that comprise legislative history for lawyers. But there are a few outstanding points that run through all of these documents.

First, the breadth of the coverage of the 1946 act that controlled information dealing with atomic energy in all its forms and uses, military and peaceful, for industrial and power uses in plenary fashion, compared with the narrow scope of the information (covered by the 1917 act) indicates that Congress understood that atomic power was a new force in American life that had multiple facets, all of which had to be controlled. The pattern of control (of which penalties were but one) deals with the infinite uses of atomic energy. The 1946 act was tailored to the subject Congress confronted in 1946. The 1917 act—insofar as information controls were concerned—was in another age and had no bearing on the subject before Congress in 1946.

Congress's preoccupation with atomic secrets comes through in some of the penalties it put into the 1946 act. In 1946, Congress wanted the death penalty to be imposed under carefully prescribed conditions, one of which was a jury recommendation to that effect, in *peacetime,* whereas the most severe peacetime penalty possible under the 1917 act was twenty years. In 1946, Congress wanted the distinction between "official secrets" and atomic information developed in private, unofficial research (a distinction that existed under the 1917 act) abolished. In 1946, Congress wanted offenders who intended to injure the United States to be treated far more severely than those who intended an advantage to a foreign power; those intentions were equated under the 1917 act. In 1946, Congress intended that no prosecution could commence for atomic spying except by direction of the attorney general of the United States, and then only after the Atomic Energy Commission had consulted with the Department of Justice on the gravity of the offense;[26] prosecutions under the 1917 act commenced on the decision of any U.S. attorney in any federal district in the land.

When it put all of these concepts into the law in 1946, Congress was closing the books on the 1917 act in cases of atomic spying: simultaneously, it was creating an ornate and judiciously crafted statute, with its penalties reflecting considerable care, to be applied to this new Frankenstein of criminality. Part of this new statute dealt with the requirement of a jury recommendation for any death penalty; part of the new statute required that this penalty be imposed only on proof of an intent to injure the United States. If this was less draconian than the 1917 statute, it reflected the compromise with the scientists. That compromise, part lenient and part severe, is what Congress intended to apply, and to apply exclusively, to prosecutions for atomic spying that occurred after August 1, 1946. And it applies equally to conspiracies to spy for atomic secrets extending past August 1, 1946.

Unfortunately, substantial portions of the 1946 act were not as carefully drafted as were the penal provisions. For instance, what is the true meaning of Section 10(b)(6) that preserves the provision of other laws? And in many places, the two acts simply conflict, with no guide as to which is to control. It is impossible to declare categorically that in all such situations the 1946 act controlled. That is also simplistic and unacceptable. But withal, there are many things clear about Congress's intent in passing the Atomic Energy Act of 1946 for anyone interested in reading it.

Perhaps the best commentary on these clear points is by James Newman, the same James Newman who was whisked from a Cape Code beach on June 17, 1953, by the Department of Justice to be present at the Rosenberg hearing before the Supreme Court on the following day, the same James Newman who wore a borrowed suit much too large for him at the hearing before the Supreme Court because he had no time to pack in Massachusetts; the James Newman who personally responded to a question asked by a justice during the argument on June 18, in an episode unique in the Court's history because this James Newman was not a lawyer for either side in this case, the same James Newman who held the post of special counsel to the Senate Special Committee on Atomic Energy during the gestation of the Atomic Energy Act of 1946, and who, ten months later, on May 7, 1947, wrote the only article in the legal literature that shed any light on the many legal problems created by that act,[27] including its relationship to the 1917 Espionage Act. In June 1953, the Newman article remained the sole source of illumination to be found anywhere on these matters. It is truly a significant document.

Newman's article first states that decisions under the 1917 act are of little value in interpreting the 1946 act because "it was the clear intent of Congress, as evidenced by the drastic penalties to treat atomic energy as a special and unique category."[28] Having been present throughout all of Congress's deliberations when it enacted the 1946 act, Newman knew well that Congress felt it was dealing with "a special and unique category." And when it came to the secrecy sections of the 1946 act, Newman wrote of Congress's recognition that the provisions of the 1917 act were wholly inadequate:

In the earliest stages of drafting legislation for the development and control of atomic energy, it was realized that the provisions of the Espionage Act were unsuited in several aspects for dealing with the secret data of theoretical and applied nuclear physics.[29]

Newman's article then directly addressed the crucial question that surfaced in the Rosenberg case six years after his article was published. It is significant that in six years no one had published a word that cast any doubts as to the accuracy or authenticity of Newman's views. Newman probed the question of congressional intent with regard to offenses that appeared to be punishable under both laws. He stated:

It is reasonable to suppose that Congress did not intend to give the prosecuting attorney the option of moving under the Espionage Act instead of the Atomic Energy Act where an offense involving information relating to atomic energy is specifically described in the latter and only broadly and generally encompassed by the former.[30]

Newman is just as precise in his discussion of Section 10(b)(6), which supposedly "preserved" the 1917 act and made it applicable to offenses such as the Rosenbergs':

And, in stating in Section 10(b)(6) that the applicable provisions of other laws were not to be excluded, it meant to guard against possible omissions rather than to give a prosecutor the option of proceeding under the other laws against offenses fully covered by the Atomic Energy Act.[31]

No pro-Rosenberg zealot wrote those words. The author was brought by the Department of Justice to the Supreme Court hearing on June 18 for the unique experience of responding to a justice's question when he had no status in the case. And these were the words written by that author in 1947, three years before anyone had ever heard of Julius or Ethel Rosenberg.

The most remarkable thing about the Newman article was its use during those last two days of the Rosenberg case. The majority referred to it as having been cited by the Rosenbergs in their first petition to the Supreme Court in 1952. Its use in 1952 was on a totally different point, which had nothing to do with the deliberation before the Court in 1953. Astonishingly, the majority also cited the article in support of its holding that Section 10(b)(6), the provision that "preserves" other laws, made the 1917 act applicable to the Rosenbergs. Newman's article took quite the opposite view. Moreover, only Justice Frankfurter, who termed

Newman a "specially qualified student of the Act,"[32] dealt in any detail with the contents of the article. The majority preferred to distort the article and ignore its contents. It was as if the pope pronounced a papal bull without reference to gospel.

One of the points that the government relied on most heavily in its briefs seeking the vacating of the Douglas stay was the point that the conspiracy involving the Rosenbergs also involved nonatomic spying (the Sobell-Elitcher-Rosenberg conduct concerning naval information). The government's argument ran that regardless of whether or not the 1946 act applied to the atomic espionage of the Rosenbergs, the broad conspiracy of which the Rosenbergs were charged covered areas not touched by the 1946 act (disclosure of nonatomic information), and that, accordingly, their prosecution and conviction under the 1917 act was proper.

The answer to that argument is that the basic thrust of the Rosenberg prosecution *was* atomic spying. The 1946 act applied to that spying. Evasion of the 1946 act by linking a conspiracy to divulge atomic information with a conspiracy to divulge nonatomic information was a prosecutorial gambit designed to prevent the application of the 1946 act to conduct that it plainly intended to cover. As such, the joinder of a conspiracy to perform nonatomic spying was a transparent effort to defeat the congressional intention to enforce and punish atomic espionage (and the conspiracy to perform it) under the 1946 act. Any other result would allow a prosecutor to search and find evidence, any evidence of nonatomic espionage, and then include it in an indictment so as to avoid the invocation of the 1946 act. Defeat of plain congressional intent by such maneuvering was attempted successfully in the Rosenberg case. But the result was just that: defeat of plain congressional intent.

Finally, the dissent of Judge Jerome Frank is relevant. Judge Frank ruled that whether there were two conspiracies (one involving atomic spying and the other involving naval espionage) or one overall conspiracy was a jury question that Judge Kaufman did not allow the *Rosenberg* jury to decide.[33] But the jury issue that Judge Frank pointed to was a major one if Congress's intent was to be followed. The *Rosenberg* jury should have been allowed to determine whether the joinder of the Sobell-Elitcher conspiracy with the Greenglass-Gold conspiracy was supported by the facts and Judge Kaufman should have himself decided, before giving that issue to the jury, that the joinder was in plain violation of Congress's intent to punish atomic spies under the Atomic Energy Act of 1946. Obviously, Kaufman did neither.

What was the question before the Supreme Court on June 19, 1953?

Everything that has just been said, and everything that the Supreme Court did and said on Friday morning during that June week, went straight to the heart of what *seemed* to be the argument before the Court. But was it?

It was not. What Douglas had done and what the majority of the Supreme Court ardently wished to undo involved a very different point. Douglas had simply said two days before that the intervention of the 1946 act was sufficiently new and complicated to require careful briefing and argument, neither of which had been possible. The majority did not answer this. They went beyond that point and decided that Douglas, whose point was the need for more study, was wrong. More than that, the majority ruled that Douglas was not only wrong but also that his contention was insubstantial and unworthy of consideration.[34]

There is a world of difference between these questions. Douglas, Farmer, and Marshall may well have been wrong on the points they were arguing. No one had ever examined them before. But, by that same token, no one could dispute that the intervention of the 1946 act was new; it was conceded that the Marshall-Farmer point had never been raised before. Nor could anyone argue that its effect on the case would be insubstantial; it controlled the life and death of two human beings. Was the Farmer-Marshall-Douglas point itself frivolous? Therein lies the nub and impropriety of the majority.

What the majority did was to deny all practice within its own Court; it deemed briefs filed two to three hours before argument, less than twenty-four hours after notice (that argument would take place), as full briefing of a new, major, and complicated legal point. The majority refused to expose this new point to the traditional test given any new argument—careful briefing, argument, and decision before two layers of lower federal courts before the nine justices of the Supreme Court would even look at it. The majority instead ordered argument minutes after it had received briefs in a break with everything the Supreme Court had ever done as a court.*

The majority of the Supreme Court went on to hold that what Marshall, Farmer, and Douglas had articulated was so irrational as to be frivolous. To do so is to impose a tremendous burden on those who point the accusing finger of frivolity. It means that there is literally no one wearing judicial robes who would give the point the slightest currency.

The majority never spoke to this precise point. The majority announced its view of the law but expressed not one word about the absence of decisions in lower federal courts, and the absence of adequate briefing or decent argument. Yet the adequacy of briefing and argument was the issue before them, not whether Douglas was wrong or right.

Moreover, the majority opinion places great weight on the fact that this new point of law came from outsiders with dubious status in the case. The author of this wisdom was Justice Jackson, and it does no credit to the majority that they consented to adopt his views so unblinkingly. By the time Jackson had written those words, Bloch had embraced the Farmer-Marshall argument,[35] so that Jackson, the model of elegant rectitude, was simply wrong. Beyond that, even if Bloch had not destroyed Jackson's position, the Rosenberg case was a capital case. As said earlier, it did Jackson and his five brothers no honor to hide under legalisms when two lives were at stake. Yet there exists in the majority opinion a long discussion on "status" (who may argue for the Rosenbergs and who may not)—legally wrong and in human terms antediluvian.

---

* The government filed a brief in support of reconvening the Court on the afternoon of June 17. Thus it filed two briefs—but both within one day of oral argument, and the second within hours of argument.

Was the Farmer-Marshall point substantial?

It certainly was.

The Rosenberg case was the first view that the Supreme Court or any federal court had taken of the knotty interaction between the 1946 Atomic Energy Act and the 1917 Espionage Act.

Normally, when it is the first time around for such legal problems posed by new statutes, the Supreme Court will grant full review, "certiorari," on that ground alone. Commentators on Supreme Court practice uniformly deem such "first-time" views of new statutes a prime ground for full Supreme Court review, even when such review is not made more compelling by the additional complication of relating the new statute to an older one with similar provisions. If the Farmer-Marshall-Douglas point had been made in the trial court before Kaufman, and then reviewed by the Second Circuit, it is almost certain that the Supreme Court would have taken the case for full briefing and argument—especially in a case involving the death penalty. But the majority of the Court found that the procedural irregularity in the manner in which the case came to them was too much to swallow. And the way it came to them was too much to swallow because, among other things, it came to them in violation of their own wholly irregular and private agreement.

Specifically, the questions that should have been decided on their merits before the Rosenbergs could die were precisely the kinds of questions normally accepted by the Supreme Court and ruled on following careful briefing and argument. What did Congress intend when it enacted the penalties found in Section 10 of the 1946 act? None of the materials, such as hearing testimony, committee reports, and floor debates by the Seventy-ninth and Eightieth Congresses, were ever looked at in those two hectic days, June 18 and 19, when the Court vacated the Rosenberg stay.

Did Congress intend to commit nuclear secrecy to the whim of individual prosecutors? If so—and the majority of the Supreme Court said this *was* so—the scientists had suffered a defeat more shattering than anyone among them had ever dreamed. Newman described it aptly:

The control of information provisions of the Atomic Energy Act were not merely designed to plug certain gaps in the Espionage Act;

they were designed with the object of satisfying as far as possible the desires of scientists to escape the stultifying restrictions on the exchange of information to which they had been subjected by the Manhattan District.[36]

If all of this went out the window and the scientists (and the interchange of ideas so cherished by them) were all swept back under the Espionage Act (so detested by them), the scientists deserved to be heard. One of the most prominent briefs in any proper review of the Marshall-Farmer point would have come from the Federation of Atomic Scientists. These views were never sought or heard on June 18 and 19, 1953. And a Supreme Court decision inimical to the scientific community was handed down without a word from that community simply because there was no time.

Moreover, the fledgling Atomic Energy Commission would have its views about being ignored in the prosecution of atomic spies. The 1946 act gave the new agency a prominent role in deciding how important the unlawful disclosures were before the attorney general could prosecute. The division of responsibilities sought by the scientists under which the AEC took this role was a cardinal feature of the legislative history of the 1946 act. To decide anything, the Court should have known this. It did not, on June 19, 1953, for lack of time.

Even a week's time would have been little enough, given the complexity of the relationship between the 1917 act and the 1946 act. Vinson and the Court had decided that July 6 would have been a proper date for argument on the Saypol point—before Douglas reversed his ground on May 23 and took Saypol's conduct out of the case. Allowing forty-four days (from May 23 to July 6) made sense if reason and deliberation were to be brought to any of these issues. Permitting but one day (June 17–18) precluded reason and deliberation. The Rosenbergs were entitled to both.

Among the questions left unanswered on June 19, 1953, was the meaning of Section 10(b)(6), the "preserving" section. Did Congress intend that the section have the destructive effect on the 1946 act that the majority gave it, or did Congress have a totally different reason? Section 10(b)(6) alone was a sizable Pandora's box. It would have justified Supreme Court review in a minor case involving unlawful disclosure of peaceful atomic research by a scientist operating under the disclosure regulations of the AEC. A death penalty case involving the first look of the Supreme Court at Section 10(b)(6) would have been at the top of any certiorari list for the Court, had the matter come to it that way.

It is again meaningful to examine the Newman article. It reflected the concern in 1947 of a careful lawyer who had observed the development of a major new act flawed by imperfections. Newman stated:

It is evident . . . that the information section of the Atomic Energy Act does not wholly supplant Title I of the Espionage Act; neither can it be maintained that it merely supplements the Espionage Act. The relation of the provisions of the two statutes was apparently not adequately studied at the time of their drafting, with the result that there are areas in which the Atomic Energy Act appears to supplement the Espionage, areas in which it appears to duplicate it, and areas in which it seems to contradict.[37]

Without Newman saying so, that is the definition of a proper Supreme Court question: Given certain facts before the Court, did the 1946 act supplement or contradict the 1917 act, and if it did the latter, what did Congress intend to be the result? Newman himself was quite explicit, indeed, about the need for Court interpretation of the differing penalty provisions of the two acts—the issue squarely raised by the Rosenberg case: "*Differing penalty provisions:* The difference can only be resolved by judicial decision."[38]

There had been no judicial decisions between May of 1947, when the Newman article appeared, and June 19, 1953. Thus, what this "specially qualified student of the [1946] Act" foresaw as a compelling need for judicial interpretation, the majority of the Supreme Court found "not substantial" and "further proceedings to litigate it . . . unwarranted."[39]

Newman's concern about the inconsistencies between the two statutes pervades his article. He recognized the difficulty in resolving these inconsistencies by recourse to "repeal by implication." Newman was perfectly aware of *Borden,* although quite possibly not aware of its imperfections as a precedent. But he wrote of *Borden* and the two acts. Newman said that repeal by implication might very well resolve these conflicts and in important areas:

Nonetheless, we cannot wholly discard the possibility that in certain areas of conflict—notably those where the same action is subject to wholly different degrees of punishment in the two Acts—the courts may hold that a repeal by implication has been effected.[40]

Newman is clearly saying here that in *some* situations a repeal by implication could very well have been what Congress intended in 1946 and intended in precisely the situation that triggered the Rosenberg dispute. By contrast, the Supreme Court, without bothering to look at any legislative history and with a ritualistic nod at *Borden,* rejected Newman's conclusion out of hand. Certainly, this issue deserved more careful examination. Bad drafting, inconsistencies with the 1917 act, and the monumental importance of the new act itself, all leap out of Newman's article:

. . . there remains a formidable problem in integrating and reconciling the provisions of the two Acts. For the Atomic Energy Act clearly cannot be considered to have supplanted the Espionage Act, and on certain major points, the two measures appear to be directly in conflict. Skillful administration and careful judicial consideration will be needed to reconcile the apparent inconsistencies and to effect the evident intent of Congress—regardless of the labyrinth of confusion that inadequate drafting has created.[41]

No such careful judicial consideration occurred between May of 1947, when these words were written, and June 19, 1953, when the Supreme Court acted finally in the Rosenberg case. The Supreme Court's act on that day bore no relation to "careful judicial consideration." The majority of the Supreme Court specifically held that no careful judicial consideration was required.

The only way that the Supreme Court could permit execution of the Rosenbergs on June 19, 1953, was to find the Marshall-Farmer-Douglas point insubstantial and frivolous. If there was anything frivolous at all in the last two days of the Rosenberg case, it was the opinion of the majority of the Supreme Court of the United States. Newman's words, written in 1947, damn the majority more completely than anything that could be written about this case. And no one should forget that the majority was also disposing of two human lives.

Improprieties During the Last Week

We come now to the judicial antics that occurred inside the Supreme Court during the last week of the Rosenberg case. A very strong argument can be made that the *Rosenberg* Court was wrong, dead wrong on the law. But a court can be dead wrong on the law and still give the litigants before it a fair day in that court. Did the Rosenbergs get that fair day in the Supreme Court of the United States during the last week of their life? They did not.

From the "perfectly understood" agreement among the justices reached on June 15; through the meeting convened by Justice Jackson between the attorney general and the chief justice on June 16 to discuss contingency plans to stop Douglas if Douglas acted; through the attorney general's urging on June 16 to the chief justice that the chief justice convince Douglas not to act alone but send the Farmer petition to conference (where the attorney general had the votes) and the chief justice's dutifully doing precisely what the attorney general asked him to do, the last week of the Rosenberg case was a week-long session in a select men's club—where the members of the old-boy network could say anything to anyone, agree to anything, and act in haste in total disregard of the Supreme Court's tradition of calm deliberation.[42] The last week of the Rosenberg case in the Supreme Court simply ceased being a judicial proceeding. To be sure, it had the forms and the pomp and the ceremony. But in that last week, the rights of the defendants whose lives were at stake were not given judicial treatment, they were grievously abused. Put more directly, had these events occurred in any court in this country and been discovered, prompt reversal of the underlying verdict would have followed immediately.

Did what was "perfectly understood" at the conference of justices on June 15 prejudice the rights of the Rosenbergs?

Justice Frankfurter's full quote is:

Jackson then went beyond what I had said by stating that it was perfectly understood yesterday at conference that in view of the Court's denial of habeas corpus no individual justice would overrule the Court's determination.[43]

Frankfurter not only said nothing in response to Jackson's statement, but the entire addendum of June 19, 1953, written by Frankfurter, is found in Jackson's preserved papers with a notation: "thereby making certain that the complete story is found in both records."[44]

Jackson's statement of what was "perfectly understood," quoted above, is on page 4 of the Frankfurter addendum of June 19, 1953. Both justices clearly wished the record of what transpired on June 16 (when Jackson made the statement) to be the same in records kept by each. Earlier we discussed Philip Elman, a close colleague of Frankfurter's, who recorded what Frankfurter told him of what was "perfectly understood" among the justices on June 15. It meant that the new argument faced very human, very emotional opposition when Justice Douglas surfaced it.

It was clear that Douglas knew that his stay did not have the support of the chief justice and a majority of the Court before he issued it. Douglas had isolated himself on this Court and the legal points as voiced in his stay—no matter how strong—were subject to his brethren's suspicions of Douglas's manner of doing judicial business, to say nothing of their vast mistrust of his motives.[45]

The point here is precisely the one made by Justice Jackson earlier in the case: Douglas would vote for review of issues in the Rosenberg case only when it was clear that there were not enough votes to secure that review.[46] What Jackson did not say but what is implicit in his words is that Douglas had a left wing political constituency to serve and he served it when it was clear to him that he would not have to adjudicate the *merits* of *Rosenberg*.

This view is not fair to Douglas. Whatever he had done to

isolate himself from his colleagues prior to June 17, 1953, Douglas was absolutely right in issuing his stay on that date. Douglas may well have known that the stay was a futile act and would be nullified. If so, that makes his June 17 stay even more an act of conscience. On that day, Douglas was dealing with a suspicious, restive, and hostile Court. That did not stop him.

No one reading today about the Rosenberg case can put out of his mind the persistent notion that the Supreme Court acted irrationally. If the issue was whether the Farmer-Marshall point was substantial enough to do what Douglas ordered, it is difficult to find any rationality of any kind that says it was not sufficiently substantial. And that *was* the issue; rereading of the majority opinions reinforces their irrationality.

The vote count within the Court on June 19 is graphic evidence of how the Rosenbergs were fatally prejudiced by the irregularities of the justices. Frankfurter's notes say that Burton stated in the conference of justices after the June 18 argument that he would provide a necessary fifth vote for sustaining Douglas's stay; he would at least stay the Rosenbergs' execution so that proper briefing and argument could be held on the application of the 1946 act—if there were four other votes. Frankfurter noted sadly there were only three: himself, Black, and Douglas.

That fourth vote was essential. No one could ever expect that it would come from Clark, Minton, or Reed. Those three justices never cast a single vote in support of any Rosenberg argument. Moreover, they were followers, not leaders, on that Court. Reed, Minton, and Clark would follow the lead of the chief justice in this case. They always had.

Eliminating Clark, Minton, and Reed, the vital fourth vote so privotal to sustain the Douglas stay (or to conduct rational briefing and argument on it) had to come from the chief justice or Jackson. But Jackson was the justice who arranged the meeting between the chief justice and the attorney general to plot countermoves against Douglas if Douglas acted. And Vinson was the justice who announced that if Douglas did act alone, he would convene the Court to vacate the stay. Clearly, the two justices who could provide the vital votes to force rational action on the

Court had made up their minds to oppose Douglas before Douglas acted.

This was wholesale prejudgment of the Douglas position by the chief justice, who carried the votes of the stalwarts (Reed, Minton, and Clark) with him. This was wholesale prejudgment of the Douglas position by Jackson as well, who might well have understood the Farmer argument and the Douglas stay—if his mind had been open. But Jackson's mind was not open. He was the author of the "perfectly understood" dogma that made the Douglas stay a personal breach of an understanding among the justices. And Jackson had a very large store of personal venom in his makeup. All of it had been loosed on Douglas for Douglas's earlier conduct in this case. Jackson clearly believed that Douglas played to a radical political constituency. Whatever his motive, Jackson's arrangement to have the chief justice and the attorney general meet before Douglas acted was total prejudgment by Jackson of Douglas's stay before Douglas had put a word to paper.

The key votes necessary to sustain Douglas had been cast against him a full day before he acted. They were cast by the chief justice and Justice Jackson, neither of whom had heard of Farmer's argument nor read a word of Douglas's stay opinion when they acted to defeat Douglas. The prejudgment of both justices was totally improper and the record is now clear that this prejudgment defeated Douglas before he acted. He may very well have known it.

If there is evidence that there was a private understanding among the justices on the preceding Monday afternoon not to intervene, and there is, and if there is evidence that Justice Douglas violated that agreement, and his action is his stay, the irrationality of what then occurred cannot be traced to bad lawyering by the justices in the majority of the Court, or to their innate stupidity. When the majority took its path, its members knew they were being hasty; they knew that they were deciding important questions in a slipshod manner unprecedented in the Court's entire history. And these six men knew they were doing this when human lives were at stake. The men in the majority of the U.S. Supreme Court knew precisely what they were doing, with all of the criticism, even dishonor, that might eventually come their way when history caught up with the hysteria surrounding the Court in that June week.

Yet they did it.

The result was that Douglas's stay of the execution of the Rosenbergs was vacated by votes cast before Douglas acted—in prejudgment of the stay by at least two justices. The vote of one of them—Jackson's vote—would have joined four of his brethren in directing the Court in the precise opposite direction. This prejudgment joins the other irregularities within the Supreme Court in that third week of June 1953, in a wholesale record of disregard for the rules of judicial conduct when this conduct would determine whether two human beings would live.

And the clerks, Department of Justice officials, and close observers of the Court knew then, and those surviving know today, that no one around the Court was happy with what happened. Then and now, the entire Supreme Court community made up of those same clerks, officials, and Court observers knew that something tawdry and sordid took place in the third week of June of 1953 in their beloved Court. The bad dream for those who cared is the fact that the Supreme Court became politicized in June of 1953. It entered an agreement that no Court should, and the chief justice met surreptitiously with the attorney general in aid of that agreement, and the attorney general and the chief justice engaged in ex parte conversations designed to influence the outcome of a case then being considered by a member of the Court. Justices of the Supreme Court should have done none of those things.

Specific rules governing the conduct of judges were violated. The Canons of Judicial Conduct promulgated by the American Bar Association traditionally set the rules by which judges must comport themselves. Judges everywhere—including justices of the Supreme Court—are themselves judged by their compliance with these canons. At least two were broken by justices of the Supreme Court during the last week of the Rosenberg case. The first was the flat-out prohibition of ex parte communications, discussed earlier. But there was another canon of judicial conduct that was also broken during that last week of the Rosenberg case. It is Canon 4, in effect in its present form in June 1953. It holds that judges must not alone shun impropriety, but must avoid the appearance of impropriety. It is worth quoting:

A Judge's official conduct should be free from impropriety and the appearance of impropriety; he should avoid infractions of the law, and his personal behavior, not only upon the bench and in the performance of judicial duties, but also in his everyday life, should be beyond reproach.

The basis for this canon is the fragile nature of public respect for the courts, which would be damaged not only by the fact of improper conduct by judges, but also by a public belief that improper conduct had occurred. In effect, an American judge becomes Caesar's wife when he dons the black judicial robes.

When the attorney general of the United States met with the chief justice of the United States during the afternoon of June 16, 1953, that canon was breached. No matter what the subject matter of that meeting, the visit of Attorney General Brownell to the chambers of Chief Justice Vinson while this bitterly contested case was entering its most controversial phase was a highly improper appearance. This was hardly a secret meeting; no visit of a cabinet officer to the Supreme Court can ever be secret. What came out of that meeting was not only the appearance of a deal, but a deal itself. The mere appearance of the deal violated Canon 4.

When the Court acted within one hour on Wednesday afternoon, June 17, to reconvene, it did so with haste that had no precedent before or since. It was reconvened with that haste because the Court itself had signaled to the Department of Justice that this is what the Supreme Court wanted. As earlier noted, this initiative *from* the Court was improper. Whether the signal was delivered in the Vinson-Brownell meeting the day before, or came more covertly by telephone after Douglas acted, will never be known. But the appearance of impropriety came into bold relief when the Court acted with historic haste in responding to

Brownell's request to reconvene on the day after Brownell and Vinson met to plan precisely what then occurred.

The private agreement among the justices made on June 15 is a subtler matter. There is no Canon of Judicial Conduct forbidding such agreement. There is no need for one. No judge needs a canon to know that it is his duty to hear *all* relevant parts of the case before him before he rules. This rule is basic; it ranks with the requirement that a judge must be fair and unbiased in dealing with the parties before him. The obligation of judges to hear all relevant evidence and pertinent arguments is what our adversary system rests on. An agreement made in advance to ignore all future arguments by one party nullifies the entire system. It violates the essence of our system. Any such understanding, either "perfectly understood" or agreed to in any way, places a psychological as well as legal burden on the proponent of any new argument. That is precisely what Farmer, Marshall, and then Bloch faced when they first mentioned the Atomic Energy Act of 1946 during the week of June 15, 1953. Six minds on the Supreme Court had been made up before any of the lawyers had said a word.

How serious is this litany of misdeeds? Officially, no one will ever know because none of this was ever disclosed until years after the Rosenbergs were executed. These pages make these disclosures (excepting only one) thirty-six years after the Rosenbergs died. The Brownell-Vinson meeting is the exception. It surfaced in response to a Freedom of Information suit filed by the Rosenberg children in 1975.

If these disclosures had surfaced while the Rosenbergs were still alive, there is little doubt that everything done in the Supreme Court after June 15 would have been tainted. The taint is not a trifling one. But who would have said so? Normally, the judging is from on high, with a higher court reversing a lower one for its improprieties. What lower court would judge the Supreme Court of the United States? And if some lower court did grasp the nettle, would the Supreme Court be prevented from reversing the lower court's action? What would happen if the Supreme Court refused to admit its own improprieties? If its refusal was improper and error, where could anyone go?

This is pure speculation, because the Rosenbergs died within eight hours after a combination of irregularities and inadequate briefing resulted in fatal error by the Supreme Court. There is no doubt that everyone involved, six justices of the Supreme Court and the attorney general of the United States, were guilty of irregularities. Obviously, no one did anything about it. None of the consciences of the six members of the majority ever moved the justices to talk. Silence about past decisions is an article of faith for justices of the Supreme Court. Silence about all decisions, good, bad, or awful. The silence of all parties concerned in the last week of the Rosenberg case over the thirty-six years since then is a ritualistic silence. Beneath it lies a number of uneasy consciences—that uneasiness has been stilled by death for all of the six justices who made up the Supreme Court majority; and the minority of justices, Frankfurter, Black, and Douglas, are all dead.

But there are living witnesses to that week in June of 1953 who remember the Rosenberg case. Those on the Rosenberg side recall that week with undiluted astonishment and horror. Those within the government recall the same events with queasy stomachs. Everyone connected with the case knew at its end that there was something very wrong going on in the Supreme Court of the United States.

If the Rosenbergs were guilty, why all this stirring about?

The crime of espionage is a grave one. Lawyers are notorious for finding technical flaws in any proceeding. Some undoubtedly occurred during the Supreme Court's consideration of the fate of the Rosenbergs. Notwithstanding, is not the clear, convincing guilt of the two defendants the ultimate answer to all of the questions about the case?

It is not.

First, the two defendants were very probably executed in violation of their rights. The government violated the Rosenbergs' rights by prosecuting them under the wrong statute. The Supreme Court violated the Rosenbergs' rights by giving them a woefully inadequate hearing, inadequate for any court, and tragically so for the ultimate voice of justice in our country. Not only were the Rosenbergs' rights violated, but the execution was—again, very probably—itself illegal. The only reason why these conclusions are stated with any reservations is that no court has ever said so. Now no court ever will. Observers, however, can certainly say two things that are very clear and true: that the Rosenbergs' rights were violated and their execution was illegal. The evidence is clear and conclusive.

It made no difference that the Rosenbergs were represented by counsel, that fifteen judges sat on their case and let them die, or that no one bothered to attack the flaw in the government's prosecution until the last week in a case that lasted close to three years. The government bore the responsibility for bringing this prosecution. The government bore the responsibility for seeking the execution of the two spies. The government cannot shift its responsibility onto the defense lawyers, nor onto the fifteen judges. Federal law enforcement officials are obligated to dispense justice, not to win cases. That is not a pietism. It is an article of faith within the Department of Justice under any administration. And it applies with crucial force in capital cases.

The guilt of the Rosenbergs has nothing to do with the injustice done them. The government had no right to execute the Rosenbergs. They were entitled by law to live and to be prosecuted properly, under the correct statute. What might then happen—as we point out in a following section—is pure conjecture. But the probable guilt of the Rosenbergs in the case in which they died washed no one's hands. Our legal system carries the blood of the Rosenbergs on its hands. Whether it is guilty blood, we shall never know. We can guess that it was. But that guilt must come following a proper charge, leveled as Congress intended, and in a fair proceeding.

And that guilt turns on what an unknown jury might do under a very different indictment, faced with different proof. The ultimate guilt of the Rosenbergs is an educated guess at best.

Finally, there is a message in this book directed to those who contend today that regardless of what happened within the Court, the majority of the Supreme Court reached the right legal result when it brushed aside the Douglas stay and allowed the Rosenbergs to die. The message goes to the basic elements of judging and judges. The heart of our system of criminal justice is the unbiased judge. All of the rules imposed on judges and lawyers by the canons governing their conduct seek the impartiality of judges. Judges' freedom from improper influences exerted by lawyers is a purpose of these canons. Our system of justice is designed to prevent these influences from being exerted on the judge—or judges—who make crucial decisions such as whether a defendant will live or die.

Just as essential to our system of criminal justice is the requirement that a judge must hear and consider with an open mind *all* of the arguments to be made on a point of law.

When influence from one side or the other is privately exerted on any judge (before whose court a case is pending) while he decides the case, our system has failed. When a judge hears an argument on a new and heretofore unlitigated point of law with his mind closed—regardless of the degree of prejudgment if the point is truly new—our system has failed.

The conduct of the majority of the Supreme Court, accordingly, cannot be excused by the contention that the Supreme Court would have decided the Rosenberg case precisely as it did had there been no ex parte communications. Similarly, the conduct of the majority of the Supreme Court cannot be excused by the contention that its decision not to intercede with the execution of the Rosenbergs would have been reached by the Court even if there had been no prior agreement among the justices not to intercede. The system our courts operate under does not put the misconduct of judges and lawyers on one side of a scale with the intrinsic rectitude of what those same judges ultimately decide weighed against it.

Judicial impropriety is very much like pregnancy. It is either present or it is not. And its impact profoundly affects the entire system.

When the majority of the Supreme Court did what it did in the last week of the Rosenberg case, it was subjected to improper influences. Ex parte communications and prejudgment were two forms of these improper influences. It is, therefore, impossible to justify the Supreme Court's ultimate ruling on June 19, 1953, by claiming that, notwithstanding the improprieties of certain of the justices, the result the Court reached was correct. Our system does not permit judicial misconduct along the way to *any* result, correct or incorrect, to be ignored.

In the Rosenberg case, the majority of the Supreme Court was blind to its own misconduct. It was dead wrong in the result it reached. That combination resulted in two illegal executions.

Since the "guilt" of the Rosenbergs can salve no one's concern about what happened in June of 1953, what lessons can the events in the crucial weeks of that month teach us?

Much and little.

Little can be learned because there are no simple, graphic reforms that anyone can point to as effective insurance that the events of that month will never recur. There is no formal written rule against a Court of the United States being politicized. Like so many things in the Rosenberg case, what occurred was so basic, so much an onslaught on the heart of the system of justice in our country, that no formal rules prohibiting it have ever been pronounced. One cannot pass a rule against judges' listening to pronouncements in the press, radio, and television, stating that delay in concluding the Rosenberg case was inimical to U.S. interests. One cannot prohibit justices of the Supreme Court from reading newspapers. One cannot insulate nine literate, sophisticated, and concerned men from a controversy that is raging across the world simply because its epicenter happens to be their courtroom.

How then does one prevent the recurrence of the obvious politicizing of the Supreme Court that took place? How does one insure that the fire storms of controversy set off by unpopular defendants, fueled by an incendiary spy scare, given cyclonic force by an unprecedented force of public opinion such as McCarthyism, and carried across the world by simultaneous events as were going on in Korea and Berlin, will not recur? Obviously, one cannot.

The only insurance that exists is that of probabilities. We probably will never again witness as violent a crescendo of public opinion over one subject as occurred when McCarthyism, the Korean War, the Berlin uprising, and the Rosenberg case combined in June of 1953. It was an accident of history that may never happen again.

But if it does, one cannot insulate the Supreme Court from it. There are no rules for the American Bar Association to pass, no reforms to be legislated by Congress. None of these will prevent another June of 1953. The politicizing of the Supreme Court of the United States is a malady so grievous and rare that wholesale alteration of the mechanism would be required to prevent it from happening again. The Rosenberg case stands alone as a major injustice perpetrated by a Supreme Court that had been politicized.

What does this lesson tell us? There are minor reforms that do seem called for by the events of June 1953. First, consideration of a new and valid point of law should never turn on who happens to utter it. At least this should be the rule in a case where major punishment is being meted out, and should be beyond doubt in a capital case. Since 1953, the rules of all courts have gradually been modified so that today, in practice, this result has been achieved.[47] But the federal system of courts should remove this matter from doubt.

Next, the comings and goings within the Supreme Court of chief officers of the Department of Justice should be recorded and made public when they occur. Most federal agencies have an internal rule requiring the formal recording of all ex parte approaches with the secretary of the agency. All such formal records are then made public periodically. There is no reason why the Supreme Court (and, indeed, all federal courts) should be any different. The public should not wait twenty-three years for disclosure of information like this as it did in the case of the Vinson-Brownell meeting of June 16, 1953. The old-boy relationship between the Department of Justice and the Supreme Court should be far more carefully monitored.

But there it ends. No formal rules go beyond that point. The rest lies in the uncharted realm of the conscience of each judge and of each attorney general, as impervious to legislation and rule-making as individual consciences must always be. For better or for worse, the formal insurance against evils of the Rosenberg case ends there.

Beyond that point, everything rests on the eternal vigilance of lawyers. That vigilance achieved nothing in the aftermath of the Rosenberg case. For thirty-five years, that vigilance has allowed sloppy, improper, irregular conduct in the Supreme Court resulting in two unlawful executions to remain buried. But weak as it may have been in this case, the vigilance of lawyers is all that will prevent another like it.

Yet that vigilance is sometimes paradoxical. In recent times, Americans have seen both the executive and legislative branches of the federal government marred by scandal. Watergate, from 1972 through August of 1974, and the Abscam trials of 1980, make vigilance over the president and the Congress an existing fact of political life. The executive and legislative branches of our government carry on their business before the fish-eye of millions who suspect the worst from both because the worst has happened so recently.

Not so the judicial branch. Because of its record, or because it is so capable of burying its mistakes so effectively, the federal judiciary is today sacrosanct. One major lesson to be learned from the Rosenberg case is that this imperious insulation from public inspection is unhealthy. One need not resort to the extremes of "sunshine" laws to illuminate the process of the federal judiciary to healthy inquiry. The bar, particularly, must assume nothing about the federal courts. When the federal courts render a decision that is questionable, or comport themselves in a manner that is dubious, the bar (rather than only the litigant involved) should routinely investigate. And this applies to the Supreme Court of the United States as well. Presently existing committees of national bar associations deal with the federal courts at each level—trial, appellate, and Supreme. In 1989, these groups are honorary bodies that do little but make changes in the procedural rules of each of these courts. These committees should assume broader powers approaching that of ombudsmen, and have the status in the court to do so. The term "ombudsman" implies an ongoing inspector-general acting for the public. If federal proceedings were subject to careful scrutiny as a routine matter (and they are not today; intervention of the bar in the federal court is highly unusual), a powerful check against recurrence of the events of June 1953 would come into being.

Unless, of course, the death penalty was involved. And unless there was a rush to execute the death penalty, powerful enough to prevent any bureaucracy from going into action. And unless, of course, this new mechanism became politicized along with the Court.

Ultimately, beyond all reform, beyond all rules, the solution rests with the conscience of the individual judge. If all of the circumstances of June 1953 recurred, there is no set of rules anywhere that would prevent the tragedy of what occurred within the Supreme Court in the Rosenberg case. In that very special sense, and under those very special circumstances, we become a government of men and not one of law. And in that ultimate sense, preventing a recurrence of the events of June 1953 becomes a matter of preventing those politicizing circumstances from recurring. Prevention of McCarthyism and all of the other facets of the hysteria that gripped this country (including the Supreme Court) is a political matter that should touch and galvanize the conscience of every American.

CHAPTER TEN

✦

IF THE ROSENBERGS
HAD BEEN TRIED UNDER
THE PROPER ACT

RIEFLY at the outset of the description of the Rosenberg trial, aspects of the trial were portrayed that received little attention then or since. First, the Rosenbergs were charged and convicted of *conspiracy* to spy, not spying itself. By so doing, the government made available to itself the evidence of Sobell's flight and the Rosenbergs' alleged plan to flee. All these events took place close to five years after any act of espionage by anyone. The utility of the conspiracy charge was that it made this evidence usable by the government and very damning to the Rosenbergs and to Sobell.

It is meaningful to examine the trial strategy of the government more closely to see whether, if the Rosenbergs had been properly charged and tried under the Atomic Energy Act of 1946 (rather than under the Espionage Act of 1917), the strategy would have worked.

First, to secure the death penalty, a conspiracy charge under the 1917 act required only proof that showed that the conspiracy aimed at an "advantage to a foreign power." Conclusive evidence that possession of the lens mold would be of benefit to the Soviet Union (albeit watered down by the fact that this was hardly the "secret of the bomb" as Judge Kaufman and the press viewed it) certainly was available to the prosecution. One important piece of testimony on this point was Harry Gold's statement on the stand that the Soviet people who received Greenglass's information were delighted with it.[1] There was no question that this requirement of the 1917 act could be proved by the prosecution with ease.

To secure the death penalty under the 1946 act was a very different matter. Conspiracy under *that* act had to be accompanied by evidence that the conspirators acted with intent to "injure the United States." Proof that a conspiracy to hand over atomic secrets to a wartime ally constituted injury to the United States was a tricky business, perhaps so tricky as to be impossible. By choosing the 1917 act, the Rosenberg prosecutors avoided this nettle.

Finally, if this prosecution was bent on the death penalty, the 1946 act required the jury to recommend the death penalty. Using the 1917 act meant the simpler chore of convincing a judge to mete out death rather than taking on the uncertainties of convincing twelve jurors to recommend it, as the 1946 act required. Certainly, after the case was assigned to Judge Kaufman, the choice of an act that made the death penalty a prerogative of the judge acting alone made a great deal of sense to a prosecution that clearly desired to put the defendants in the electric chair. Any thoughts of using the later act—assuming that the prosecution ever harbored any—disappeared when a notorious pro-government and notoriously tough jurist was assigned to the case. For, unlucky as the Rosenbergs were in the assignment of Kaufman as judge, the death-penalty-minded prosecution was lucky.

Thus, the prosecution chose to charge and try the Rosenbergs for conspiracy to commit naval and atomic espionage during the period from June 1944 through June 16, 1950. And it did so explicitly under the 1917 Espionage Act, alleging that the Rosenbergs, Morton Sobell, and David Greenglass and Anatoli Yakovlev (the soviet courier) had conspired to deliver and transmit to a foreign power (the USSR, which was explicitly named), with reason to believe that this would be used to the advantage of that foreign power, "accounts, writing, sketches, notes and information relating to the National Defense of the United States." The indictment made no distinction between naval and atomic secrets. It also named Harry Gold and Ruth Greenglass as co-conspirators but not as defendants. David Greenglass had entered a plea of guilty to conspiracy before the trial of the Rosenbergs and Sobell had started. Yakovlev was severed from the case; he had left for the USSR in December 1946.

At trial, the prosecution had no problems whatever with its entire stratagem. It worked perfectly. Judge Kaufman had just as little difficulty in placing all of this within one grand conspiracy to steal secrets of all kinds—naval and atomic—from the United States government.

And the defense at the 1951 trial helped. Bloch never cross-examined Gold and told the jury that Gold spoke the truth. In a second trial, Gold would be shown to be an unbalanced spinner of fanciful tales, whose appearance on the stand in the Rosenberg case was aimed at the reduction of his sentence. In a second trial, the inexplicable blunder of the *defense* moving to suppress the Greenglass sketches of the implosion-detonated bomb (on security grounds) would never occur. In a second trial, the accomplice testimony (inherently suspect because the witnesses *were* accomplices) of both Greenglasses would be attacked far more strenuously than Bloch ever did. Both were singing to save themselves: David Greenglass from the death penalty, Ruth Greenglass from an indictment she deserved. Moreover, the unnatural act of a brother testifying to put his own sister into the electric chair would be shown to be just that. Bloch never did this effectively. No one can speculate how a second jury would react to these major changes in the defense case. But the facts would be given to the jury in a very different case.

As to the law, up to this point, these pages have been free of any accusation of legal error by Judge Kaufman. He was, however, accused of error in this case by none other than his judicial brother and superior, Judge Jerome Frank, of the U.S. Court of Appeals for the Second Circuit. It was to this court that the *Rosenberg* conviction went for its first review in 1953. The three-man appellate panel confirmed the conviction, predictably found that sentencing was wholly within the province of Judge Kaufman and not reviewable by them, and, overall, affirmed the outcome of the trial.

But Judge Frank, who wrote the long and incisive opinion for the three, individually dissented on the key point of joining the naval and atomic rings into one conspiracy.[2] Because the distinction made by Judge Frank would be pivotal, if the Rosenbergs were ever to be tried again (and properly), it is worthwhile to examine what Judge Frank wrote.

Judge Frank cited two well-known conspiracy cases. In *Kotteakos* v. *United States*,[3] a number of salesmen defrauded the United States by filing false loan applications through a single broker who was also a party to the fraud. The Supreme Court held that the salesmen may have had similar ends in mind but were acting individually (as they did) and lacked the "single unified purpose" of co-conspirators. Clearly, none of the salesmen knew of the activities of the others. On the other hand, in *Blumenthal* v. *United States* (also cited by Judge Frank),[4] a number of salesmen who sold a particular brand of liquor above the wartime ceiling price, and "knew or must have known" each other's activities, were found by the Supreme Court to be part of one conspiracy to charge an illegal price for this liquor. Knowledge, thus, of the overall aim of the conspiracy is the key to charging its members with participation in it. Judge Frank held Kaufman erred for not questioning whether the naval espionage ring and atomic spying were two separate conspiracies or segments of one, and for not instructing the jury to answer that question.

To Judge Frank, this was of crucial importance to Sobell, and obviously so. For Sobell had been the victim before Judge Kaufman of the devastating Gold-Greenglass disclosures concerning atomic spying; but no one ever testified one word that Sobell knew anything about the atomic spy ring. Judge Frank's criticism was quite valid. There was no testimony that linked the two spy rings, not a word of evidence that either Sobell or Elitcher ever knew the Greenglasses or vice versa. If this was true, the Rosenberg case was very much more akin to *Kotteakos* and the fraud by the individual salesmen who knew nothing of each other, and far from *Blumenthal,* where the salesmen knew of each other's misdeeds. But Judge Frank was outvoted two to one in his court and the Supreme Court never reached the point.

If the conclusion reached earlier is correct, if Congress intended that the atomic spying that occurred after August 1, 1946 (and conspiracies to spy for atomic secrets that continued past that date), were to be prosecuted under the 1946 act and under that act alone, a second trial of the Rosenbergs would have put the prosecution in a dilemma. It seems clear that the two conspiracies, naval and atomic espionage, would have had to be severed, and in all likelihood tried separately. This result seems inevitable both from the testimony already on record and because the atomic conspiracy would have violated a different statute than did the naval spy ring.

In any such trial, the prosecution, if it still sought the death penalty, would have three hurdles it did not have in the 1951 trial. First, it would have to prove an intent by the Rosenbergs to injure the United States. Nothing like that is in the record of the Rosenberg trial. There are criticisms by the Rosenbergs of the capital system, but they fall far short of evidence that anybody's spying was aimed at injury to this country. Patently, the testimony shows an intent to benefit the USSR and nothing more. But that something more would be required in a second trial, and would be exceedingly hard to prove.

Second, the Sobell testimony and the Elitcher testimony would be much more difficult to line up with the Greenglass-Gold atomic spying ring. The difference would be that one conspiracy violated the 1917 act and the other violated the 1946 act. Tying both together as part of one large conspiracy (as was done before Judge Kaufman) is possible. But Judge Frank's dissent would be buttressed by an additional factor: the different statutes that the two rings violated. Use of the Elitcher–Sobell testimony in a second effort to put the Rosenbergs into the electric chair would be far trickier the second time around.

Finally, if the Rosenbergs were properly tried under the 1946 act and the prosecution still sought the death penalty, it would have to secure a jury recommendation to do so. By the time that any second trial took place, much of the perspective in which the events took place (described in the next chapter) would have become fully known and presumably be used by the defense.

This perspective was availabe to the defense in 1951 but never brought forward. But if the context in which the Rosenbergs and David Greenglass spied was put before twelve good men and true, and if events two thousand miles west at Los Alamos and three thousand miles east at the Bow Street Court in London (where Klaus Fuchs had been tried) were scrutinized by these good jurymen, it is exceedingly doubtful that they would ever return a recommendation that Julius and Ethel Rosenberg should die.

CHAPTER ELEVEN

✦

A DEATH SENTENCE
BASED ON IGNORANCE
OF THE FACTS

I F PERSPECTIVE is to be given the Rosenberg case, a vital
element in any such perspective is Judge Kaufman's sentence.
Judge Kaufman's reasons for ordering execution of Julius
and Ethel Rosenberg are explicit. In sentencing them to
death on April 5, 1951, Judge Kaufman pronounced these words:

I consider your crime worse than murder. Plain deliberate contemplated
murder is dwarfed in magnitude by comparison with the crime you
have committed. In committing the act of murder, the criminal kills
only his victim. The immediate family is brought to grief and when
justice is meted out the chapter is closed. But in your case, I believe your
conduct in putting into the hands of the Russians the A-bomb years
before our best scientists predicted Russia would perfect the bomb has
already caused, in my opinion, the Communist aggression in Korea,
with the resultant casualties exceeding 50,000 and who knows but that
millions more of innocent people may pay the price of your treason.
Indeed, by your betrayal you undoubtedly have altered the course of
history to the disadvantage of our country. No one can say that we do
not live in a constant state of tension. We have evidence of your
treachery all around us every day—for the civilian defense activities
throughout the nation are aimed at preparing us for an atom bomb
attack. Nor can it be said in mitigation of the offense that the power
which set the conspiracy in motion and profited from it was not openly
hostile to the United States at the time of the conspiracy. If this was

your excuse the error of your ways in setting yourselves above our properly constituted authorities and the decision of those authorities not to share the information with Russia must now be obvious.[1]

Federal judges are given wide latitude in sentencing. The 1917 statute permitted Judge Kaufman to impose death. But judges are held to their words—within the same wide latitude—when they state their reasons for imposing sentence. For the second time, Judge Kaufman's conduct rather than that of the Supreme Court must be examined. His words quoted above are extreme. They focus on the atomic espionage carried on by Julius and Ethel Rosenberg in complicity with Gold and the Greenglasses. But the Rosenbergs, Harry Gold, and David Greenglass were not the only atomic spies working for the Soviets. Far from it. To determine whether Judge Kaufman's words were true, whether he accurately described the gravity of the injury to the United States (and to the non-Soviet world) perpetrated by the Rosenbergs, the activities of the other spies must be examined. Those activities were widespread and amazingly effective. Curiously, they began within a half-mile of Judge Kaufman's courtroom, seven years before the judge doomed the Rosenbergs.

Klaus Fuchs

It was a strange night. The thin, balding man was bouncing a tennis ball aimlessly on a windy street corner during a late January twilight near Delancey Street on New York's Lower East Side. From the way he handled the tennis ball, the thin man was clearly no athlete. He appeared to be simply passing time. The street was full of rush-hour passersby. No one seemed to pay any attention while the thin man continued bouncing his ball past dusk and into the darkening and cold evening.

Just after dark, another man, this one also bald but much heavier, stopped on the sidewalk across the street from the thin man. For a full half-hour the two of them just stood there, one watching the other bouncing his little ball, stopping, then bouncing it again. Finally, as the brisk winter wind carried the ball near the gutter, the balding man went to the edge of the sidewalk, now dark and nearly vacant. He stopped bouncing his ball. He had seen the fat observer and decided that the fat man was waiting for him.

What happened then was even stranger. As if in a charade, the fat man saw that he was recognized and instantly took an odd assortment of belongings from his coat. Walking to the nearest streetlamp, he held up to the light a book with a vivid green binding and took two pairs of gloves from his overcoat and slowly counted them so that the thin, bald man across the street could watch his count. After he counted the gloves, the fat man put each pair on his hands to show that he had two left gloves and two right gloves.

The thin man had seen enough. He crossed the street and spoke briefly with the fat man. The thin, balding man with the ball showed it to his new acquaintance, as if to prove that it was a tennis ball. The fat man appeared satisfied but looked up and down the street fearfully. The street was now totally deserted.

The two men then spoke again, just as briefly. The balding man handed the tennis ball, incongruous in this dark and desolate corner, to his fat companion and together they walked away. Within a block, they hailed a taxi that took them to a dingy restaurant in mid-Manhattan. There the strange conduct continued. Both sat. Neither ate. They talked again for less than ten minutes. They ordered tea and coffee but neither drank. Then the balding man looked about again at the few diners around him, looked at the thin man, nodded in agreement, and left.

Klaus Fuchs had been told of the man with the green-bound book and two pairs of gloves by his last courier in London just before his transfer to New York and the Manhattan District Project one month earlier. The last courier, sent to Fuchs by the Soviets in England, was a woman. She told Fuchs he would have to get a tennis ball. She had been vague about addresses and Fuchs had been afraid he would miss his new American courier. But here he was, with his book and gloves, right on schedule and on the right corner. Although Klaus Fuchs did not learn his new courier's name for seven years after many meetings with him, the fat little man with book and gloves was named Harry Gold.[2]

*   *   *

Klaus Fuchs was an authentic genius. His colleagues among British and American nuclear physicists ranked him one cut below the giants, Einstein, Fermi and Bohr, but well within the next rank of intellectual pioneers on the frontier that was pierced to give the United States the atomic bomb and nuclear energy. He was an expert in the process of developing U-235 by the gaseous diffusion method, employed by the United States at the Oak Ridge, Tennessee, facility. Fuchs, a naturalized British citizen, was also a leader, both scientifically and communally, at the Los Alamos laboratory where the bomb was designed and experimentally exploded at Alamogordo in the New Mexico desert on July 16, 1945. His was a brooding mentality that stretched across the entire Manhattan District Project (as the atomic energy effort was named), ranging from the theory behind the chain reaction on which atomic power is based, through the development of U-235 as a nuclear fuel, which had put the United States years ahead of all other nations in the manufacture of the bomb, down to the design of the weapon itself. There was literally no aspect in the crash development of atomic energy during World War II that was not touched by Fuchs and many of these were influenced by his work. Fuchs, to be sure, was not an innovator. But his purity of reason, the error-free mechanism of his intellect, was an invaluable testing device on which many of the theoretical innovations in gaseous diffusion and later in the design of the bomb were evaluated. As a human being, Fuchs looked and acted like the original disembodied brain. As a scientist, he was an honored colleague to both American and British scientists in the strictly policed confines of the Manhattan District and the British code-named laboratories "Tube Alloys" at Birmingham, and later at Harwell. Fuchs was a top scientist in the development of the bomb.[3]

Fuchs was also a dedicated Communist and had been for most of his adult life. How this strange and awful combination occurred and escaped the detection of both the British and American authorities until after Fuchs had betrayed both countries is a horror story all its own, but vital to any true perspective on the Rosenberg crimes.

*   *   *

Klaus Fuchs came from the finest intellectual stock that Germany produced. His father, Dr. Emil Fuchs, was an outstanding pastor, a member of the Religious Society of Friends, at Eisenach and Kiel in North Germany. The senior Dr. Fuchs was a spokesman for the religious wing of the German Social Democratic Party. He opposed Hitler before Hitler came to power and, what is more revealing, Dr. Fuchs continued to do so long after January 1933, when Hitler became chancellor. He spent months in a concentration camp. Throughout the war, he remained a Socialist, a pacifist, and an anti-Nazi, all inside Germany. That was a unique record for a man as well known to the authorities as Dr. Emil Fuchs. But among other things, Dr. Fuchs was known for his courage.[4]

His younger son, Klaus Emil, was born in 1911. Brilliant from his earliest school days, Klaus Fuchs grew up in the academic circle that fermented so badly in the late twenties and early thirties and ended as fertile spawning grounds for young Nazis. Klaus Fuchs, first at Leipzig and then at Kiel University, went the way of his father.[5] He became a Social Democrat and a pacifist. But some time in 1932, Klaus Fuchs became disenchanted with the Social Democrats. They were, in a word, unable to stop Hitler. As Fuchs searched about himself for the answer to the greatest riddle of his time—to Fuchs and to many other intellectuals like him—that of how to defeat Hitler, the great enemy of mankind then maneuvering Nazism to power in Germany, Klaus Fuchs saw only the Communists. Like many Social Democratic intellectuals at this time, he fell prey to the Communist propaganda that the Socialists (more even than the Nazis) were the greatest moral lepers. This logical turnabout came easily for the Communist dialecticians: the Social Democrats were weak and powerless, unable to stop the Nazis. The only movement with half a chance to do so was the revolutionary movement of workers. The Socialists, in good Communist dogma of the early thirties, were worse than the Nazis because they were enlisting so many soft-minded intellectuals into a campaign that led nowhere except to the ultimate triumph of Hitler.[6]

When Klaus Fuchs joined the Communist party in Kiel in 1932,[7] he took his first move as a controlled Communist in conduct that went on without interruption for at least seventeen years. Curiously, the most important aspect of Fuch's enlistment into communism was its location. Thirteen years later, Fuchs was terrified when the British captured Kiel before the Russians could get there in the late winter of 1945. Terrified, because the Nazis kept full dossiers on Communists through the Nazi years, and in true German fashion had not destroyed them. Thus, Fuchs feared, the records proving his Communist past would fall into British rather than Russian hands and give him away.[8] Fuchs could not guess that bureaucratic bungling kept this evidence, as well as an abundance of other evidence of Fuchs's Communist ties, from the attention of British security officers until it was too late.

Fuchs developed a classic schizoid personality. By day and in the open, he became an accomplished and then premier scientist. From his bulging forehead came little innovation in his chosen field—atomic physics—but rather an encyclopedic understanding of the subject and an ability to know at any given time what the state of current understanding was, and where he and his colleagues would have to strike out in new directions.[9] The new departures were rarely his own. But the theoretical proof that came after the vast move forward was often his. He was a near-genius researcher after-the-fact, capable of understanding everything and formulating it into a program for still greater advances. At the University of Kiel and later at Birmingham University with his mentor, Professor Rudolph Peierls, a refugee just as Fuchs was, he rose fast in the new science that was kindling in the fires of the Allied war effort. That new science, atomic physics, grew to a major place in the Allied war effort in less than five years.

By night, in his heart, Fuchs was something very different.[10] He was a dedicated Communist. Klaus Fuchs was not one of the fuzzy-minded intellectuals who read *Das Kapital* and argued through the night on its dialectical nuances. He was an operative, a worker, a silent and brooding conspirator wholly indoctrinated with Party discipline, willing to do anything he was directed to do. He was directed to become a spy. He then became the most effective spy in the history of that profession.

Before Fuchs became a spy, he became a refugee. He did not flee voluntarily, although the plans for his wandering, worked out by others, reflected no willingness on Fuchs's part to endure Hitler or Nazi Germany. Rather, Fuchs became a refugee in exactly the same way he became a spy. He was organized and sent underground by the Communist party, first to France in 1932. From France, Fuchs went to England to take up a scholarship at Bristol University. The scholarship was partly his own doing; but he was aided by an organization of liberal scientists who were hard at work arranging for the escape and resettling of outstanding German scientists. That organization, the Society for the Protecting of Science and Learning (SPSL),[11] was peopled by the best-willed and most articulate of British anti-Nazi scientists. It was exploited by Fuchs, just as he exploited his family connections and his university status in earlier years. Fuchs used the society to get his scholarship at Bristol.

From Bristol, it was a quick jump to another scholarship at the University of Edinburgh.[12] In 1937, he was awarded his Ph.D. in mathematical physics. Fuchs was moving up the ladder fast. His reputation as perhaps the most promising young man in the new science of atomic physics was spreading across the English academic community. True to his schizoid nature, Fuchs never left Party discipline in this period. He kept his ties and met with Party couriers regularly. There was no participation in public discussions or anything so open. There was contact, and there was discipline, and, in its midst, there was Fuchs, the good Party soldier.

In 1939, the war began. For a time, there was confusion with the official British views of the Communists. This was the time, 1940, of the Nazi-Soviet pact and the phony war. The Communist line was that the English and the French were imperialistic, antiproletariat. Fuchs himself acted in a singular fashion. Called before the British Alien Tribunal in 1939, Fuchs claimed membership in the German Social Democratic Party as proof of his anti-Nazi beliefs. Fuchs was permitted to continue working at Edinburgh and stayed there until the Nazi invasion of the Low

Countries. Then, in 1940, the government's General Order covering all enemy aliens included Fuchs. In 1940, he was interned, along with a number of alien scientists, and sent to a camp in Canada on the Plains of Abraham just outside Quebec.[13]

Here occurred a series of incidents that gave great pain to the security people who finally brought themselves, ten years later, to examine Fuchs's conduct. In the Quebec camp, Fuchs befriended one Hans Kahle, an avowed Communist who had fought in the Spanish Civil War. Kahle led an outspoken Communist section in the camp. Those who recall the camp also recall Fuchs's identification with this section. Significantly, Fuchs joined a discussion group of Communists that met under Kahle. Fuchs did nothing to conceal his Communist views.[14] It is astonishing that no one raised this fact until after his conviction as a spy twelve years later.

Not astonishing, given the changed complexion of public opinion after the German invasion of the Soviet Union in June of 1941, was the permission granted to Fuchs to return to England in 1942. There were no security procedures in effect at the level of work that Fuchs assumed at Glasgow University. There were no apparent security procedures operating to probe left wing scientists in the British atomic effort in the ten years that followed. Fuchs returned to Glasgow and soon came to the attention of Professor Peierls at the University of Birmingham. Peierls had known of Fuchs for some time, and a close camaraderie developed between the two refugees. Peierls was much older and became a father figure for Fuchs, who transferred to Birmingham and worked intimately with Peierls.[15] Fuchs became an affectionately regarded and unofficial member of the older scientist's family. Fuchs's perfidy was also a betrayal of Peierls's trust in Fuchs and Peierls's family's love of Fuchs. It added a personal dimension to the fabric of treachery that the young scientist perpetrated on his country and his friends during the next eight years.

For Fuchs now became a British citizen. It suited his purpose and it suited the purposes of his Communist directors. In June of 1942, Fuchs secured two sponsors and took an oath of allegiance to the Crown.[16] Just a month before, Fuchs had signed the customary security undertaking at the University of Birmingham, apparently the only such document that Fuchs was ever called upon to sign. On both occasions Fuchs lied. His allegiance remained what it had always been: to his Communist apparatus. For the next eight years, while Fuchs was rising through the ranks of atomic scientists in the United States and Britain, he maintained continuous contact with Communist couriers, supplying them with a greater wealth of scientific information than had ever before passed from spy to courier.

In December 1943, Fuchs went to the United States, as did Peierls, to work in the newly formed Manhattan District Project, the effort begun a year before, which controlled development of the atomic bomb. Fuchs lived in New York from December 1943 until August 1944 and worked in laboratories at Columbia University.

And, also, in mid-winter in early 1944, Fuchs bounced a tennis ball on a street on the Lower East Side of New York City and met his fat American courier, Harry Gold.

British treatment of its atomic scientists was very different from that of American officials. The leading British scientists were free to roam at large over the entire spectrum of atomic research carried on in the United Kingdom.[17] The purpose of this freedom was to encourage the free exchange of ideas that the British called on for their contribution to the bomb. The American security philosophy was quite different. It largely came from a stolid, stout Army officer, General Leslie Groves, who became the senior officer in charge of the Manhattan District Project soon after it was created. Groves never quite understood the spirited, independent academicians he had technical charge of. But he was an Army man and he understood what security required. Accordingly, the Manhattan District was compartmentalized; its scientists were restricted (as far as this was possible) to a need-to-know range of technical information surrounding their own specific labor. It was an Army man's attempt to try and cope with the free spirit of the men who were working on the biggest military secret of all time.

Curiously, an exception to the compartmentalization was made for British scientists at work in the United States. And following an agreement between the two governments in 1943, there were a number of leading British scientists at work in the Manhattan District. Peierls and Fuchs were two—and to the great discomfort of all those who learned the true facts about Fuchs in 1950, Fuchs was given access to all technical information, no matter whence it came within the Manhattan District.[18] He could look at anything, and did. And, of course, he reported it all to his Soviet masters.

By far the most important secret that he passed on was the monumental step toward the bomb achieved when the Americans developed the gaseous diffusion process for isolating uranium-235, the explosive used in the bomb. The precious U-235 had to be isolated from the vastly more abundant U-238. In the first two years of the project, the major obstacle appeared to be the isolation of enough U-235 to place in a usable explosive. Only U-235 would develop a chain reaction; in lay terms, only U-235 would explode. But it was exceedingly hard to produce. There were three laboratory techniques for isolating the U-235 known at the beginning of the war: electromagnetic, centrifuge, and gaseous diffusion. The failure of Germany to develop a bomb can be ascribed to a large extent to their persistence in the first two techniques, which never succeeded. But gaseous diffusion worked. The Americans developed it and from it produced U-235 in amounts sufficient for the A-bomb used at Hiroshima. Fuchs was right in the middle of this development. He passed on all of its technical data to the Soviets.[19] The significance of these disclosures was overwhelming. To understand why this was so, some details of the process should be explained.

Development of chain-reacting U-235 from relatively plentiful U-238 is like diamond mining, except that it is all done in laboratories and plants equipped with the most sophisticated and expensive equipment known to Western science. It is not an exaggeration to state that hundreds of millions of dollars were expended by the United States in the development of the gaseous diffusion process. A very great part of that money was spent in perfecting it so that small amounts of the exceedingly rare, enriched, pure U-235 would be produced. That volume, in the case of each individual U.S. bomb, had to be enough to reach critical mass so that a chain reaction would occur. After spending those hundreds of millions of dollars in the middle of the war, after harnessing American and British scientific resources and the awesome industrial resources of the United States to perfect the gaseous diffusion process, the Americans achieved success. Because of Klaus Fuchs, the Soviets got massive technical information on gaseous diffusion for nothing. To be sure, the Soviets then had to build their plants. But the mammoth expenditure of funds required to perfect the process amounting to those hundreds of millions of dollars was cut into a fraction by Fuchs. Fuchs delivered information on gaseous diffusion to the Soviets that, quite literally, was of priceless value. He did so when the process was perfected to a degree that it was capable of producing enough U-235 for a workable bomb within weeks of Fuchs's betrayal.

Moreover, Fuchs not only handed over scientific details of the perfected process in mid-1945, but he kept the Soviets abreast of all the developments leading to the achievement of an efficient U-235-producing process in the preceding four years. This gave the Soviets another great advantage: they knew where the problems, the "bugs," in the process were located; they knew how the bugs had been eliminated and could install the gaseous diffusion process—as they did—with confidence that it would not only produce U-235 for bombs, but that it also could do so without the fear of a disabling breakdown.[20]

It was a vastly complicated procedure. U-235 differs from U-238 in its lighter molecular weight. The difference is so minute that ordinary methods of diffusing or separating the molecules will not work. To screen the molecules of the lighter U-235 from the heavier molecules of U-238, great quantities of the more plentiful U-238, pure uranium, as it is found in nature and then refined, are rendered into a gaseous state. This process of converting metal into gas involves a technology using extremely high temperatures and pressures under difficult control conditions. Once converted, the gaseous uranium is then forced through a series of porous membranes under high pressure. The theory is that the heavier molecules of U-238 will move more slowly through the membranes and will slowly separate themselves from the lighter molecules of U-235. To do so in any effective way, miles of tubes containing these porous membranes must be used. These tremendously elongated tubes containing the porous membranes are called "cascades." The gradation of the uranium molecules is so slight that several thousand successive stages of passage of the uranium gas through the membranes must be used to produce a minute quantity of the lighter residue, U-235. All the miles of tubing must be enclosed in an airtight container called a "diffuser." To illustrate the sophistication of the separation process, each membrane through which the uranium gas is forced must contain a vast number of microscopic holes bored into it. In order to trap the lighter U-235, the membranes must contain millions of these microscopic openings per square inch. Miles of these are involved, all in tubelike passages enclosed in the airtight diffuser.

The problem of the welds in these tubes, so as to insure absolute airtightness, was immense. The air pumps, the coolants used to prevent the high pressures and the high temperatures of the diffusion process from exploding and destroying itself, absorbed hundreds of scientists for years. The American effort in gaseous diffusion was divided into two parts: the so-called SAM group and the group that was installed at the Kellex Corporation. Although Fuchs was nominally attached to the Kellex group (and after the return of Professor Peierls to England in 1941, Fuchs headed this group), it was typical of the omnipresence of British scientists in the Manhattan District that Fuchs was intimate with both groups. The chief of the SAM group, Karl Cohn, later described Fuchs's knowledge of the SAM work as "enormous," adding that "one would have to search diligently in the records of treason to find a case more far-reaching and of permanent effect."[21] The head of the Kellex group, Manson Benedict, was more graphic: "[Fuchs] was in possession of information which, if transmitted to the Russians, would have saved them years of development effort."[22] It was and it did.

*　　*　　*

Therein lies the significance of what Fuchs did for his masters. There is grave doubt that the Soviet Union, expending its lifeblood in battle to survive the Nazi invasion, would have been able to put together the industrial know-how to create a workable gaseous diffusion process at all until after the Nazi defeat in 1945. Starting in 1945 meant starting four years after the Americans had started, and starting with an industrial plant that was substantially wrecked by the invaders.

Gaseous diffusion of U-235 was as much an industrial triumph as it was a scientific feat for Americans. As such, its achievement was a mass achievement of the Manhattan District Project and not that of one man, Klaus Fuchs. Thousands of Americans worked on gaseous diffusion; millions of 1940–45 U.S. dollars were spent on it. The breadth of the industrial achievement involved hundreds, if not thousands, of industrial breakthroughs. No one man, not even Klaus Fuchs, could conceivably be privy to all of these accomplishments.

Moreover, it is clear from what we know of the wartime history of Soviet nuclear science (as outlined in a later section) that the theory of gaseous diffusion was thoroughly known to the Soviets, who had expert nuclear scientists at their disposal.

But it must never be forgotten that in 1944 and 1945, when Fuchs made his major disclosures, the Soviets were directing all of their industrial resources to the defeat of the Nazis using conventional methods of warfare. Soviet records themselves reflect that very little was left over to develop an atomic bomb, which the Russians knew in theory could be built.

Accordingly, everything that Cohn and Manson said of Fuchs's exploits remains true. Instead of beginning gaseous diffusion in 1945, instead of beginning the process with an industrial capacity battered by the most destructive force in history, instead of being forced through years of slow trial, slow error, toward eventual success, the Soviets were handed key industrial secrets of the gaseous diffusion process intact, operative and immensely useful in producing U-235 in quantities large enough for an atomic bomb, by Klaus Fuchs in his conduct that culminated in September 1945. How much time did the Soviets gain from the Americans because of Fuchs? No one can be sure.

Perhaps the most precise measurement is that of Manson Benedict, who was close enough to Fuchs and his conduct inside the Manhattan District Project to provide an educated measurement. Benedict's view is that Fuchs saved the Soviets "years of development effort."

We know that the Soviets were delighted with Fuchs's disclosures. Their delight and what we have learned since indicate that Soviet science and industry were already at work, but far behind the United States in 1945. That gap closed almost totally when Fuchs's final disclosures were made in 1945 and 1946. And since all experimentation leading to successful production of bomb-size quantities of U-235 became wholly unnecessary, the Soviets took giant steps forward and exploded their own bomb in September of 1949.

As every scientist who ever commented on Fuchs had agreed, Fuchs's betrayal had monumental significance. It shortened the U.S. monopoly in atomic weaponry to four years. It gave the Soviets the ultimate weapon at the beginning of the Cold War. And as highly knowledgeable Americans have commented, it was an act of Olympian perfidy, felt across the world and for many years. The Joint Committee on Atomic Energy report states:

It is hardly an exaggeration to say that Fuchs alone has influenced the safety of more people and accomplished greater damage than any other spy not only in the history of the United States but in the history of nations.[23]

No David Greenglass could approach the scientific comprehension required to do what Fuchs had done. In cold fact, Greenglass's treachery was of another order, as knowledgeable scientists have contended with near uniformity. It took the rhetoric of Judge Irving Kaufman to elevate Greenglass's treachery (and treachery it was, even of a different order) to that perpetrated on the West by Klaus Fuchs.

It is a strange and almost impossible speculation: the question of who is more guilty, whose sin is more egregious and deserves less compassion than other sinners and criminals. Yet judges do it all the time. The meting out of sentences is precisely that exercise. "To make the punishment fit the crime," says the Mikado in Gilbert and Sullivan. Judges have done this since Western law began.

All of Fuchs's misdeeds were a matter of record before Judge Kaufman when he sentenced Julius and Ethel Rosenberg to death. Fuchs's sentence (fourteen years, the maximum that a British judge can impose for violation of the Official Secrets Act) was a matter of public record. The scientific community knew as well then as it does today the awful perfidy of Fuchs as well as the far lesser dimensions of what David Greenglass did. Not a word of this was given to Kaufman. The American scientific community might have feared putting the details of Fuchs's disclosures before an American court. But Bloch never made any attempt to do so. When Kaufman spoke of Greenglass's betrayal as putting the bomb in the hands of the Soviets, he may really have thought that this was true. It was not, far from it.

If Fuchs had not betrayed the gaseous diffusion process and perhaps a good deal more (for Fuchs was never confined to gaseous diffusion in his roamings over the secrets of the Manhattan District, could meander almost at will over the entire atomic bomb project, collect precious scientific data, and give it away), the Soviets would not have paid much attention to David Greenglass. There is, indeed, evidence that Fuchs provided the Soviets with the concept of a lens mold used in the plutonium bomb dropped on Nagasaki—developed by the scientists at Los Alamos—which was simply confirmed by Greenglass's subsequent sketches,[24] drawn with the crudeness of a machinist who knew little or nothing about implosion or any other triggering device.

In proper perspective, Fuchs was—for the Soviets—the Nobel of atomic weaponry. Fuchs provided the Soviets with invaluable scientific data on the greatest explosive device in history. Fuchs gave them the greatest explosive device in history and saved them years of experimentation and mountains of money that the postwar Soviets might never have been able to commit to the task. And if the Soviets did, the date of the atomic parity would have been years after 1949. How many years? No one knows. But these were vital years in U.S. foreign policy. Major portions of the Cold War would have been battled on the diplomatic fronts of the world with the United States holding a monopoly in atomic weaponry. What that would have meant to Dean Acheson and John Foster Dulles is for historians to tell us.

And in all this, what was David Greenglass? To the Soviets, he was at most a draftsman working in Alfred Nobel's machine shop. His rough design for a lens mold for the new weapon had value, but trained nuclear scientists had to address this problem, not a machinist. And first there had to be a bomb.

Fuchs and Gold were orderly in their drops. There were more meetings in New York after the two men had established contact on the cold winter night on the Lower East Side.[25] In mid-June, they met again at Woodside in Queens and Fuchs promised Gold that he would deliver to him a design of the atomic bomb. At the end of June, they met near Borough Hall in Brooklyn and Fuchs turned over designs that he had prepared. In July, the two met in Central Park and were together for an hour and a half in a stroll through the park.[26]

Then the meetings stopped. In their last meeting in July, in Central Park, Fuchs had agreed to meet with Gold at the Brooklyn Museum with a backup plan to meet back in Central Park if the Brooklyn meeting was aborted.[27] Gold always provided for a backup meeting in case he felt he was being followed to the first meeting. But Fuchs missed both meetings. Gold became disturbed and did something very foolish for a courier. He went to Fuchs's apartment on West Seventy-seventh Street and asked the doorman if anything had happened to Fuchs. He was told simply that Fuchs had gone away.[28]

Gold became so distracted that he reported Fuchs's disappearance to his Soviet chief, Anatoli Yakovlev, on the Soviet consulate staff in New York. Yakovlev then went through his dossier on Fuchs and found Fuchs's sister's address in Cambridge, Massachusetts, where she was living with her husband. Kristal Fuchs could tell Gold only that her brother had gone off "somewhere in the Southwest." But Kristal Fuchs did say that her brother would be visiting with her and her family in Cambridge the following Christmas. Gold gave Kristal Fuchs a telephone number—again breaking courier practice—and told her to ask her brother to call him at Christmastime.[29]

Fuchs had, in fact, been transferred to Los Alamos along with his mentor, Professor Peierls, who had returned from England. When Fuchs visited Cambridge in January of 1945, he dutifully telephoned Gold and arranged to meet with him in Cambridge. They met at Fuchs's sister's flat. There Fuchs told Gold a great deal about the new explosive device and what it could do. The description was quite broad and Gold was impressed. He asked Fuchs to put all this on paper and Fuchs agreed.

Days later, Fuchs and Gold met again in downtown Boston. Fuchs had transcribed most of his oral disclosures onto paper. He described (in his papers) the plutonium bomb in contrast to the earlier conceived U-235 bomb, and Fuchs described in detail—in papers given to Gold in January of 1945—the implosion lens that would be used in detonating the plutonium bomb.[30] Gold was very curious about these details and pressed Fuchs for more. Fuchs promised more, and agreed to deliver the next shipment of data to Gold at the Castillo Bridge in Santa Fe, New Mexico, at four o'clock in the afternoon on the first Saturday in June 1945.[31]

Since Julius and Ethel Rosenberg were executed for disclosure of information concerning the implosion lens to the Soviets, a comparison of what Fuchs disclosed and what Greenglass disclosed, and when each made the disclosures, becomes relevant.

At some time in January 1945, Fuchs had his two meetings with Gold in Boston. Out of them came written details of the implosion lens, from Fuchs, a scientist who understood every detail of the bomb from the nature of the explosive through how it was manufactured down to the process by which it was detonated. In that same month, 230 miles south, David Greenglass, on leave from Los Alamos, met with Julius Rosenberg in the first of three disclosures made by Greenglass. Greenglass made a series of sketches of the lens mold that he had been working on in his machine shop in Los Alamos and gave them to Rosenberg, along with a list of possible recruits for espionage at the Los Alamos site.[32] But Greenglass's description was that of a

machinist with no knowledge of what the lens mold could be used
for. The testimony at trial is quite clear: it was Julius Rosenberg,
not David Greenglass, who knew that an atomic bomb was being
prepared at Los Alamos. It was Julius Rosenberg who told David
Greenglass this vital information in January of 1945, not vice
versa.[33] Whatever information Greenglass gave Rosenberg was a
machinist's version of a sophisticated scientific imploding device
far better described to Harry Gold days earlier by a scientist who
fully understood what it was being used for; Greenglass had not
the first clue about its use until Rosenberg told *him*. And, quite
clearly, Rosenberg's information had first come (via Harry Gold)
from Fuchs.

How did these disclosures fit into the larger picture of what
was really happening at Los Alamos? It is not easy to complete
this picture because forty-four years later, all the details of the
production of the bomb are not clear in information available to
the public. But a good deal is. It has been published in a series of
technical histories, of which *The Secret History of the Atomic Bomb,*
edited by Anthony Cave Brown and Charles B. McDonald,
is one.

David Hawkins (who wrote the history of the Los Alamos
project in the Brown-McDonald book and was the official
historian of the Los Alamos installation) discloses that late in 1944
the designs for a series of lens molds were "frozen."[34] This meant
that the authorities at Los Alamos made a decision that this design
was it: the project would go forward with a particular lens mold
design rather than alternative basic designs. This design concept
was, thus, the information that Fuchs disclosed to Gold in Boston
and, almost simultaneously, Greenglass put in his sketch for Julius
Rosenberg in New York City. But the historians add an additional fact that is quite relevant. The problems in making the lens
mold design workable within the bomb remained immense from
late 1944 through the middle of July in 1945. Five new buildings
for lens testing were constructed at Los Alamos between December 1944 and March 1945. Engineering on perfecting the lens
mold had become a bottleneck,[35] whose solution in 1945 the
historians describe as "one of the primary accomplishments of the
period."[36] It was much more than giving a series of lens molds to

a machinist and asking him to machine them down. Fuchs was a major scientific participant in this breakthrough. Greenglass drew rough and inaccurate layman's sketches of experiments along the way. Therein lies the difference between what Fuchs understood and what Greenglass sketched. That difference is relevant to what each gave away.

The critical nature of this engineering increased as the days in 1945 passed, long after the disclosure in January. At Los Alamos, there was literally a crash program in development of the lens molds. The historians add: "Even so, the bottleneck remained, and it was only a matter of days that enough final full-scale lens-molds were obtained for the Trinity test."[37]

That test occurred in the New Mexico desert on July 16, 1945. What both Fuchs and Greenglass had disclosed six months earlier had been thoroughly modified in the intervening time to make the implosion device workable inside a bomb. And, of course, Greenglass, in January, had not known that it was to be used in a bomb until Rosenberg told him.

The next episode of spying in tandem occurred in June of 1945. Again, the common ingredient in both meetings was the fat little courier, Harry Gold. He met Fuchs first, at the designated spot on the Castillo Bridge in Sante Fe. Gold arrived first. Fuchs drew up a few minutes later in his Buick. They were together only a short time. Fuchs again gave Gold a batch of papers.[38] Fuchs told Gold that tremendous progress had occurred on the bomb, and that a test explosion would take place in the desert near Alamogordo during the following month, July. Gold and Fuchs agreed that the next meeting would be near a church just outside Santa Fe on September 19.

Gold then went back to the bus station in Santa Fe and took the bus to Albuquerque, sixty miles from Santa Fe. It was on this trip to visit the Greenglasses that Gold identified himself with a section of the Jell-O box that fit exactly with another section that Julius Rosenberg had given Greenglass in New York the preceding January.[39] Rosenberg had told Greenglass that the courier would use the sections of the Jell-O box to identify himself. He did so on June 2 at the Greenglass apartment in Albuquerque. At the Rosenberg trial, Greenglass described what he then did and told Gold:

Q. Tell us exactly what you did.
A. I got out some 8 by 10 ruled white paper, and I drew some sketches of a lens mold and how they are set up in an experiment, and I gave descriptive material that gives a description of this experiment.
Q. Was this another step in the same experiment on atomic energy concerning which you had given a sketch to Rosenberg?
A. That is right, and I also gave him a list of possible recruits for espionage.[40]

Immediately thereafter, Greenglass repeated that these sketches and descriptive material "concerned" experimentation on the atomic bomb. Clearly nothing had been finalized about the lens mold by the first week of June. We know from the historians that the redesigning of the detonating device went on to within days of the July 16 test explosion. Greenglass's contribution to the Soviet store of knowledge on June 2 was defined by the following colloquy, this time between Judge Kaufman and Greenglass:

Q. Were there constant experiments going on?
A. Constant.
Q. And the sketches in 6 and 7 [copies made by Greenglass of what he had given Gold on June 2, 1945] were what were considered an advance on these sketches marked as Government's "Exhibit 2"? [Copies made by Greenglass of what he had given Julius Rosenberg in January of 1945.]
A. Yes.
Q. Well, let us eliminate the "advanced"; they were just another step?
A. That is right.[41]

By the beginning of June of 1945, Greenglass had sketched the lens mold for the Soviets (without knowing how it was to be used) and had then sketched an "advance" made in the continuing experimentation on it. Fuchs, on the other hand, had given a detailed description of the same device to the Soviets five months earlier, and had related it to the overall design of the bomb. There is evidence that the June discussion between Fuchs and Gold included talk of the lens mold, but details are inconclusive.

*　　*　　*

The third episode in simultaneous disclosure to the Soviets took place in September of 1945. Greenglass was back in New York then on another furlough from his activities at Los Alamos. This time the intermediary was Julius Rosenberg. Greenglass's testimony at trial was that what he disclosed in September had more to do with the overall nature of the Nagasaki bomb—the plutonium bomb dropped by the U.S. Air Force on Nagasaki in August of 1945—which differed substantially from the bomb that Julius Rosenberg had described to Greenglass eight months earlier. But Greenglass then repeated his description of the lens mold to Rosenberg, and again drew a sketch of it. He also delivered a batch of papers, in Fuchs's style, to the interested, solicitous Rosenberg. These papers, Greenglass recalled on the stand, dealt with the final structure of the bomb, the various compartments that were built into it, and the dynamics of how it was detonated. Greenglass proffered a cross-section sketch of the plutonium bomb.[42]

The government had a few doubts of its own concerning the importance of the testimony (wholly apart from what Fuchs had disclosed—which never was mentioned once during the Rosenberg trial). In the Rosenberg trial, the prosecution brought Walter Koski, a professor at Johns Hopkins University, to the stand. Koski was one of the scientists at Los Alamos who had worked on the implosion lens. He was put on the stand to tell the jury just how significant the sketches made by Greenglass were in the total order of things at Los Alamos. On cross-examination, Emanuel Bloch felt he was on to something and asked:

Q. Well, let us satisfy everybody, I will tell you what I am driving at, Dr. Koski: Is it not a fact that scientists would not consider Government's Exhibits 2, 6, and 7 [the Greenglass sketches], whether or not two of them relate to a lens and one of them relates to some kind of cylindrical apparatus, until the scientists knew the dimensions of the lens or the cylindrical apparatus?

A. This is a rough sketch and of course is not quantitative but it does illustrate the important principle involved.

Q. It does, however, omit the dimensions?

A. It does omit dimensions.

Q. [by the Court] You say it does, however, set forth the important principles involved, is that correct?

A. Correct.

Q. [by the Court] Can you tell us what that principle is?

A. The principle is the use of a combination of high explosives of appropriate shape to produce a symmetrical converging detonation wave.

Q. Now, weren't the dimensions of these lens molds very vital or at least very important with respect to their utility in terms of the success in your experiments?

A. The physical over-all dimensions that you mention are not important. It is the relative dimensions that are.

Q. Now the relative dimensions are not disclosed, are they, by these exhibits?

A. They are not.[43]

What the court and jury were being told was that the significance of the Greenglass disclosures was their "illustration of the important principles involved." But that principle, described as "the use of a combination of high explosives of appropriate shape to produce a symmetrical converging detonation wave"[44] described nothing more or less than the phenomenon of implosion using some form of lens mold. Fuchs had disclosed that principle to Gold in January 1945, six months before the Greenglass disclosures of June 1945, and contemporaneous with Greenglass's sketching of the device for Julius Rosenberg without even knowing it was to be used in a bomb.

In September 1945, there was also a Fuchs-Gold meeting as previously arranged, near a church on the road out of Santa Fe. It was a long meeting. Fuchs delivered to Gold a fat package of written information. In it, he set forth the size of the bomb—a vital point only guessed at by Greenglass, who, of course, had to guess, while Fuchs knew.[45] Fuchs also gave Gold a description of each of the parts of the bomb, setting forth dimensions. The written material included what the substance in the bomb was, how the bomb had been put together, and, most importantly in relation to the Greenglass disclosures, a scientific discussion of how it had been detonated. It was a scientist's report in contrast to a machinist's speculation. It was, indeed, the whole works.[46]

In addition, Fuchs spoke glowingly of the Alamogordo explosion on July 16. Fuchs told Gold it could be seen more than two hundred miles away.[47] On the negative side, Fuchs told Gold that the security people had finally intervened to deny him anything except on a need-to-know basis. He told Gold that the spirit of cooperation between the American and British scientists had eroded to distrust, a note that Gold may well have passed on to his superiors, precipitating later action by them.[48] Finally, Fuchs told Gold he was being transferred back to England.

Gold then made arrangements with Fuchs for contact with a courier in London. Fuchs seemed disturbed about the future. He feared that his father might surface in England and leak facts about Fuchs's Communist record in Germany before the war. Finally, the capture of Kiel by the British scared Fuchs. He told Gold that this might lead to uncovering his past.[49]

This meeting was the last that Fuchs and Gold ever had.

Greenglass later testified to the security provisions at Los Alamos that graphically placed himself near the bottom of the pecking order of personnel within the project. He testified that the scientists on the project wore white badges. The "White Badges" knew practically everything.[50] Fuchs was a "White Badge," singularly enhanced by the freedom that British "White Badges" possessed to roam unchecked through the scientific data within the Manhattan District Project. Wearers of blue badges, however, were something very different. Greenglass testified: "Now, the blue badge was the one you were supposed to wear if you could know what you were working on but nothing further."[51]

Greenglass was obviously a "Blue Badge." That he knew more is testimony to his ability to get around the security precautions. But he never had the ambit of a scientist, never understood what the scientists did, and never could betray what a scientist could. That is especially true if that scientist was Klaus Fuchs.

Nothing of the significance of Klaus Fuchs's disclosures in comparison with Greenglass's was mentioned during the Rosenberg trial. There was no testimony regarding the substance of or gravity of what Fuchs had done. And no one ever argued this point to Judge Kaufman.

The broad provisions of the Espionage Act of 1917 were clearly violated by what David Greenglass did. But the significance of what Greenglass betrayed through Julius and Ethel Rosenberg, in comparison with what the Soviets had already learned from a far more rewarding source, Klaus Fuchs, makes Judge Kaufman's sentence a repudiation of hard facts. Those facts were available when Judge Kaufman sentenced Julius and Ethel Rosenberg. He was never given them. Foremost among them are two: It was Klaus Fuchs and not David Greenglass who gave the Soviets major secrets of the bomb; and Klaus Fuchs—whose betrayal of the West was catastrophic in comparison with Greenglass's transgressions—was sentenced to imprisonment of fourteen years.

A caveat is required here. Fuchs's confession to the British in the Bow Street Court was simply a recognition of the disclosure of information in violation of the British Official Secrets Act. What that information was did not become public with the confession or incarceration of Fuchs. But the American scientific community, and certainly those scientists who had worked at Los Alamos, knew full well in April of 1951 precisely how devastating Fuchs's spying had been. Those same scientists were perfectly capable of testifying how insignificant, by comparison, Greenglass's disclosures were. Before April 5, 1951, when the Rosenbergs were sentenced, these scientists were qualified and, with near unanimity, willing to testify that Fuchs may have "given the Soviets the bomb"; but that Greenglass was incapable of doing anything remotely comparable. Why this testimony was not put before Kaufman is another of the continuing mysteries of this case.

Regardless of this caveat, it seems entirely clear today that it was Klaus Fuchs who gave away the major technological information involved in producing the bomb. Greenglass knew nothing of this. On a lesser level, it was Fuchs who provided the scientific details of how the plutonium bomb was detonated. Greenglass may also have done so; but Greenglass's contribution was to illustrate for the Soviets the principle of implosion. Fuchs had done that eight months before.

All of Judge Kaufman's rhetoric was misapplied. Greenglass was guilty of a major crime, but not the crime that Kaufman accused him of. Klaus Fuchs was. It was a gross miscarriage of justice to execute the Rosenbergs for disclosing what Fuchs had already given to the Soviets. The miscarriage was aggravated because Fuchs's disclosures were so significant and Greenglass's betrayals had become—because of what Fuchs had done—little more than scientific redundancies. All of this information was available to the Rosenberg defense team before the Rosenbergs were sentenced.* None of it was put before Kaufman before he passed sentence.

If all of this information was available to the Rosenberg defense and none of it was argued to Kaufman, does the judge bear any onus for the miscarriage? He does. It was Judge Kaufman who accused the Rosenbergs of putting the bomb in Russian hands years before scientists predicted they would have it. The judge made this determination by himself. No one on the witness stand told him so.[52] It was an utterly false conclusion. Kaufman must bear responsibility for it alone.†

---

* There were major problems in outsiders (such as Bloch) even communicating with atomic scientists in 1951. Approval from the AEC was required for such communication. Regardless of the difficulties involved, the testimony of the scientists was relevant during the trial and crucial for sentencing. The fact is, notwithstanding the difficulties in securing this testimony, the Rosenberg defense neither produced any of the scientists nor put on record the government's constraints that made it difficult to do so. It is not clear today that the scientists (or the government) could have successfully resisted a subpoena by the defense. Bloch's failure to take these steps is consistent with his inexplicable motion to suppress Greenglass's supposed "sketch" of the lens. While consistent with each other, both tactical moves made no sense in 1951 and less today.

† Beyond the scope of this book but very much a concern to all of the Western allies was Fuchs's extensive knowledge of the thermonuclear device—the H-bomb. No less an authority on the H-bomb than Dr. Edward Teller acknowledges that Fuchs was a brilliant scientist from whom Teller himself learned a great deal. Teller also acknowledges that Fuchs made a substantial contribution to the development of our own hydrogen bomb. It must be assumed that all of Fuchs's knowledge of the thermonuclear bomb was turned over to the Soviets. (Interview with Stanley Blumberg, biographer of Dr. Edward Teller, December 20, 1988)

Bruno Pontecorvo and Allan Nunn May

Two other scientists must be examined briefly if any full perspective of the gravity of David Greenglass's disclosures to the Soviets can be made. The two scientists are important because another arm of the American government has itself ranked these two scientists (along with Fuchs and David Greenglass) in the infamous pantheon of atomic spies. For all of them, Fuchs, Greenglass, and the two additional scientists, Bruno Pontecorvo and Allan Nunn May, betrayed their country and the United States–United Kingdom alliance on behalf of the USSR, and did so at about the same time. What Pontecorvo and May did is relevant in comparative terms: How serious were their derelictions, and what happened to them?

Bruno Pontecorvo was a brilliant Italian physicist.[53] He studied in the new field of atomic science at universities in Rome and in Paris before the war. When the Nazis invaded France in May of 1940, Pontecorvo escaped through Spain to the United States. First he was employed by an American oil firm in Oklahoma, and then, when his training and reputation became known to the authorities at the Manhattan District, Pontecorvo was assigned to the atomic energy team working at McGill University. He was then assigned to the atomic energy project at Chalk River, Canada, and stayed there through 1948. In that year, Pontecorvo became a British citizen. In the same year, Pontecorvo returned to England and became the principal scientific officer at Harwell Laboratory, the chief atomic research facility in the United Kingdom.

Pontecorvo's major contribution to the development of the bomb lay in the development of production techniques for generation of plutonium. Plutonium became a major source of fissionable material for explosive use, rivaling U-235 and then duplicating U-235 after the Hiroshima bomb. The Nagasaki bomb was a plutonium bomb. The American plant at Hanford, Washington, which produced (and still produces) plutonium, drew heavily on design research led by Pontecorvo. Pontecorvo also did a considerable amount of research on the heavy-water technique for isolating U-235 from U-238.

More significant and disturbing was Pontecorvo's pioneering work—before 1940—on tritium, the raw material used in the manufacture of the hydrogen bomb. Pontecorvo, like Fuchs, held knowledge that crossed into development of both the atomic and hydrogen bombs.

Pontecorvo never had any direct contact with the design of the atomic bomb. His work was one step removed, at the level of scientific research into fissionable (and later fusionable) materials for use in the explosives in the atomic and hydrogen bomb. Pontecorvo was a scientist of first rank. Some of his scientific associates in Canada believed Pontecorvo of higher rank than Klaus Fuchs because Pontecorvo was an innovator, possessed of a mentality that broke through scientific frontiers on the way to new and more powerful weapons.

In the late 1950s, Canadian and American security officials came to believe that Pontecorvo was in direct contact with Soviet couriers in Canada from 1943 onward. In September of 1950, Pontecorvo, his wife, and their three children disappeared while on a European vacation. They had gone from France to Sweden and then to Finland, and then to Moscow during that month. In Moscow, Pontecorvo holds a major scientific post and is an honored member of the Soviet scientific community.

Allan Nunn May was a lesser light, but still of considerable scientific importance. May was a natural-born British scientist, who joined the British atomic effort in the spring of 1942.[54] May was posted first at Cavendish in England and then, in January of 1943, was transferred to the Anglo-Canadian atomic research team at McGill University in Montreal.

Like all of the British scientists, May was eclectic in his knowledge of the wartime atomic energy project. He visited the reactor pile in Chicago on many occasions; he understood the nature of the plutonium production problems, and had a working knowledge of what was transpiring at Oak Ridge and Hanford without being intimately involved in either project on a working basis.

In late 1944 or early 1945, May met a Soviet military officer in

Montreal and began betraying what he knew. He did so regularly, writing comprehensive reports to his Soviet couriers, reports that covered everything that he knew about the multifaceted atomic energy effort, which, as a British scientist, May was uniquely privileged to receive and which he assiduously proceeded to pass on to his courier.

In the last days of 1945, a Soviet code clerk, Igor Gouzenko, at the Soviet embassy in Ottawa, attempted to defect to the Canadian authorities. For days, Gouzenko was ignored as a crank. Finally, Gouzenko convinced the Canadians that he was what he purported to be. Gouzenko took with him a number of papers that incriminated others. One of those who was incriminated was Allan Nunn May. Upon arrest in England (where he had become a lecturer at Kings College, Cambridge, in September 1945), May disclosed that he had been a Communist before the war and had retained his allegiance to the Party throughout. May confessed and was sentenced to ten years at the Wakefield Prison in Yorkshire.

Fuchs, Pontecorvo, May, and Greenglass were all brothers in infamy. The brotherhood, as do most, has degrees of un-worthiness. Two arms of the American government declared themselves on who stood where in this ladder of crime. One was a judge in New York, Irving Kaufman, pronouncing a death sentence without benefit of any scientific information relevant to the crime of atomic spying on which he was passing judgment. The other was a committee of the Congress, the Joint Committee on Atomic Energy, speaking with the benefit of all such information. The contrast in these findings is noteworthy.

The second arm of the American government very interested in the Rosenberg case in April of 1951, the month in which Judge Kaufman sentenced the Rosenbergs to death, was the newly created Joint Committee on Atomic Energy of the Congress. In that month, the staff of the committee prepared an appraisal of the damage done to the U.S. atomic energy program during the war by the series of betrayers whose spying had been confirmed. And there was, indeed, quite a number.

The committee study is a public document. It examines the history of atomic espionage as it had become known to American authorities from the trials and defections beginning with Nunn May and ending with the Rosenbergs. The committee study was circulated after the Rosenberg trial was completed. The study quotes liberally from the Rosenberg transcript.

Although the purpose of the committee study was not to rank atomic spies, it did precisely that. And it made this ranking with greater understanding of the scientific importance of the various spies' disclosures than anyone ever attempted. The Joint Committee had available to it the vast resources of its scientific consultants, the facilities of the Atomic Energy Commission, and excerpts from the files of the FBI. It knew more about the details of atomic spying than anyone sitting in Judge Kaufman's courtroom, far more than the judge himself.

In the foreword to the study, the committee states its conclusion regarding the relative importance of the atomic spies.

The individuals who had access to classified atomic information and who are definitely known to have conveyed such information to the Soviet Union* while employed on the project are three in number. To list them in the estimated order of their importance, they are: (1) Dr. Klaus Fuchs, the German-born British scientist who worked at the key Oak Ridge, Tenn., process laboratory during World War II; (2) Dr. Allan Nunn May, the British scientist who was arrested and convicted in connection with the Canadian spy exposés of 1946; and (3) David Greenglass, an American citizen, who as an Army technical sergeant, performed weapons work at Los Alamos during World War II.[55]

Of Fuchs, the study stated the following:

It is little appreciated that Fuchs is not only the great betrayer of weapons data but also the great betrayer of the theory underlying the only Oak Ridge production method in use today.[56]

Fuchs, the study concludes,

took part in the making of the earliest atomic bombs; he was privy to ideas and plans for improved atomic weapons, and he possessed insight into the thinking of the period as regards the hydrogen bomb. . . . He

* Pontecorvo is treated separately.

had shipped to Russia the most sensitive information, including extensive quantitative data in written form, regarding the Oak Ridge gaseous diffusion process, the weapons work at Los Alamos, British activities at Harwell, and other projects located in the United States, Canada and the United Kingdom.[57]

The study further concludes:

It seems crystal clear that Fuchs was the most damaging [of all the spies listed in the Joint Committee report] because no information surrounding the various Los Alamos weapons center and, likewise, no information involving what is now the sole Oak Ridge production process were withheld from him; and the evidence is plain that he effectively placed in Soviet hands the data at his command.[58]

Pontecorvo's betrayal was somewhat harder to appraise because he had never been tried. But the committee study states:

In any event, as of September, 1950, the Soviets acquired in Pontecorvo not only a human storehouse of knowledge about the Anglo-American-Canadian atomic projects but also a first-rate scientific brain.[59]

Nunn May's rank as a betrayer is given him because

he worked closely with the wartime Metallurgical Laboratory in Chicago, visiting there on three occasions; and, as a result, he understood a number of the problems overcome in constructing the Hanford, Washington, plutonium piles. . . . He confessed to writing an overall report on atomic energy as known to him and transmitting it to the Soviets.[60]

Greenglass is described as:

Only he is an American citizen; and he also stands alone as the only non-scientist in the group.[61]

Of Greenglass's activities, the committee study states:

Greenglass was in a position to furnish Russia with mechanical details of bomb gadgetry and weaponeering *that might have supplemented the data divulged by a theoretical physicist such as Klaus Fuchs* (emphasis supplied).[62]

The study then supports its conclusion regarding Fuchs with the declaration:

It is hardly an exaggeration to say that Fuchs alone has influenced the safety of more people and accomplished greater damage than any other spy not only in the history of the United States but in the history of nations.[63]

The spies are then ranked:

The relative importance of the four betrayers is a matter of judgment and, in part, speculation. It seems crystal clear that Fuchs was the most damaging because no information surrounding the wartime Los Alamos weapons center and likewise, no information involving what is now the sole Oak Ridge production process were withheld from him; and the evidence is plain that he effectively placed in Soviet hands the data at his command. Pontecorvo, May and Greenglass all rank well below Fuchs in importance, and how they rank among one another is particularly speculative. It may be pointed out, however, that Pontecorvo is considered by some to be an even abler scientist than Fuchs. . . . Moreover, he has devoted himself to atomic energy problems since 1934, and the classified data known to him is fresh and recent. For these reasons, Pontecorvo may be plausibly rated as the second deadliest betrayer, though considerably less deadly than Fuchs.[64]

Then the report deals with Greenglass:

David Greenglass' ranking below the other spies is well documented.

David Greenglass was a 23-year-old machinist, with no real scientific training, during the period of his main espionage activity at Los Alamos.[65]

The theatrical quality of what Greenglass did in relation to its real worth is highlighted by the study:

The diagrams and written explanation of the Nagasaki-type atomic bomb that he gave to courier Harry Gold have a theatrical quality and, at first glance, may seem the most damaging single act committed by any of the main betrayers. But, on one occasion, Greenglass met with a Russian official in New York and was asked to supply a mathematical formula concerning high-explosive lenses used in the Nagasaki weapon. Not being a scientist, Greenglass lacked capacity to furnish this information—although, in all probability, Klaus Fuchs could have and did furnish it thereafter. By the same token, the bomb sketches and explanations that Greenglass—as a virtual layman—could prepare must have counted for little compared with the quantitative data and the authoritative scientific commentary upon atomic weapons that Fuchs transmitted.[66]

The committee ranked Greenglass last among spies because

Greenglass' value to Russia in generally corroborating Fuchs' statement and perhaps in supplying miscellaneous information which Fuchs omitted is not to be discounted. It is even possible, moreover, that Greenglass—in the narrow but important field of his own work upon high explosive lens molds—was able to convey practical data and know-how beyond Fuchs' understanding. Yet, everything considered, Greenglass appears to have been the least effective of the four spies, ranking behind Allan Nunn May in this regard. Had there been no Klaus Fuchs, Greenglass would take on far greater importance.[67]

The committee study states of Greenglass:

Needless to say, this evaluation does not detract one iota from the horror of this man's crime nor lessen his legal and moral guilt.[68]

No one can deny Greenglass's guilt. But Judge Kaufman took pains to ascribe to him and to the Rosenbergs "conduct in putting into the hands of the Russians the A-bomb years before our best scientists predicted Russia would perfect the bomb."[69]

The statement was in error, total error. That statement might well have applied to Fuchs. It might well have applied to Pontecorvo. It could even have applied to Nunn May. But it could never have applied to Greenglass and therefore never to the Rosenbergs. Our own Joint Committee on Atomic Energy reached this conclusion in April of 1951, in the same month that Judge Kaufman passed sentence on the Rosenbergs. Judge Kaufman must bear responsibility for this error.

One additional and vital element of perspective must be added in order to determine whether Judge Kaufman's sentence was justified by fact, scientific or any other. And that element of perspective is provided by what American scientists who were involved in the development of the atom bomb believed the Greenglass disclosures to be, and what these same scientists were convinced that the Greenglass disclosures were not.

Obviously at the root of this question is Greenglass's testimony. Greenglass drew sketches of the implosion lens that he had worked on in the machine shop at Los Alamos and offered them into evidence. He also testified as to the operation of these implosion lenses in the plutonium bomb. Greenglass then proffered a sketch from memory of the plutonium bomb itself, and testified concerning the sketch. These were the disclosures that were made by Greenglass to the Rosenbergs that directly resulted in Judge Kaufman's sentence. The significance of these disclosures was the subject of the testimony of government witness Major John Derry, an engineer, but not a scientist.

It is striking to quote Judge Kaufman's sentencing speech in contrast to the sworn trained and expert scientific testimony that deals with the same subject: the Greenglass testimony. Judge Kaufman stated:

> But in your case, I believe that your conduct in putting into hands of the Russians the A-bomb years before our best scientists predicted Russians would perfect the bomb has already caused, in my opinion, casualties exceeding 50,000 and who knows but that millions more of innocent people may pay the price of your treason. Indeed, by your betrayal you undoubtedly have altered the course of history to the disadvantage of our country.[70]

It is unfortunate that the testimony of scientists who were involved in the development of the bomb at Los Alamos was not presented at trial before Judge Kaufman.* Certainly, after publication of the Smyth Report in 1945, there was minimal, if any, security value in the Greenglass disclosures in April of 1951. Yet, inexplicably, the Rosenbergs' own counsel, Bloch, moved to suppress the Greenglass sketches of the plutonium bomb and Greenglass's testimony concerning it on security grounds. Why Bloch did so will forever remain a mystery.

Why, too, the members of the scientific community at Los Alamos were not called in to give the lie to the importance of the

---

* As earlier noted, securing such testimony was not without difficulties in 1951. But the Rosenbergs, as criminal defendants, had certain rights to obtain it. The government may well have resisted the defense effort to subpoena the scientists, but whether it would have succeeded is very unclear. The fact is that Bloch never attempted to secure such testimony, relevant at trial and essential for proper sentencing.

Greenglass disclosures is another mystery. The fact of the matter is that three outstanding scientists, Philip Morrison, Henry Linschitz, and Harold Urey, each intimately connected with the development of the bomb and each with outstanding scientific prestige in nuclear science, did offer sworn testimony that belied the government position on the Greenglass disclosures. But this testimony came in a posttrial motion submitted by defendant Morton Sobell some fourteen years after the Rosenbergs had been executed. This sworn scientific testimony damns the government position at trial and totally destroys the factual basis for the Kaufman sentence. Fourteen years late it may be, but for any perspective of the egregious error made by Judge Kaufman in sentencing the Rosenbergs to death, the Morrison, Linschitz, and Urey affidavits are both fascinating and essential. Their conclusions are unanimous.

Morrison, an eminent physicist who served at Los Alamos throughout, stated under oath:

The entire testimony of Greenglass concerning the bomb is confused and imprecise. It is both quantitatively and qualitatively incorrect and misleading. The errors are further compounded by erroneous mislabelings of portions of the cross section [of the bomb itself].[71]

Morrison further noted that Major Derry (the government's key witness in evaluating the Greenglass disclosures)

had neither the scientific background to equip him with knowledge of the design and construction of the atomic bomb, nor was he closely associated with the technical aspects of the project.[72]

Describing Greenglass's sketch of the bomb itself, Morrison testified:

If, in truth, Major Derry had occasion to see the actual atomic bomb under development at Los Alamos "many times," as he stated, he ought to have added "and it did not look like that." In reality, such an inside view cannot be obtained. It is doubtful that such a sketch was to be found anywhere on the project, as Major Derry apparently testifies. . . . The drawing [Greenglass's sketch] was completely insufficient and could not be used for any construction purposes in that it lacked any detail.[73]

Morrison finally concluded that no scientist could perceive (from Greenglass's testimony and sketch) what the actual construction of the bomb was.[74] And Morrison's affidavit ended with his sworn statement that Greenglass's sketch was a "caricature" of the bomb rather than any true depiction.[75]

Henry Linschitz (who worked as a scientist at Los Alamos from November of 1943 on), who assembled the test bomb at Alamogordo and then moved on to the bomb assembly group at Tinian Island, summarized the Greenglass disclosures as follows:

Before bomb construction can even begin, a nation must build a full-fledged atomic energy industry and obtain an adequate supply of fissionable material. To do this unaided requires a research, development and construction effort measured in hundreds of millions of dollars. This is the major task in bomb development. Absolutely none of the requisite scientific and technological information needed for plutonium is conveyed in the Greenglass testimony or drawings introduced at the Rosenberg-Sobell trial.

The information in question purporting to describe the construction of a plutonium bomb was too incomplete, ambiguous and even incorrect to be of any service or value to the Russians in shortening the time required to develop their nuclear bombs. This conclusion is even more firmly established, in view of the information presumably given by Klaus Fuchs. The statement made by Judge Kaufman, when passing sentence on the Rosenbergs, regarding the technical importance of the information conveyed by Greenglass has no foundation in fact. Rather, it expresses a misunderstanding of the nature of modern technology, a misunderstanding which, in this case, has had tragic consequences.[76]

Harold Urey, a Nobel laureate, who was active in a variety of functions in the work of preparing materials for the bomb, stated under oath:

I have read the statements of Henry Linschitz and Philip Morrison in regard to the diagram and statements of David Greenglass and find these statements to be reasonable and convincing to me. Their statements in regard to the great complexity of the problems are certainly correct. The value of the Greenglass sketch and statement, if they were transmitted to the Soviet scientists and engineers, would be of very minor importance.[77]

Professor Urey went further:

I do not approve of transmitting any classified information to unauthorized persons but the severity of the sentences on the Rosenbergs and
Sobell were justified on the basis of the value of the information
allegedly transferred. I believe that the statements made by Linschitz and
Morrison are eminently reasonable and convincing.[78]

These affidavits, albeit fourteen years too late, state the
scientific facts concerning the Greenglass testimony. They stand
in stark contrast to the totally unsupported myths that moved
Irving Kaufman to sentence the Rosenbergs to death.

Dr. Linschitz speaks of Klaus Fuchs. Before we leave Klaus
Fuchs, a curious denouement to his spying activities occurred just
months after his conviction and then another in 1959, nine years
later. After Fuchs was convicted of violation of the Official
Secrets Act in March of 1950, his case came before a tribunal of
the Law Courts on December 20, 1950. The issue was whether
Fuchs's British citizenship should be denied not alone because of
his spying but because he had withheld vital information concerning his Communist ties when he swore allegiance to the Crown in
1938.

Fuchs's reaction to the petition of the attorney general, who
had brought the matter to the Committee of the Lords, was
singular. Although there was reason to believe that at the time of
his conviction Fuchs had recanted his communism, the strenuous
petition submitted by Fuchs on his own behalf speaks tellingly of
what Fuchs wanted his future to be. He pleaded full loyalty to the
Crown. He argued that if denial of his British citizenship was to
be deemed punishment of him, he had already been sentenced to
the maximum sentence permissible under the law—fourteen
years.[79] Moreover, Fuchs argued that the British Nationality Act
of 1948 specifically excluded punishment of the naturalized citizen
as a basis for revoking citizenship. Fuchs then went on to say that
the real issue was his present loyalty to the Crown, not his loyalty
during his spying. He stated that his disloyal conduct had ceased

in 1949, and that in his subsequent actions he had cooperated fully with the British authorities in making full disclosure to them and to the American FBI regarding his past espionage. Fuchs contended that what he had done since 1949, and particularly what he had done since his conviction, indicated quite fully where his present loyalties really lay.

Acting, however, under a provision of the act of 1948 that provided that citizenship could be revoked if "it was not conducive to the public good" to preserve it, the committee recommended that Fuchs's British citizenship be revoked. And it was.[80]

In 1959, Fuchs, having been a model prisoner, was released for good behavior. He could well have remained in England because he was now stateless. His former residence was now in East Germany and according to his beliefs as espoused in the 1950 petition, he had no desire to return there. He was not a political refugee, and could have remained on in England indefinitely.

On June 22, 1959, Fuchs boarded a Polish plane and flew to East Germany, where he joined his father in the town of Schönefeld. Until his death in 1988, he was a member of the faculty of an East German university and had eminence as a socialist scientist of the first rank.[81]

It also now appears that there is some question regarding Fuchs's cooperation with the American authorities. In this country, it was concluded that Fuchs first identified Gold. English records indicate, however, that only after the FBI showed movies of Gold to Fuchs, growing out of an investigation begun on information received from others, did Fuchs identify Gold. These records reflect that Fuchs identified Gold on the day that Gold was arrested in the States, on the information supplied by others.[82] Fuchs's dishonesty included intellectual dishonesty. He was a servant of the Soviet apparatus and remained so until his final defection—from his own statements made to the Committee of Lords nine years before—in 1959.

To Irving Kaufman, the Rosenbergs and David Greenglass represented the single leak that betrayed the bomb. What recorded history tells us is that the Klaus Fuchs, Bruno Pontecorvo, and Allan Nunn May betrayals demonstrated that Kaufman was woefully in error.

Atomic Spies Five, Six, and Seven

It might have been worse. There were no less than three other atomic spies at work at Oak Ridge, Columbia University, and Chicago whose betrayals have never been measured. Each of them, known to U.S. authorities at the time as spies, could have been as devastating to the secrecy of the bomb as was David Greenglass. These three are separate and in addition to Klaus Fuchs, Bruno Pontecorvo, and Allan Nunn May. Assuming that Fuchs, Pontecorvo, and May are ranked as offenders one, two, and three, and David Greenglass as putative offender number four (as the Joint Committee ranked him), we now have offenders five, six, and seven. Greenglass's disclosures may belong even farther down the ranking.

For this purpose, Alfred Dean Slack must at least start as spy number five. Slack was, at least, charged, tried, and convicted for his spying. It began sometime in 1936, when Slack, an engineer at the Holston Ordnance Works in Kingsport, Tennessee, began to deliver information to a courier named Richard Briggs. Slack was no Communist. He did his spying for money. This information was little more than industrial espionage while Briggs was a courier. By 1941, the Tennessee plant had been absorbed into the Manhattan District. Slack became a department supervisor in what became known as the Oak Ridge plant. That plant was the first installation that developed the process for producing U-235 by the gaseous diffusion method. Before this occurred, Richard Briggs had been replaced as Slack's courier by none other than the ubiquitous Harry Gold.

In 1943, Gold pressured and bribed Slack to deliver to him samples of "RDX," a nonnuclear explosive being developed at the plant where Slack was employed. Gold's method was much more strong-armed than his later technique in handling either Fuchs or Greenglass. He continually threatened Slack with disclosure. What Gold wanted was a sketch of the manufacturing process used to develop RDX inside the plant. He finally got it—along with samples of the explosive—from the intimidated Slack.

RDX was not nuclear material and was unconnected with the Manhattan District Project. But Slack was certainly a paid Soviet spy; he also had been employed at the Oak Ridge plant.

Slack was then caught. He was arrested on June 15, 1950, the same day the FBI picked up David Greenglass. The newspapers erroneously tried to connect the events. A federal judge in Tennessee gave Slack fifteen years for his spying activities on behalf of the Soviets. Within months, the case was forgotten.[83]

Spies six and seven will go unnamed in this narrative. They were never charged or tried. Their place in history is etched out in the published statements of the House Un-American Activities Committee, and it is for that reason that they are not named herein.[84] But the dossiers kept by that committee on six and seven are quite interesting.

Six began work as an atomic scientist—on the recommendation of a leading scientist in the Manhattan District—in the SAM laboratory in New York City. He worked on the SAM version of gaseous diffusion. Six also worked on the heavy-water alternative to gaseous diffusion in the production of U-235. From September of 1943 through April 25, 1944, Six worked at the Metallurgical Laboratory in Chicago, an advanced lab in the Manhattan District gaseous diffusion effort.

During this entire period, according to the committee's records, Six was in continued contact with one Alexander Adams, who was a Soviet courier. Adams had entered the United States fraudulently in 1938. Also during this entire period, Six held a commission in the Army reserve, a commission that Army intelligence tried (unsuccessfully) to revoke for Six's known participation in Communist party activities wholly separate from his contact with Adams. While the investigation was still pending, Six continued his work at Chicago within the Manhattan District. The Army solved Six's security problem in a curiously practical way. It got him out of the Manhattan District by calling him to active duty and making him a property control officer at White Horse, in the Yukon.

While Six was in the Yukon, Manhattan District officials found that an important notebook of data was missing. They ordered Six's residence in Chicago to be searched, unsuccessfully. Finally, the Manhattan District authorities dispatched a team to the Yukon, visited Six, and retrieved the notebook.

The saga does not end there. On the first day after Six was called into active service (April 19, 1944), Adams met with Six in Chicago, now that his usefulness to the Soviets was ended. Six then went to Cleveland and met with Spy Seven, who was then on detached duty from the metallurgical lab in Chicago, working on what the committee termed an even more secret phase of atomic activity than was proceeding at the Chicago lab. At the Cleveland meeting, which was fully reported by Seven, Six told Seven that he had agreed to provide Adams with comprehensive data regarding the bomb (identifying it as such), and recruited Seven to take his place as Adams's man at the lab in Chicago. In the clandestine pattern that surfaced later in the Rosenberg case, Six gave Seven a key that Seven was to use to identify himself to Adams. Seven told the House Committee that at the Cleveland meeting Six made it quite clear that Adams was a Soviet spy. Thereafter, Seven did meet Adams. Thereafter, Seven did correspond with some frequency with Six's wife, whose illegal activities, according to the committee, went on full force while Six was exiled in the Yukon.

Seven then decided to pull out. He went to the committee and recanted fully. Six was subpoenaed by the committee but took the Fifth Amendment repeatedly and divulged nothing.

The Joint Committee was moved to the following conclusions:

While military and civilian investigative agencies knew of contact between [Seven] and Adams, no effort was made to remove [Seven] from highly secret chemical research.

The committee stated:

The meeting in Cleveland between [Six] and [Seven], the conversation which transpired, the letter from [Seven] to [Six's wife], and the subsequent contact between [Seven] and Adams in Chicago represent a clear case of a conspiracy between [Six], [Seven] and [Six's wife] to divulge secret and classified information relating to the atomic bomb project to a Soviet espionage agent. The committee recommends immediate prosecution of the conspirators.

That was in 1948. None of the three (including Six's wife) was ever charged.

The Joint Committee report in 1951 made one other surprising disclosure. It disclosed that during the war the United States shipped to the Soviet Union—with full knowledge and approval of our War Department and, presumably, our officials in the Manhattan District—1,444.2 pounds of uranium, all through Great Falls, Montana, the wartime air gateway to the USSR. The uranium went in three shipments, two in 1943 and one in 1944. In addition, 1,100 grams of heavy water were shipped via the same route, with the same approval, to the Soviet Union between June 1943 and June 1944.[85]

Apparently all of these shipments were made before the Manhattan District changed its mind regarding the importance of these materials and banned their export.

None of this material had any use, for the United States or for the USSR, except in the development of atomic weaponry. We now know that these shipments were useful in the development of the Soviet atomic bomb. But our own officials did little to maintain the American monopoly in atomic weaponry with these shipments.

Donald Maclean

Before leaving the subject of the relative destructiveness of the various spies employed by the Soviet Union to ferret information from the American atomic bomb project, the name of Donald Maclean must be mentioned. Maclean had his own share of notoriety (wholly apart from atomic matters) because of his flight from England in the company of Guy Burgess in 1951. The defection of the two highly educated members of the British

Foreign Service to the Soviets came after they were warned of trouble by Kim Philby. Philby was the "third man" who informed Maclean of his impending confrontation with MI-5, the British counterintelligence service, while Philby himself continued to serve his Soviet masters in Washington (from where his warning came) until he defected from Beirut to Moscow in 1962.

Maclean's role in atomic spying is but one chapter of his devotion to the Soviet cause from the time that he left Cambridge in 1934. The son of a distinguished lay preacher and moralist, Maclean was nurtured in the midst of the British establishment. It is difficult to determine whether Maclean, Burgess, or Philby came from the highest pedigreed stock within the British elite. They all were bred and educated impeccably, as was the "fourth" man, Anthony Blunt, who surfaced twenty years after the Burgess-Maclean defection. All four had been at Cambridge during the same period in the early 1930s, when (as it later appeared) hidden adherence to communism was part of the effete fashion of the undergraduates who were bored, bright, spoiled, and ideologically undirected. Maclean's wealth came from his father's position as an outstanding solicitor in Cardiff. His social standing also came from the causes championed by his father, who was co-founder of the National Society for the Prevention of Cruelty to Children, and from the elder Maclean's election to Parliament in 1908 as a Liberal. Maclean senior became a stalwart of the Liberal party and its national leader in 1918.

The significance of all this lies in the British tendency during World War II to accept family pedigree in place of the most rudimentary investigation of individuals who were invited to join the Foreign Service. This was true of Maclean (and equally true of Burgess, Philby, and Blunt), whose activities at Cambridge before they came to London and the Foreign Service (in 1934) would have raised eyebrows from any security officer even then. Maclean's homosexuality was not quite so notorious as Burgess's (no one was ever quite so notorious as Burgess, whose Foreign Service career stands as a triumph of the wartime British belief that highly bred and carefully educated young men are incapable of treason), but Maclean's sexual tendencies and drunkenness were known to the Foreign Service community very soon after he joined it. Maclean served in London and then abroad in Paris, coming to Washington in February 1947. He left Washington in 1948. Maclean had been a spy for the Soviet Union at least ten years before he arrived in Washington. What Maclean then did for his Soviet masters during his year and a half in Washington has never been either disclosed in detail nor evaluated.[86] But the public record nonetheless contains damning evidence.

By the time Maclean arrived in Washington in 1947, both London and Washington were in a legal quandary. Under no less than three agreements between the governments, full and complete exchange of atomic secrets between the United States and Great Britain was obligatory. The Quebec Agreement of 1943 was the first of these accords; but far more important were private agreements between Roosevelt and Churchill (executed at Roosevelt's home at Hyde Park in September 1944) and a later personal accord signed by Truman and Attlee in 1945. The formal body that served as funnel for the exchange of this information was called the Combined Policy Committee. It should surprise no one that Maclean was chosen as British secretary of this body, positioned so that all major atomic information exchanged between the two governments went through his hands.[87]

On a less formal basis, it was under the umbrella of these agreements that Klaus Fuchs was able to operate with total impunity. Similarly, these accords made access to American atomic information possible to Bruno Pontecorvo, the brilliant scientist and Soviet spy.

But the passage of the Atomic Energy Act of 1946 ended all that. What had heretofore been legal seemingly was banned by the new act. But new enactments are like new executives, they must be seasoned by use. It later turned out that the passage of the 1946 act had little effect in preventing Maclean from serving up to his Soviet masters vast and vitally useful information on the U.S. atomic and nuclear efforts. Some of these disclosures might even have been legal; for some reason, the 1946 act did not forbid disclosure of declassification procedures for atomic information nor, astonishingly, the means of access to raw materials used to produce the bombs (atomic or nuclear) or patents used in the production of the bomb. Maclean was not a stickler for any of these subtleties. What he learned about the American atomic bomb, legally or illegally, he passed on to the Soviets.

In February of 1956, five years after Maclean and Burgess had defected, the Senate Internal Security Subcommittee formed a committee to determine the extent of the leakage caused by Maclean while he was in Washington. The creation of this senatorial subcommittee was a result of the British White Paper of 1955 on the Burgess-Maclean defection, which made no mention whatsoever of Maclean's access to atomic information while in Washington. In consequence, Senator Eastland of Mississippi, who chaired the subcommittee, wrote the State Department a lengthy letter seeking the department's position on the damage done by Maclean. The department's reply contained the following statement:

In February, 1947, Maclean was designated by his Government to act as the United Kingdom's secretary on the Combined Policy Committee which was concerned with atomic energy matter and composed of representatives of the US, UK and Canada. In this position he had an opportunity to have access to information shared by the three participating countries in the fields of patents, declassified matters, and research and development relating to the programme of procurement of raw material from foreign sources by the Combined Developed Agency, including estimates of supplies and the *modus vivendi* concerning atomic energy matters followed by the three governments. After January, 1948, Maclean in his official capacity had access to information relating to the estimates made at that time of uranium for the atomic energy programmes of the three governments, requirements of uranium for the three governments for the period from 1948 to 1952, and the definition of scientific areas in which the three governments deemed technical cooperation could be accomplished with mutual benefit.[88]

This information was exceedingly useful to the Soviets. There can be no doubt that Maclean passed every bit of it on to them.

What was especially valuable to the Soviets was the information on U.S., Canadian, and British requirements for uranium for the four years from 1948 to 1952.[89] It gave the Soviets, more than any other information, a firm basis for the calculation of how many atomic bombs the United States, Canada, and Great Britain were to produce during that period.

But Maclean's activities were not limited to his official role. Months after passage of the Atomic Energy Act of 1946, which ostensibly banned this practice, Maclean secured a pass to the main Atomic Energy Building in Washington, which he could use at any time. Moreover, Maclean's pass permitted him to roam the AEC headquarters unescorted, a privilege specifically denied personages as exalted as J. Edgar Hoover.[89a] There was full knowledge that Maclean invariably used this pass after hours, when a minimum of AEC personnel were in the building.

Maclean made a dozen visits to the AEC headquarters under this pass, unescorted and after hours. What he learned there turned on what was lying about in various offices. To this day, no one knows how much leaked out of the headquarters of the agency itself. Finally, months after Maclean's voyaging through the AEC building had commenced, his pass was quietly withdrawn.

But it was an article of faith at the time that full and free exchange between the United States and Great Britain of atomic information was serving the interests of the United States. What Maclean found and passed on no one knows. It is no solace to anyone surveying this spectacle to learn that Maclean was recalled from Washington to London because of a drinking problem.

Where does one place Maclean among the spies during that heyday of freely licensed, near-routine espionage of America's atomic secrets? The best evidence came in a speech made by Secretary of the Army Wilbur M. Brucker, on February 17, 1956. The speech was the first public assessment by an American official of the damage done to American interests by Burgess and Maclean. Burgess's own activities were serious enough to warrant misgivings within our State Department. Brucker put it more succinctly: "Burgess and Maclean had secrets of priceless value to the Communist conspiracy."

Placing Maclean alongside David Greenglass is very much like ranking Benedict Arnold with the battlefield spies during our own revolution. Maclean was a man authorized by intergovernmental practice, if not by law, to examine every bit of atomic information this country possessed. He did so for close to two years. There is also no doubt that whatever Maclean examined went directly into Soviet hands. When all of this happened, in 1947 and 1948, U.S. atomic policy was in critical straits. Not only was the number of atomic bombs possessed by this country of strategic importance to our foreign policy in 1947 and 1948, but the hydrogen bomb was also under development. The Soviets were able to track these matters on a daily basis from a source that was officially sanctioned by the U.S. and British governments, and thus unimpeachable, a source no one ever detected or ever suspected until that source, Maclean, defected to Moscow three years later.

What Donald Maclean did occurred from two to three years after the Fuchs betrayal and the perfidy of David Greenglass. But Judge Kaufman pronounced the Rosenbergs as bearing responsibility for the Korean War, which began in 1950. It is fair to say that those words might have applied to Donald Maclean far more accurately than they did to David Greenglass or Julius or Ethel Rosenberg, whose disclosures of atomic secrets had been completed by 1945.

There is irony in Kaufman's accusation of the Rosenbergs' responsibility for the Korean War. In the same State Department response to Senator Eastland's inquiry as to the damage caused to U.S. interests by Maclean, the State Department voluntarily revealed that U.S. efforts to localize the Korean War in 1950 and 1951 were known to Maclean, then in Cairo, having been incomprehensibly promoted to chief of chancery at the British embassy in Egypt. The State Department revealed that Maclean probably was privy to Washington's decision not to cross the Yalu River between China and North Korea if the Red Chinese invaded North Korea.[90] That information went from Maclean straight to Moscow and thence to its then-ally, Peking. General MacArthur and his chief of intelligence, General Willoughby, were convinced that American policy had been leaked to the Communists. Just before he died, General MacArthur complained that the Chinese not only knew of this policy but also all of the details of what the UN forces would and would not do in Korea.[91] Maclean and his protector, Philby, who followed Maclean to a high post in Washington in 1950, were positioned to reveal this information to Moscow and Peking. The State Department believes that Maclean did so. Kaufman picked the wrong spy, or spies, on which to blame the American bloodshed in Korea.

Just as Judge Kaufman chose the wrong thief of the atomic bomb itself, he strayed irrationally in accusing the Rosenbergs of having anything to do with the Korean War. That accusation might well have been made of Donald Maclean, whose disclosures informed the Soviets of American atomic power in the late 1940s, and in 1950, when Korea was invaded. Swept by the passion of his time, Judge Kaufman was wrong in accusing the Rosenbergs of the two historic betrayals (the theft of the A-bomb and the resultant Communist aggression in Korea), which impelled the judge to sentence the Rosenbergs to death.

Fatal Error and Morton Sobell

To this point, the case against Morton Sobell (the Rosenbergs' co-defendant) has not been discussed. Any discussion of the error committed by Judge Kaufman in sentencing the Rosenbergs must include the reflection of that error in the sentence given Sobell.

There is, to begin with, a major question as to whether Sobell should have been tried with the Rosenbergs. Appellate Judge Frank ruled that the issue of whether the Sobell-Elitcher conduct was part of the same conspiracy with the Greenglass-Rosenberg atomic espionage should have been decided by the jury. And, we have indicated, in any putative retrial, it would have been difficult indeed to join Sobell with the Rosenbergs because the retrial would have proceeded against the Rosenbergs under one statute (the 1946 Atomic Energy Act), whereas a second Sobell trial would have necessarily been brought (as was the first) under the 1917 Espionage Act.

But Sobell was victimized in a far more realistic sense. He was given a sentence of thirty years; a good portion of that sentence was served in our Devil's Island, Alcatraz. It is a fair inference from the sentencing remarks of Judge Kaufman that the severity of the Sobell sentence was a reflection of the judge's belief—right or wrong—that the Rosenbergs put the atomic bomb in Soviet hands. It is a fair inference from that same sentencing speech that Judge Kaufman believed that Morton Sobell was part and parcel of the same conspiracy and therefore had to suffer the same harsh fate that the judge meted out to those who were responsible for betraying our atomic secrets.

No one at trial (or since) has ever contended that Sobell had anything to do with atomic espionage. But linking his activity with the Greenglass-Rosenberg conspiracy—as Kaufman did—exposed Sobell to the same excessive punishment that was given the Rosenbergs. If David Greenglass was a third-rank spy in terms of damage done to our security (as now seems apparent), everyone connected with Greenglass deserved punishment commensurate with that rank. And, pointedly, an admitted outsider to the venomous plot to put "into the hands of the Russians the A-bomb" (and Sobell was such an outsider) deserved lesser punishment. Sobell, accordingly, may not have suffered fatal error. But in the sentence given him, he suffered something far worse; the living hell of a thirty-year sentence (part of it at Alcatraz) for being tangentially and dubiously linked to atomic espionage in Judge Kaufman's personal myth that the Rosenbergs betrayed our most precious military secret.

Atomic Expertise of the Soviets

In the welter of unauthorized disclosures concerning our development of the atom bomb, it is relevant to evaluate the scientific information held by the Soviets themselves, without regard to what they secured through spies. Although the substantive information available to the West is limited, there is a fair measure of it. It is summarized very succinctly in the article "Entering the Nuclear Arms Race: The Soviet Decision to Build the Atomic Bomb," by David Holloway, which appeared in the May 1981 edition of *Social Studies of Science*. Holloway describes three separate Soviet decisions that bear on the development of the Soviets' bomb.

The first, an essentially negative decision, came as a result of earlier, intensive interest by Soviet scientists in the possibility of chain reactions. N. N. Semenov, of the Soviets' Institute of

Physical Chemistry, received the Nobel Prize in 1956 for work he did in the 1930s on chain reactions. Semenov, in 1940 and 1941, led the group of Soviet scientists in a drive to secure additional government funding for what Semenov clearly described as an atomic bomb. The government, however, appeared to be preoccupied with other matters and made no response to Semenov's request.[92] The invasion of the Soviet Union on June 21, 1941, brought substantially all nuclear research in that country to a halt. Americans, however, should have no doubt that Soviet scientists were fully aware of the possibilities of an atom bomb as far back as 1941. As Holloway states:

Petrzak [another Soviet scientific leader] was later to claim that, had it not been for the war, Soviet physicists might have achieved a chain reaction before Fermi did in Chicago in December of 1942. It is impossible to know whether or not they would have done so, but the claim is not a wild one.[93]

The reason was:

Soviet physicists did not lag behind their American, British or German counterparts in their thinking about nuclear fission.[94]

Contrary to the simplistic notion that American spies "put into the hands of the Russians the A-bomb," the advanced state of Russian scientific thinking about an atom bomb in 1940 and 1941 must be accepted as a reality. Obviously, vast other challenges took the industrial wherewithal away from atomic energy when the German invasion occurred. But a major cadre of Soviet scientists were on the frontiers of scientific thought and experimentation on the feasibility of a chain reaction and a bomb before, or roughly at the same time that, the Manhattan District produced its chain reaction at Stagg Field in Chicago in December of 1942.

The second Soviet decision was a much more positive one. At the end of 1942, the Soviet State Defense Committee issued a decree setting up a laboratory within the Academy of Sciences and naming I. V. Kurchatov as scientific director. Not until February or March of 1943, however, did Kurchatov settle in Moscow to begin substantive work on the uranium problem.[95] Orders for uranium nitrate and uranium oxide were placed with the United States.[96] The scientists that were gathered were small in number;

at the end of 1943, there were only fifty people working in the laboratory. But their activities were precisely parallel to those of American scientists and, indeed, it was the interruption of scientific conversation with the Americans on nuclear matters that convinced the Russians that an American atom project was in being—long before Klaus Fuchs told them so. The chief purposes of the Soviet laboratory were to achieve a chain reaction in an experimental pile using natural uranium; to develop methods of isotope separation and to study the configuration of a bomb.[97] Use of heavy water as moderator, use of an electromagnetic isotope separation process and use of gaseous diffusion were defined as research goals, and work proceeded.

What is significant is that in 1944, Kurchatov repeated to the government (in his report to it) that although a chain reaction was possible, he asserted that great difficulties, both industrial and research, remained before it could be achieved.[98]

The final Soviet decision concerning the bomb is one that was most open. Whether Stalin knew of the details of the bomb from Fuchs (and others) in August of 1945, Truman did address the subject (in somewhat elliptical terms) to Stalin at Potsdam in August of 1945. By November, Molotov had declared: "We will catch up on what we must and we will achieve the flowering of our nation. We will have atomic energy, and much else."[99]

Kurchatov was then asked (in August of 1945) how long it would take the Soviets to develop their own bomb. Five years was the response, as Holloway notes.[100] In fact, the first Soviet test took place four years to the month after the August 1945 meeting.

What this history tells us is that there were no scientific secrets that Americans held alone while we were developing the atomic bomb. The Soviets were working in tandem on their project while we were. The major difference was the amount of money, manpower, and industrial effort that we could put to the task as compared to the Soviets. And, in that race, the contribution of Klaus Fuchs in disclosing the industrial know-how of gaseous diffusion to the Soviets saved the Soviets enormous amounts of money and industrial resources, both in short supply in the Soviet Union during and after its exhausting defeat of the Germans.

*   *   *

A major purpose of this book is to place the Rosenberg case in perspective. One context for perspective is the degree of punishment meted out to the various spies involved in atomic espionage.

- Klaus Fuchs got fourteen years.
- Bruno Pontecorvo was never caught.
- Donald Maclean defected to the USSR and was never caught.
- Allan Nunn May got ten years.
- David Greenglass got fifteen years in return for becoming a government witness against Julius and Ethel Rosenberg.
- Ruth Prinz Greenglass was never charged.
- Alfred Dean Slack got fifteen years.
- Spy Six and Spy Seven were never prosecuted, although their supposed atomic spying was known to U.S. authorities and both were in the United States.
- The American officials who shipped uranium salts and heavy water to the Soviets were never investigated.
- Julius and Ethel Rosenberg received the death penalty and were executed.

If there was substantial overkill in the sentencing of the Rosenbergs in April of 1951, why did it occur? By far the biggest reason for the death sentence was the government's desire for it. Why the government wanted so badly to send the Rosenbergs to the electric chair is more complicated. Anyone reading the transcript of the trial and the other information available to the government, such as the study of the Joint Committee on Atomic Energy, reaches the conclusion that the government (in this case, the Department of Justice and U.S. attorney Saypol and his staff) knew very well that in David Greenglass and his sister and brother-in-law they had small potatoes before them. It is clear that the prosecution communicated with Atomic Energy Commission personnel, and had been informed that the real traitor was in jail in England more than three thousand miles away, months before the Rosenberg trial began. Why, then, did the prosecution work so hard for the death penalty?

There are at least two reasons. The first is that the government did not really want to kill Julius Rosenberg, it simply wanted to scare him to death. Knowing their quarry well, the Department of Justice worked hard on Julius prior to his execution. The head of the Bureau of Corrections, James Bennett, visited both Rosenbergs at Sing Sing in the last weeks before their death to inform them that the Department of Justice was prepared to intervene officially on behalf of clemency if the Rosenbergs would recant and divulge what they knew.[101] Ethel Rosenberg was as unyielding on the day she died as she was when sentence was pronounced. But Julius Rosenberg might have been another matter. Bennett arranged for a private line to be opened from Sing Sing to Washington. It was never used.

Recent stories have surfaced, contending that the entire prosecution of the Rosenbergs was simply a prelude to additional disclosures by federal officials of wrongdoing involving espionage during the war. The entire Bennett effort (which was rebuffed, with bitter comments made about it by Ethel Rosenberg in her last letters) failed. But it gave credence to the idea that the death penalty was used by the Department of Justice as pressure on the Rosenbergs to recant and implicate others. If the government did use the Rosenbergs as cat's-paws, whom was it after?

By 1951, the government had not one but three government witnesses who had either spied at Los Alamos or had been couriers in a spy ring. It had David Greenglass singing to save his skin; it had Harry Gold, for better or for worse; and, most importantly, it had Klaus Fuchs. A delegation from the FBI met with Fuchs in early 1951 to try and pick his brains on other spies, and Fuchs was proud of the cooperation he gave the American official police.

While it may be clear that the Soviets had splintered their spying operations at Los Alamos so that individual spies might not necessarily know of others, it is also true that Harry Gold served not only as David Greenglass's courier, but also as Klaus Fuchs's. If there was another top-level spy at Los Alamos, the probabilities are that either Fuchs or Gold knew of him. Certainly, in the technical disclosures given by Fuchs to Gold it is likely that Fuchs would have learned of other technical information given to the Soviets. His relationship with Gold was free and open, and Gold ate up every word. If Gold was receiving information from others, Fuchs would have known it. If another top-level spy was inside of Los Alamos, the questions posed by Gold to Fuchs would have been penetrating. Fuchs clearly would have been able to guess it. More important, Fuchs revealed no second major spy. If one existed and Fuchs knew of him, there is every reason to believe that Fuchs would have revealed him. It was Fuchs's pattern in 1950 and 1951 to do so. He fingered Gold—albeit at a time when Gold was already identified by others. By the time of his trial in 1950, Fuchs was a played-out case. His revelations of 1944 and 1945 were now six years old. Earthshaking as these disclosures were during the war, by 1950, they were part of a scientific conversation going on all over the world—including the Soviet Union—because of Fuchs. By 1950, there was little reason left for Fuchs to remain silent. His zeal to cooperate with Western authorities offered him every reason to reveal any spy known to him. He never did anything like that. Even in light of Fuchs's final turnabout in 1959, his revelations in 1950 make it probable that Fuchs would have revealed another atomic spy if Fuchs knew of him.

While one cannot wholly discard the notion that the U.S. government was probing for other atomic spies when they sought the death penalty for the Rosenbergs, the logic of events in 1951 points in another direction. Julius Rosenberg also was involved in conspiring to in Washington. When the government sought to scare Julius Rosenberg to death, it could very well have been looking for information about another spy in Washington, active in the naval spy ring that was relegated to the background by atomic espionage in the Rosenberg case.

Another motive of the prosecution in seeking death for the Rosenbergs is very plausible. Faced with the terrible realization that the American effort to produce the atomic bomb had been successfully penetrated by Soviet spies from its inception, the Department of Justice badly needed a scapegoat. It could not get its hands on Klaus Fuchs. Our extradition treaty with England (where Fuchs was apprehended) did not provide for extradition to this country of persons accused of violating our espionage laws. It is also quite likely that the Department of Justice was quite content not to have to prosecute Fuchs in this country. The revelation of how feckless and inept our own security forces had been in trusting the British to clear British scientists working in this country would have embarrassed every ranking official in the Manhattan District, civilian and soldier alike. The revelation of how astonishingly blind the British security forces were to the known facts concerning Klaus Fuchs would have added further embarrassment. Very little of this came out of the surprisingly brief and sparsely reported Fuchs trial in England. That sleeping dog was far better left undisturbed.

What the Department of Justice needed was a spy or group of spies who looked as if they had handed over the bomb, who could fill the role of betrayers of atomic secrets to the Soviets, and whom the American public would accept as the prime villains in betraying to the Soviets the bomb years before the Soviets would have developed it themselves. In the heyday of the McCarthy times in the early 1950s, the Rosenbergs and David Greenglass qualified admirably. Without examining the facts too careful-ly, the American public could easily believe that what David Greenglass and his relatives did was nothing more nor less than deliver the bomb to the Soviets. This would work only if the Rosenberg defense did not give lie to this exaggerated and oversimplified tale. The defense never did. The scheme would work particularly well if the judge was of a mind to accept the mythology as propounded by the Department of Justice. Judge Kaufman did so, hook, line, and sinker. All of this was vastly aided by the American public's willingness to believe almost anything that was said about Communists in the early 1950s. Julius and Ethel Rosenberg were certainly Communists. Their conduct at the trial made them admirable and credible scapegoats.

For years, it was common belief in this country that the Rosenbergs gave the Soviet Union the secret of the atomic bomb. The success of the Department of Justice effort to bury Klaus Fuchs and point the finger at the Rosenbergs is measured thereby.

The ultimate triumph of this exercise came in the sentencing of the Rosenbergs to death. Americans had to believe that no American judge would put two spies into the electric chair unless these spies truly betrayed the bomb. If this was a prosecution game, it was played with consummate skill and ruthlessness. It is difficult to believe today that officials of the Department of Justice and members of the prosecution team did not understand the true significance of the Rosenbergs' crimes in the perspective, for example, of the conclusions of the Joint Committee on Atomic Energy. The cynicism that pervaded the drive for the death penalty is another part of the tragedy of this case.

Curiously, in all this, the unlovely conduct of Irving Kaufman emerges unscathed. He was wrong in his facts, probably politicized by the times in pronouncing death, but he did not commit any legal error or any irregularity in so doing.* He had the widest kind of latitude under the Espionage Act in 1951. Quite probably, he did not exceed that latitude in imposing the death penalty. Not until 1972 did the Supreme Court rule that the kind of unbridled latitude of trial judges to mete out the death penalty was unconstitutional. That was nineteen years too late to do the Rosenbergs any good.

The Rosenberg case, as controversial as it was, was also a major miscarriage of justice. No one can be proud of what American justice did in the Rosenberg case. It deserves a special place in the conscience of our society.

---

* Roy Cohn, in his 1988 autobiography, claims numerous ex parte communications with Judge Kaufman during the Rosenberg case. But Cohn had an aggrandized notion of his own prowess and achievements, and Cohn's respect for the truth was far from absolute.

NOTES

Chapter One

1. Two judges of the U.S. District Court had reviewed the case prior to June 13, 1953. Two panels of the U.S. Court of Appeals for the Second Circuit had done so, but the panels were not always made up of the same three judges: our count is that four judges of that court had sat on it prior to June 4, 1953; all nine justices of the Supreme Court had sat on it on numerous occasions prior to June 1953; the total number of judges who had done so prior to June 1953 appears, therefore, to have been fifteen.

2. Irwin Edelman of Los Angeles.

3. Atomic Energy Act of 1946, effective August 1, 1946, Ch. 724 60 Stat. 755.

4. Espionage Act of 1917, Public Law No. 24, Sixty-fifth Congress, approved June 15, 1917.

5. Justice Douglas, 346 U.S. 310, June 19, 1953.

6. Justice Black, 346 U.S. 296, June 19, 1953; Justice Frankfurter, 346 U.S. 301 (1953).

7. Chief Justice Vinson, Justices Reed, Clark, Minton, Jackson, and Burton; majority opinion is at 346 U.S. 277 (1953).

8. The original indictment in the Rosenberg case was issued on August 17, 1950.

9. Memorandum of Justice Frankfurter on Nos. 111 and 607 in October 1952, dated June 4, 1953, found in the Frankfurter papers kept in the library of the Harvard Law School (FF Papers).

10. A memorandum and an addendum to it produced by the FBI in the Freedom of Information action brought by the Rosenberg children; both are dated by the FBI June 17, 1953; they go from the chief of the New York offices of the FBI to a senior FBI official in Washington. In the memorandum, a telephone call by Judge Kaufman to the FBI New York office on June 17 reports information on this meeting (between the attorney general and the chief justice) received by him from assistant U.S. attorney Kilsheimer, a member of the prosecution team; in the addendum dated the same day by the FBI, New York FBI supervisor McAndrews reported "that Judge Kaufman had very confidentially advised that at the meeting between the Attorney General and the Chief Justice Vinson last night, Justice Vinson said that if a stay is granted he will call the full Court into session Thursday morning to vacate it."

10a. See chapter 6, note 2.

11. FF Papers, addendum dated by Frankfurter June 19, 1953, p. 4; see also quotation from oral history of Philip Elman prepared by Columbia University, Norman Silber, interviewer.

12. Supreme Court records reflect a filing by the Justice Department seeking a special term at or about 5:00 P.M. on Wednesday, June 17, 1953. Chief Justice Vinson acted on this petition at 6:00 P.M.

13. Walter and Miriam Schneir, *Invitation to an Inquest* (New York: Pantheon Books, 1965, 1983), and John Wexley, *The Judgment of Julius and Ethel Rosenberg* (New York: Ballantine Books, 1955, 1977).

14. Louis Nizer, *The Implosion Conspiracy* (New York: Doubleday, 1973) and Jonathan Root, *The Betrayers* (New York: Coward-McCann, 1973).

Chapter Two

1. Tr. 1579 (all trial transcript references are to the complete edition of the original trial transcript made available by the National Committee to Secure Justice in the Rosenberg Case).

2. Tr. 1612.

3. David Greenglass: Tr. 394–406, 438–66, 489–500; Ruth Greenglass: 677–787.

4. Tr. 398 et seq.

5. Tr. 438–39, 428, 460, 495, 498, 510.

6. Tr. 459–60, 497–99.

7. Tr. 826–27.

8. Tr. 428–90, 495, 498, 510.

9. Tr. 830 et seq.

10. Tr. 831.

11. See Tr. 1051–59, 1282–86, 1293, 1307, 1311–43, 1398–1410.

12. Tr. 470–84.

13. Tr. 903–15.

14. Tr. 210, 236, 256–357.

15. Tr. 236–37.

16. Tr. 260–61, 848–55.

17. Tr. 1148–59.

18. Tr. 524–28.

19. Tr. 523–24, 650.

20. Tr. 857–67, 919–30.

21. Tr. 857–67, 919–38.

22. Tr. 938 et seq.

23. Tr. 705–7.

24. Tr. 1054–55, 1136, 1209–11, 1332.

25. Tr. 500 et seq.

26. Tr. 1479.

27. Tr. 1–3.

Chapter Three

1. These events (of Saturday, June 13, 1953), were reported in the *New York Times* the following day.

2. 195 F. 2d at 611; rehearing denied April 8, 1952.

3. FF Papers, memorandum on petition filed by the Rosenbergs on June 7, 1952, p. 3.

4. Ibid., p. 4.

5. 200 F. 2d at 670.

6. Ibid.

7. 200 F. 2d at 670.

8. FF Papers, memorandum on Rosenberg petition filed March 30, 1953, on the Saypol point, p. 4 (dated June 4, 1953).

9. FF Papers, Appendix IV to the foregoing memorandum, written by Justice Douglas, dated May 22, 1953.

10. FF Papers, memorandum (dated June 4, 1953) on Rosenberg petition of March 30, 1953, p. 7.

11. Ibid.

12. Ibid.

13. Ibid., p. 8.

14. Ibid., p. 9.

15. The events in New York City on June 13, 14, and 15 were recounted by Farmer in a personal interview with the author in Nashville on August 15–16, 1988.

16. Petition filed by Farmer with Judge Kaufman, June 13–14, 1953, p. 17.

17. Ibid., p. 18.

18. Farmer letter to Judge Kaufman, dated June 14, 1953.

19. Farmer letter to Bloch dated June 13, 1953.

Chapter Four

1. 345 U.S. 965, 989 (June 15, 1953), 1003.

2. Ibid.

3. Ibid.

4. On June 15, Vinson, Reed, Clark, and Minton voted against a stay, now joined by Douglas; Frankfurter and Jackson voted for granting a stay until oral arguments could be heard; Black voted for a stay, but if no stay could be secured, for oral arguments; Burton voted for oral arguments and then defected and voted against a stay.

5. 294 U.S. 103.

6. Order of Judge Irving Kaufman, June 15, 1953.

7. FF Papers, addendum dated June 19, 1953, p. 1.

8. Ibid.

9. Ibid.

10. 346 U.S. 271–72.

11. Ibid.

12. FF Papers, addendum of June 19, 1953, p. 3.

13. Interview with Farmer, Nashville, August 15–16, 1988.

Chapter Five

1. Interview with Farmer, Nashville, August 15–16, 1988.

2. Ibid.

3. Belmont to Ladd, memorandum dated June 17, 1953, paragraph 2.

4. Canon of Judicial Conduct, American Bar Association, 1953.

5. Rule 3.5(b), Model Rules of Professional Conduct, passed by House of Delegates, American Bar Association, August 2, 1983. Canon 3 of Professional Ethics, which prohibits lawyers from making ex-porte communications to judges, was adopted by the American Bar Association in August 1908 and was in effect in 1953.

6. This disclosure came in consequence of the Freedom of Information suit commenced by the Meeropol children on July 14, 1975.

7. FF Papers, addendum of June 19, 1983, p. 3.

8. Ibid.

9. Ibid.

10. FF Papers, addendum of June 19, 1953, p. 4.

11. Philip Elman, an Oral History, interviewed by Norman Silber, Columbia University, Vol. 4, p. 226.

12. Ibid.

13. Ibid.

14. Ibid., pp. 4, 227.

15. Ibid.

16. FF Papers, addendum of June 19, 1953, p. 5.

Chapter Six

1. FF Papers, addendum of June 19, 1953, p. 4.

2. Ibid., p. 7.

3. Ibid.

4..If the records of the Federal Bureau of Investigation and the private papers of Justice Frankfurter are to be believed. There is no reason to doubt either source.

5. 346 U.S. 317 (June 17, 1953).

6. Ibid.

7. Ibid.

8. Ibid.

9. Ibid.

10. 346 U.S. 318 (June 17, 1953).

11. 346 U.S. 318–319.

12. 346 U.S. 319–320.

13. 346 U.S. 321.

14. The impeachment resolution was reported in the *New York Times* on Thursday, June 18, 1953.

15. The events at the offices of the Bar Association of New York were reported in an interview with Farmer in Nashville on August 16, 1988.

16. *Harvard Civil Rights Law Review* 11 (1976):514.

17. Douglas's reaction is recorded in his autobiography, *The Court Years* (New York: Random House, 1980), p. 81.

Chapter Seven

1. Szilard's experiences before the House Committee are described in Robert Jungk, *Brighter Than a Thousand Suns* (New York: Harcourt Brace Company, 1956), p. 235.

2. 60 Stat. at Large, 765.

3. 60 Stat. at Large, 766 (Section 10[a][2], Atomic Energy Act of 1946).

4. Ibid., Section 10(a)(3).

5. Farmer-Marshall petition filed with the Supreme Court, June 16, 1953, pp. 5–8.

6. Ibid., p. 4.

7. Ibid.

8. Ibid.

9. Ibid., pp. 4–5.

10. Ibid.

11. James B. Newman, "Control of Information Relating to Atomic Energy," 56 *Yale Law Journal* 769 (May 1947).

12. Application of Department of Justice to Convene Court in Special Term, filed June 17, 1953, at 13; the brief filed by the government two to three hours before argument on June 18 is unfortunately not in the Supreme Court files. It is clear, however, from oral argument that it raised no points that were not covered in the lengthy, more comprehensive petition filed by the government on June 17.

13. Ibid., p. 7.

14. Justice Jackson pointed out this possibility during oral argument, *New York Times*, June 19, 1953, p. 12.

15. Ibid., reported in the same article.

15a. Marshall's conduct and Farmer's statement were recounted in an interview with Farmer, Nashville, August 16, 1988.

16. *New York Times*, June 19, 1953, p. 12.

17. Senior government officials working on the Rosenberg case have no recollection that any recording of the oral arguments on June 19, 1953, was made. None has been found.

18. *New York Times*, June 19, 1953, p. 8.

19. Ibid.

20. Ibid.

21. Ibid.

22. Ibid.

23. Ibid.

24. Ibid.

25. Ibid.

26. Ibid.

27. Ibid.

28. Ibid.

29. Interview with Philip Elman, 1981, in which this event was reported. Newman was forced by the abruptness of his trip to borrow a suit coat from Elman.

30. *New York Times*, June 19, 1953, p. 8.

31. FF Papers, Frankfurter's handwritten interlineation on p. 7 of the majority opinion by the chief justice on June 19, 1953.

32. Ibid.

33. Burton's notes to himself in his papers, dated June 19, 1953. Burton indicated a willingness to shorten the Douglas stay and conduct briefly oral arguments on an expedited basis before the Supreme Court. He was voted down (Burton Papers, Library of Congress).

34. FF Papers, addendum dated June 19, 1953, p. 6.

35. *New York Times*, June 18, 1953.

36. Ibid.

37. Reported by Marshall Perlin at an interview with the author on August 24, 1988.

Chapter Eight

1. 346 U.S. 273 at 277.

2. 346 U.S. 273 at 293.

2a. 346 U.S. 273 at 322.

3. 346 U.S. 273 at 301.

4. 346 U.S. 273 at 297.

5. 346 U.S. 273 at 310, 311.

6. 346 U.S. 273 at 322.

6a. 346 U.S. 273 at 322.

7. Ibid.

8. Interview of Marshall Perlin by author, August 24, 1988.

9. All of the events in New Haven were re-created by Marshall Perlin in an interview with the author on August 24, 1988.

10. Quoted in the *New York Times,* June 20, 1953, p. 1.

11. Ibid., p. 6.

12. Ibid.

13. Ibid.

14. Ibid.

15. The executions are described in detail in the *New York Times,* June 20, 1953, pp. 1, 6.

16. *New York Times,* June 20, 1953, p. 6.

17. Ibid.

18. Robert and Michael Meeropol, *We Are Your Sons* (Boston: Houghton Mifflin, 1975), 232.

19. *New York Times,* June 20, 1953, p. 8.

20. Ibid., June 20, 1953, p. 8.

Chapter Nine

1. See dissenting opinion of Justice Black at 346 U.S. 297 (footnote therein).

2. Ibid.

3. 346 U.S. 298.

4. 346 U.S. 290 (opinion of Justice Jackson in which majority concurred).

5. Tr. 5–6.

6. 346 U.S. 295–296.

7. It did until June 16, 1950; Tr. 5–6.

8. Section 10(b)(1), Atomic Energy Act of 1946, 60 Stat. at 766.

9. Section 2, Espionage Act of 1917.

10. Section 10(b)(4), Atomic Energy Act of 1946, 60 Stat. at 767.

11. Section 10(a)(2), Atomic Energy Act of 1946, 60 Stat. at 766.

12. Compare Section 2 of the Espionage Act of 1917 with Section 10(a)(2) of the Atomic Energy Act of 1946.

13. Section 10(a)(2), Atomic Energy Act of 1946, 60 Stat. at 766.

14. Newman, "Control of Information," 56 Yale Law Journal at 784.

15. Section 10(b)5(A), Atomic Energy Act of 1946, 60 Stat. at 767.

16. Newman, "Control of Information," 788.

17. *U.S.* v. *Yuginovich,* 256 U.S. 450 (1921).

18. Ibid.

19. *Norris* v. *Crocker,* 13 How. 429 (U.S. 1851).

20. *Ferch* v. *People,* 104 Colo. 471, 74 P. 2d 712 (1937).

20a. See *Winston* v. *State,* 186 Ga. 573, 198 S.E. 667 (1939) and *Marion* v. *State,* 16 Neb. 349, 20 N.W. 289 (1894).

21. 346 U.S. 294.

22. Section 10(a)(2), Atomic Energy Act of 1946.

23. 346 U.S. 294.

24. 308 U.S. 188 at 198. Notwithstanding, both the government and courts have customarily cited *Borden* for its dictum, that is, the presumption against repeal by implication.

25. 308 U.S. 188 at 198–199.

26. Section 10(b)5(A), Atomic Energy Act of 1946, 60 Stat. at 762.

27. 56 *Yale Law Journal* 769 (May 1947).

28. Ibid., 783.

29. Ibid., 790.

30. Ibid., 797.

31. Ibid., 798.

32. 346 U.S. 308, Footnote 4.

33. 195 F. 2d at 600.

34. 346 U.S. 289; the majority ruled concerning the applicability of the 1946 act: "We think the question is not substantial. We think further proceedings to litigate it are unwarranted."

35. In addressing the Court on June 18 Bloch recognized the argument and admitted openly that he was not prepared to make it.

36. Newman, "Control of Information," 790.

37. Ibid., 798.

38. Ibid., 799.

39. 346 U.S. at 289.

40. Newman, "Control of Information," 799.

41. Ibid., 791.

42. This "club" has to include Jackson and Vinson; whether it should include the majority of the justices who nullified the Douglas stay turns on the degree that the majority was influenced by what was "perfectly understood" by the justices on June 15. That will never be known, but the term must exclude Black, Douglas, and Frankfurter because regardless of what was "perfectly understood" on June 15, the three justices voted their consciences in their dissents on June 19.

43. FF Papers, addendum, June 19, 1953, p. 4.

44. Papers of Justice Robert Jackson, on file at the Library of Congress.

45. "Cold War Justice: The Supreme Court and the Rosenbergs," by Michael Parrish, in the October 1977 issue of the *American Historical Review,* takes this position; the article itself is as incisive a study of the Supreme Court's conduct in the Rosenberg case as can be found anywhere.

46. Jackson did tell Frankfurter that "every time a vote could have been had for a hearing, Douglas opposed a hearing in open court, and only when it was perfectly clear

that a particular application would not be granted, did he take a position for it" (FF Papers, addendum of June 19, 1953, p. 4).

47. This is only partially true. It is true in the sense that the rules permitting the filing of "amicus curiae" briefs have, by practice, become far more liberal at the trial court level than they were in 1953. But there remains a substantial body of opinion that heartily agrees today—in 1988—with Justice Jackson's complaints that Farmer and Marshall had no status to make their argument in *Rosenberg*. This is true even though Bloch himself had adopted the Farmer-Marshall points in arguments before the Court on June 18; Jackson, in his opinion written on June 19, had his point pulled from under him by Bloch the day before. Yet there are those who agree today with what Jackson wrote on June 19, 1953.

Chapter Ten

1. Tr. 831.
2. 195 F. 2d 583, at 601.
3. *Kotteakos* v. *U.S.*, 328 U.S. 760, cited by Judge Frank at 195 F. 2d 601.
4. *Blumenthal* v. *U.S.*, 332 U.S. 539, cited by Judge Frank at 195 F. 2d 601.

Chapter Eleven

1. Tr. 1614–1615.
2. This episode is described in Montgomery Hyde, *The Atom Bomb Spies* (New York: Ballantine, 1980), 105.
3. Fuchs's credentials and standing in the Manhattan District Project are described in detail in *Soviet Atomic Espionage*, published by the Joint Committee on Atomic Energy of the Congress, April 1951, 1–28 (hereinafter Joint Committee Report or JCR).
4. Hyde, 97–98, JCR 17.
5. Hyde, 97.
6. JCR, 18–19, quoting Rebecca West, "The Terrifying Import of the Fuchs Case," *New York Times,* March 4, 1951.
7. JCR, 19, quoting West's article.
8. Hyde, 111.
9. An evaluation of Fuchs's capabilities while at Harwell (the British nuclear laboratory); the setting for this description is Hyde, 114, quoting the official historian of the British Atomic Energy Authority.
10. Hyde reports that Fuchs signed the British Official Secrets Act in May of 1941 and maintained contact with his Soviet courier from at least 1941 on (Hyde, 102–3).
11. Hyde, 99.
12. Ibid., 100.
13. The British Enemy Aliens Tribunal had unconfirmed Gestapo reports that Fuchs had been a Communist since 1932, but an absence of confirmation and Fuchs's professional reputation brought about his return to England in 1942 (JCR, 20).
14. "Being among Germans again, he [Fuchs] reverted to his Communist past and dropped his concealment of his Communist beliefs. He used to attend the weekly discussion meeting of a group of Communists or fellow travellers which was formed in the camp. The leader of the group was Hans Kahle, a German Communist who had commanded the Eleventh International's Brigade in the Spanish Civil War" (Norman Moss, *Klaus Fuchs, a Biography* [New York: St. Martin's Press, 1987], 26–27).

15. JCR, 21, quoting the Rebecca West article in the *New York Times.*

16. Hyde, 102; Fuchs formally became a British citizen on August 7, 1942.

17. Letter of Karl Cohen to Senator McMahon, dated March 18, 1951, quoted at JCR, 22–23.

18. General Groves, chief of security for the Manhattan District, relied on the British investigation of British personnel working within the Manhattan District Project (Hyde, 105–6).

19. An evaluation of the damage done by Fuchs's disclosures, indicating their enormity, is found in the letter of Karl Cohen, director, Atomic Energy Division, Manhattan District, to Senator McMahon, dated March 19, 1951 (JCR, 22–23).

20. The advantages given the Soviets by Fuchs's disclosures are summarized in a letter from Manson Benedict, head of the process development division of Kellex Corporation (the name given the unit that developed the gaseous diffusion process), dated March 19, 1951, to Senator McMahon (JCR, 23–24).

21. Letter of Karl Cohen to Senator McMahon, dated March 19, 1951.

22. Letter of Manson Benedict to Senator McMahon dated March 19, 1951.

23. JCR, 5–6.

24. Tr. 819.

25. Hyde, 107.

26. Ibid.

27. Ibid.

28. Ibid.

29. Ibid., 108.

30. Ibid., 109.

31. Ibid., 109.

32. Tr. 496, 497.

33. Tr. 491, 494.

34. Anthony Cave Brown and Charles B. McDonald, *The Secret History of the Atomic Bomb* (New York: Dial Press, 1977), 493.

35. Ibid., 496.

36. Ibid., 494.

37. Ibid., 496.

38. Tr. 877.

39. Tr. 821–823.

40. Tr. 459.

41. Tr. 466.

42. Tr. 498, 500.

43. Tr. 482.

44. Tr. 482.

45. Hyde, 111.

46. Hyde describes the disclosures made by Fuchs at this meeting: "Fuchs had written down all he knew, and the information was vital" (Hyde, 111).

47. Tr. 837.

48. Tr. 836.

49. Tr. 838.

50. Tr. 618–619.

51. Tr. 618.

52. Neither government witness Derry nor Koski offered testimony that supported

Judge Kaufman's conclusion. Both dealt with Greenglass's sketches and disclosures that scientific testimony available in April 1951 would have demonstrated to be inaccurate, and inadequate to base any conclusion as to putting the bomb in anyone's hands. Judge Kaufman reached his own conclusion—but not on the *Rosenberg* record.

53. The details of Pontecorvo's defection are set forth at JCR 2, 38–48; see also Hyde, 154–71.

54. The details of Nunn May's defection are set forth in JCR 2, 49–60.

55. JCR, Foreword, iii.

56. JCR, 1.

57. Ibid.

58. JCR, 6.

59. JCR, 2.

60. Ibid.

61. JCR, 3.

62. Ibid.

63. JCR, 6.

64. Ibid.

65. JCR, 7.

66. Ibid.

67. Ibid.

68. Ibid.

69. Tr. 1614–1615.

70. Tr. 1614–1615.

71. Affidavit of Philip Morrison, Appendix 339a–348a, Docket 791, October Term, Supreme Court, 1967, at 345a–346a.

72. Ibid., 346a.

73. Ibid.

74. Ibid.

75. Ibid.

76. Affidavit of Henry Linschitz, Appendix 314a–338a, Docket 791, October Term, Supreme Court, 1967, at 337a–338a.

77. Affidavit of Harold Urey, Appendix 413a–414a, Docket 791, October Term, Supreme Court, 1967, at 413a.

78. Ibid., 413a–414a.

79. Hyde, 148–49.

80. Ibid.

81. Ibid.

82. Hyde, 146–47.

83. Slack's case is discussed by Ronald Radosh and Joyce Milton, *The Rosenberg File,* (New York: Holt, Rinehart and Winston, 1983), 151–53.

84. The HUAC summary of the facts concerning Six and Seven are found at JCR 163–70; neither Six nor Seven was prosecuted; accordingly, their identities are not published herein. (HUAC's "Report on Soviet Espionage Activities in Connection with the Atom Bomb," September 28, 1948; Eightieth Congress, 2nd Session; the report was clearly taken from raw HUAC files.)

85. JCR, 184–90.

86. Hyde has recorded some of Maclean's activities in Washington, p. 115.

87. Maclean's activities as liaison between the United States and the British in transmitting atomic data is described in Hyde, 115.

88. Response of Department of State dated February 21, 1956, to letter of Senator Eastland. Quoted in Bruce Page et al., *The Philby Conspiracy* (New York: New American Library, Signet Books, 1969), 193.

89. Hyde, 115.

89a. Ibid.

90. See n. 88, above; the portion of the State Department response cited here is found at Page et al., *The Philby Conspiracy*, 195.

91. Richard Rovere and Arthur Schlesinger, Jr., *The MacArthur Controversy* (New York: Farrar, Straus, 1955), 259.

92. Holloway, 169.

93. Ibid.

94. Ibid.

95. Ibid., 175.

96. Ibid.

97. Ibid., 177.

98. Ibid., 178.

99. Ibid., 185.

100. Ibid.

101. The Bennett effort and the Rosenberg reaction are described in *We Are Your Sons*, 207–18.

INDEX

269